The Baby's Coming

A Story of Dedication by an Independent Midwife

VIRGINIA HOWES

with Charlotte Ward

headline

First published in 2014
by HEADLINE PUBLISHING GROUP

1

Cataloguing in Publication Data is available from the British Library

978 1 4722 1173 6

Typeset in Adobe Garamond by Palimpsest Book Production Limited,
Falkirk, Stirlingshire

Printed and bound in the UK by
CPI Group (UK) Ltd, Croydon CR0 4YY

HEADLINE PUBLISHING GROUP
An Hachette UK Company
338 Euston Road
London NW1 3BH

www.headline.co.uk
www.hachette.co.uk

www.kentmidwiferypractice.co.uk

Disclaimer

In order to protect the privacy and, in some cases, the medical confidentiality of the people concerned, certain characters have had names and other details changed, and some characters or their stories are composites of several different experiences. Everything that is in the book happened in real life, but the details may be slightly different from the way they are told in this book.

Acknowledgements

When I read about the struggles some writers have getting a book published I have to pinch myself to believe that at my first attempt I have become an author! I would not, however, have done so without the help of my management team, Pat and Ceri, who saw promise in my work the very first time I approached them; or Emma, Jo and Emily from Headline Publishing, who kept my feet on the ground but my head in the air with excitement.

With this book all finished I still miss Charlotte (and her dog) and the many laughs we had as she helped to weave my stories into the timeline of what has been the trials and tribulations of my life, it was a great journey and one which made me recall times, people and places long forgotten. I look forward to being your midwife one day, Charlotte.

I wish I could have written more about the professionals who have had such a positive influence on my learning throughout my career (and about those who didn't). Thanks go to Dr Haken Coker in Turkey for allowing me to use his name in this book and I hope his childbirth education programme *Birth With No Regrets,* goes from strength to strength. I want to thank Sue Eve who was my supervisor for many years, as well as every one of my independent colleagues who I know I can count on whenever they are needed, and of course my friend and colleague Kay who has supported me (and vice versa) through thick and thin both during work times and the difficulties of everyday life.

Of course I want to thank every single one of the women included in this book for allowing me to include their stories. I also want to thank all those women whose stories have *not* been used (I may just start on my second book soon) because you are all in there too, between the lines, between the passing weeks and years. I still think of every single one of you and if anyone reading this has been a client and we have lost touch please find me in on Facebook or Twitter and say 'hi'.

Most importantly I want to thank my family: my lovely mum, my nieces and my beautiful children, not only for being the best grown-up kids there could ever be, but also for allowing me to achieve the most wonderful thing any mother, grandmother and midwife could dream of: to be midwife at all of her grandchildren's home births. What could be better? What could possibly surpass that in life?

Lastly I want to thank Sean for all his love and support through the good times and bad of my career, for his help, his love and his push for me to write this book. He is such a handsome man, witty, charming, talented, smart, clever and so affectionate. (Hmmm? He wrote the last sentence but as I always I like to find the funny side of things I am leaving it in!)

Prologue

Knocking on my daughter's front door, I tapped my foot agitatedly; every cell of my body pounding with maternal instinct to get inside and check all was well.

As her partner Robert let me in, I rushed through to the kitchen to find a heavily pregnant Sophie standing next to the counter, her hands on her hips and her legs straddled apart like she was about to perform a squat.

Her eyes were glued downwards as she stared in disbelief at the stream of water trickling from her body to form a puddle on the floor.

Immediately I morphed into a no-nonsense midwife.

'Here,' I said, grabbing the mop and pushing it into Robert's hands.

'Sophie, why are you just standing there?' I asked, bending down to study the liquid. 'Come on, chop, chop! You're about to become a midwife yourself so you know this is normal. The water is clear, your baby is due and well grown so everything is fine. Go on upstairs and get yourself cleaned up.'

Sophie had gone into labour a week before her due date after we'd enjoyed a day as a family at a car race meeting. In hindsight, considering Sophie had spent the day traipsing tirelessly up and down steep, grassy banks to visit the toilet, it was really no surprise that all that ascending and descending had brought on the labour.

But when Robert called to alert me, at 9pm, a mere hour after we'd arrived home, the news caused me to spring from the sofa like a startled cat. I'd never been more surprised or excited.

'Put her on the phone,' I'd demanded, my heart beating fast.

'Hi Mum!' Sophie's voice filtered down the line, a mix of nerves and excitement.

'Is it really your waters, Sophie?' I'd questioned. 'Are you sure?'

'Mum, there is no doubt!' she'd exclaimed in a high-pitched tone. 'I'm flooding the place!'

'OK, I'm on my way.'

I'd quickly grabbed my equipment bag, keys and phone and hurtled out the door, arriving at my daughter's home in under three minutes.

Now reassured that everything was normal, I watched amused as Sophie waddled across the room with her legs apart, gingerly holding the soggy material of her leggings away from her.

'Make sure you put heavy pads on because there will be more fluid to come,' I called out as she began to climb the stairs.

After helping Robert clean up the kitchen floor I headed upstairs where I found Sophie in a clean nightie. I tucked her into bed, bringing the duvet up to her chin.

'Try and get some sleep while you can – before the contractions start,' I whispered softly, stroking her long, dark hair. 'I'll be back as soon as you need me.'

'Thanks, Mum,' Sophie said, smiling appreciatively and suddenly looking a lot younger than her 25 years. It felt like only yesterday that I'd been tucking her into bed each night with a 'straddle and a coke' (a cuddle and stroke) – her words for me holding her in my arms and gently stroking her arms and face. Now my 'baby' was going to have her very own baby. And as both her mum and midwife I was going to be there for her every step of the way.

Returning home, feeling tired after a busy and exciting day, I quickly got ready for bed. Best to get some rest while I can, I reasoned. I suspected it would only be a few hours before Sophie called on me. Putting on my pyjamas I clambered into bed. I was asleep as soon as my head hit the pillow.

Awakening to a shrill sound, I stirred, trying to steer my brain through the fog. Sophie? But as I blinked sleepily I realised it wasn't the telephone but rather the morning chorus of birds chirping outside. I sat up with a start. Sophie hadn't called. What time was it?

Grabbing my phone I stared at the display in disbelief, already 8.30am and no call. I immediately scrolled down to Sophie's number and pushed the call button.

'Hello,' answered a tired voice. 'Oh, Mum, I've had a horrible night.'

'Why?' I barked. 'Are you having contractions? Why didn't you call me?'

'No, Mum, I haven't felt a thing,' she said. 'But this bloody water keeps coming out of me. I've had the worst night ever. It feels like I've got a soggy nappy on!'

'OK,' I laughed. 'I will come over very soon.'

Quickly flicking through my diary I cancelled all my appointments for the next few days and set off to see my daughter.

I'd hoped things would get going pretty swiftly but, despite Sophie having contractions on and off throughout the day, by that evening everything had once again calmed down and there was no sign of active labour commencing.

As I returned home to bed, I found myself restless and anxious. With Sophie's waters having broken and no regular contractions, there was a small chance of infection. I'd feel a lot more at ease once active labour was underway.

'Her waters are clear, her temperature is normal and she's a healthy woman carrying a healthy baby,' I chastised myself, urging my brain to think like a midwife and switch off the 'apprehensive mother' mode.

I must have drifted off at some point as the loud ring of my telephone at 6.15am caused my heart to pound in my chest. Grappling with the receiver I held it to my ear, blinking as the dawn light began to creep through my curtains.

'It's started now, Mum,' Sophie said, her voice breathy with excitement and nerves. 'I had a huge contraction at 6am and another nine minutes later. The last one was only five minutes ago.'

'OK, darling, I am coming now,' I said, having already begun to dress. After 32 hours, the wait was over. My grandchild was on its way at last.

Arriving at Sophie's house, I found Robert filling the water pool in the front room and a rather sorry-looking Sophie leaning over the edge of the sofa holding a hot-water bottle to her tummy and tears streaming down her face.

'Don't cry, darling,' I said, feeling my own stomach convulse with the discomfort of seeing my child in pain. Suddenly I could understand why people question whether a mother is the correct person to act as caregiver in a situation like this. But when Sophie had announced her pregnancy she'd immediately asked for me to be there, to care and champion her as she had her much-wanted water birth at home. Yes, I was emotionally involved, but that wasn't going to affect my ability to care for her. I'd be mother, midwife, comforter and rock all rolled into one.

'Come on, Sophie,' I said, as she continued to sob. 'You knew this was going to be tough. But you will be OK. You are OK. Now let's get you over to the toilet.'

Guiding my still-sniffling daughter to the bathroom, I supported her petite frame as she sat on the loo and used the position to rock through the colossal contractions.

After the original delay everything was moving fast and just over four hours from that first contraction at 6am, I could see something building in her. Her body was starting to heave downwards.

'Time to get in the pool, I think,' I said as I helped her up off the toilet and into the front room.

Sophie took off her nightie and submerged herself into the warm, soothing water.

'Where's Robert?' she asked.

'I'll go and find him,' I said.

Going upstairs I was stunned to see Robert cleaning the bathroom with gusto. Knowing Robert's usual intense aversion to household chores that was really saying something about his nerves.

'She's in the pool now, Robert,' I told him, keeping a straight face before heading back downstairs.

'He's coming now,' I reported back to Sophie. A few minutes later a pale-faced Robert ambled down the stairs to join us.

Having spent the last three years training to be a midwife, Sophie was well used to delivering babies but as her own child descended down through her pelvis with uncontrollable force she was fearful just like any other first-time mother.

'Mum, please help me. Make it stop,' she said, gripping the sides of the pool, her eyes full of panic.

'Please, my darling, have confidence, you can do this,' I said, doing my best to calm her. 'It won't harm you and soon you will have your darling baby in your arms.'

As I stroked her hair, my eyes fixed on her anguish-filled face, there was a sizeable lump in my throat. With Sophie's eyes closing as the contractions momentarily subsided, I glanced down at my tightly clasped hands now white with tension. I vowed to keep a smile plastered to my face to reassure both Sophie and Robert that all was well.

Six more rounds of contractions came and went before I caught a glimpse of the wispy blonde hair at the top of the baby's head.

'I can see the baby, sweetheart,' I said. 'It's coming, darling! You're nearly there.'

As Robert and I peered into the pool we watched as a small face appeared upside down in the water, tiny bubbles spiralling up from its mouth as the pressure of being in the birth canal squeezed amniotic fluid from the baby's lungs.

We held our breath as with one final push, the baby squeezed and manoeuvred through the tiny space of his mother's body and broke free into the water, little limbs flailing.

Reaching through her legs, Sophie immediately scooped up the baby bringing him up through the water to the surface with ease. A little boy!

'Hello, baby,' Sophie cried, wet hair plastered to her smiling, euphoric face.

I watched awestruck as the baby's skin started to change colour and he let out the faintest, tiniest squeak – barely a cry but enough to acknowledge he was breathing, healthy and fine.

Throwing my arms around Sophie and Robert I began to cry quietly, warm tears of relief and ecstatic happiness trickling down my cheeks.

'Jesse, this is Noonie,' Sophie whispered later when, all wrapped up warm on the sofa, she passed my grandson to me. Gently holding him in my arms, I gazed at the beautiful boy, the newest addition to our family – baby of my baby, flesh of my flesh.

Throughout my whole career as a midwife there had never been a more perfect moment than this . . .

Chapter One

Lying on my back I gripped the bars of my hospital bed, clenching my jaw as I felt the pain of a contraction throbbing in my back.

'Oh my God!' I thought. 'I never imagined it would be as bad as this.'

I was alone in a birthing suite at All Saints' Hospital in Chatham, Kent, having been brought in the night before – ten days overdue – to be induced. It was July 1976 and I was giving birth to my first baby at the age of 17.

Prior to the intense pain, I'd been excited, smiling and chatting to a kindly student midwife who was there throughout my labour.

I was one of the youngest mums giving birth that day but this was no unplanned teenage pregnancy. My desire to have a baby had been burning away since the age of 12 when I'd been told I might never have children.

I'd learnt this very adult news after going to hospital with stomach pain caused by a ruptured cyst on my right ovary.

After having surgery to remove my damaged ovary, I'd awoken feeling sore and unlucky but by far the worst pain was my prognosis.

Around two weeks after the operation I was laying on the sofa at home snuggled under a blanket watching TV when my mum, Lillian, came into the room, gently shifted my legs and sat down next to me.

'I need to talk to you,' she said, her face serious. 'After your operation the doctor told me you might have some problems with your periods. They might be every other month because your right ovary is gone.'

'Does that mean I can't have babies?' I asked.

'We don't know,' Mum said. 'Your other ovary might take over but we'll have to wait and see.'

Afterwards I lay on the sofa feeling dazed and unsure of what was going on. I'd already had a lot of contact with babies as my brother Stephen had two daughters – Karen, three, and one-year-old Diane.

I loved being an aunty and was never happier than when spending time with my nieces. As I chased Karen around the garden and nursed baby Diane on my knee, I already had that warm, maternal longing to have a baby.

My recovery after the operation was slow and it was made even worse when I suffered complications because of an abscess on the wound. It was ten weeks before I could return to school.

I was a year into my education at grammar school but, despite being confident and bright, I found the strict regimes of my new school hard to deal with. I'd always been top of my class at primary school but, after having so much time off, I was now behind with my work and struggling to catch up. I wasn't offered any help and if a teacher reacted negatively towards me I'd rebel against them. More than once I had a blackboard rubber thrown at me. It was a shame because if a teacher praised me I'd work really hard but being so ill left me lacking in energy and enthusiasm to prove I could do well. Instead I was lazy with my homework and made minimal effort in class.

I was never in a gang or group and, feeling like a bit of a square peg in a round hole, I rebelled in my own way, objecting to the rules for rules' sake by refusing to do my homework, change for physical education or bunking off school to stay at home and read. I'd always been a book worm and would stay up late into the night gripped by the storyline of a good book. My other passion was riding and occasionally I'd go to the local stables after school or at the weekend to have riding lessons. It was my dream to have a horse but, while my parents indulged me a lot, they drew the line at buying me a pony!

While my adolescent friends spent break times chatting about boys and fashion or fantasising about meeting their music idols, such as Marc Bolan and David Bowie, I had other dreams.

All I wanted was to leave school and be a mum. The sooner I could get married and find out if I'd be able to have a baby the better.

Over time my periods returned but the fact I only had one ovary still felt like a worrying disadvantage. My longing to be a mum only intensified when my aunt Edna, my mum's sister, had a baby boy called Andrew.

Suddenly I was spending as much time as I could at her house carrying Andrew around on my hip pretending he was my baby. I also fed him, took him out in his pram and changed his nappy. Aunt Edna didn't mind at all, having had two babies close together later in life she found having an extra pair of hands very helpful.

I was 14 when I met Mark who, in perfect keeping with the life I'd imagined for myself, would marry me and father my first child within three years.

I'd been getting off the bus and on my way to take my dog, Kimmy, to an obedience class when I'd noticed a good-looking blonde boy grinning at me as he ambled past. As I returned his smile, he doubled back to talk to me.

'What's her name?' he asked, running his hand over Kimmy's black fur.

'Kimmy,' I said as my pet licked his fingers appreciatively.

'Can I walk with you?'

'OK,' I agreed.

Mark told me he was 18 and worked at the local dockyard. He lived in Chatham a few streets from the road I'd been born in and we later discovered he'd been the milkman's boy who delivered our family's milk years before.

When I came out of the obedience class 30 minutes later I was pleased to see he'd waited for me. He even caught the bus home with me and walked me to my front door, a route that took him a fair bit out of his way.

We agreed to meet the next day, with Mark inviting me to tea at his house. Poking my head shyly round the door, I'd been shocked to find his mum had laid on a spread of jelly and ice cream as if I were someone really special.

I introduced Mark to my parents soon after and they did not appear to be bothered by the age gap until a year later when my dad, Charlie, discovered that the relationship had gone beyond a kiss goodbye at the front door. This resulted in a huge family argument and me declaring, 'I love him! We're going to get married when I'm sixteen!'

'No you're not!' Dad shouted back.

'I'm not sure who I'm more angry with,' Mum barked at Dad and I during the resulting showdown. 'You for breaching her trust or you for having underage sex!'

'It's illegal!' Dad continued. 'I've got a good mind to report Mark to the police.'

By now I was crying. 'Please don't!' I sobbed. 'I love him! We're going to get married when I'm sixteen!'

'No you're not!' Dad said. 'And you're not sleeping with Mark again.'

That was the end of the discussion for now but when I turned 16 and left school, having gained no qualifications, to take a full-time job in the newsagent where I'd worked for two years, I approached Mum again.

'I want to get married,' I said.

'You're too young,' came the inevitable reply.

'No, I'm not,' I argued. 'I want to have a baby and if I'm going to get married before that happens then I need your permission.'

I really didn't want to disappoint my parents and I continued to beg and plead until eventually Mum gave in. She loved me very much and wanted to make me happy; in turn, my dad idolised her and she could always talk him round.

With my parents' blessing Mark and I set the date for 26 April 1975 – two months after my 16th birthday. I didn't want a big fuss – as long as it was a white wedding attended by friends and family I was happy.

We chose a local church, St Philip and St James', I asked a neighbour to make my dress and chose my nieces as bridesmaids.

Back in 1976 girls often had to get married in dubious circumstances and I was proud I was doing it right.

'I'm not pregnant!' I'd tell anyone who'd listen.

But as soon as my marriage certificate was signed, sealed and delivered it was time to start making babies!

Mark and I lived with my parents for four months before moving into a new two-bedroom rented home in Lordswood, four miles from Chatham and close to where my folks lived.

We were both working and used our own money to furnish the house ourselves with furniture picked from catalogues that we could pay off monthly. I was very independent and the only things I turned to Mum for was the use of her twin-tub washing machine. I was very proud of my home and kept it spotless.

In September 1975, a month after we'd moved in, I realised that I'd missed two periods and went to the doctor. He instructed me to pee in a urine cup and return a week later, when I sat in the surgery waiting room fidgeting impatiently. Finally my name was called.

'We have your test results back,' he said. 'You're pregnant.'

As a massive smile spread across my face, I could have kissed him! I felt like I'd won the football pools. I was so happy.

My pregnancy progressed very normally, although I did suffer a bad bout of morning sickness. For weeks all it took was the chemical 'new carpet' smell at home to set me off and there were plenty of other everyday scents that instantly made me gag.

One cold, rainy, winter morning as I travelled to work on the bus, I found myself squashed up against the window. With every stop the bus got increasingly hot and steamy as more and more commuters piled on board and suddenly the stuffy smell of stale coats began to overpower me. I felt a sickness starting low in my stomach.

'Oh God, I'm going to be sick,' I thought.

There was nowhere to escape and the bus was so crowded that I couldn't even lean forward to be sick on the floor. As the bile rose in my throat all I could do was clamp my gloved hand against my mouth and swallow the contents back down again. Thankfully, I only had to endure that for a few weeks but now when the women I care for tell me their own morning sickness stories I am always transported back to that awful vomit moment!

Unlike today, I had no internet, TV shows, books or magazines to educate me about pregnancy and childbirth, and as my bump grew I didn't know what to expect. The only information I got was from other pregnant friends, who knew little more than I did.

At hospital check-ups I was weighed, measured, prodded and poked with no explanation why and I didn't think to ask any questions. All I knew was that I was having a baby and I was going to breastfeed as my mum had. It wasn't really an informed choice as all I knew was that it would help me lose weight!

If I had aches or pains I'd go to Mum for advice and I loved it when she told stories about her own pregnancies with Stephen and me.

My brother had arrived while Dad was away in the Navy and Mum, a very naive 17-year-old, had gone into hospital completely clueless as to how her baby would be born. Would it arrive via the stork or did she pick it up from the cabbage patch?

'I was in the toilets at the hospital when I asked another pregnant woman how my baby was going to get out,' she said. 'She just looked at me and laughed, before telling me: "The same way it got in!"'

I also loved Dad's story of how he'd been there to see my birth – something that was highly unusual for 1959, when men were normally banned from the room until baby arrived.

'Of course your mum started to get strong contractions half an hour after the midwife left,' he told me rolling his eyes. 'She said to me: "Quick, Charlie, go and catch up with the midwife!" so I left the house and started running up the road to find her. I ran and ran until I spotted her on her bike cycling along a road parallel to the one I was on. I was running and yelling down each alleyway but she couldn't hear me! Finally, just as I was about to collapse she looked my way and I yelled: "Lillian's in labour!"'

By the time Dad got home, Mum was in active labour upstairs and the head was already showing.

'Fat lot of good he was,' Mum said, finishing the story. 'He ran up to me, pulled the blanket over me and said, "Cover yourself up!" The doctor and midwife arrived then and your dad stayed in the room to watch his "Little Peach" being born. He was the talk of the estate!'

As my stomach ballooned, I began the highly anticipated countdown to my due date. But, to my disappointment, it came and went. I tried everything – hot baths and spoonfuls of gooey castor oil – to bring it on but frustratingly ten days past my due date, still nothing had happened.

Finally I went into hospital on a Wednesday night so I could be induced the following day. There I lay in bed stroking my swollen stomach and savouring the feeling of kicking inside me. It blew my mind to think that very soon I'd have a baby of my own.

Throughout the night I awoke feeling discomfort and twinges of pain in my back and by the next morning it was obvious that I was starting to have mild contractions. But when I told the midwife she seemed uninterested.

'Let's get you off for your bath,' she said. 'Then we can induce you.' In hindsight, it's obvious to me that I was showing all the signs of being well on my way to a natural labour and I really didn't need to be induced. I should have got up out of that bed and walked out, but being young I did exactly what I was told.

I had been denied breakfast and I was starving! Denying women in labour food and drink, except for sips of water or sucking on ice chips, was normal practice in 1976, although there was no evidence to support doing so, and this continued until I was a qualified midwife. However, as it has since been discovered by research, women who were starved in this way would smuggle in food. I had been given a box of chocolates the night before by a visitor and, without the midwife knowing, I gobbled chocolates every time her back was turned.

At 10am I was taken to a small room for my induction where I lay on my back on the bed as the midwife put a drip into a vein in my arm.

'There you go. Shouldn't be long now,' she said. 'I'll be back in a bit.'

Although at first my contractions seemed mild, by 11am they were coming on in great whopping waves that shocked the life out of me. I gritted my teeth silently and gripped the bed bars as each contraction hit with the feeling of an intense, deep period pain – only 100 times worse.

All the pain was in my back, probably because I was lying down the whole time. I didn't know then that it would be easier if I got up and moved around. I just followed the midwife's lead and accepted that lying on my back was what I should do.

After a while Mark arrived wearing a gown and a mask that could not hide the huge Cheshire Cat grin on his face. I was also pleased to see the smiling, youthful face of a student midwife, who was only a few years older than me and seemed a lot warmer than the more senior midwife who'd hardly cracked a smile all morning.

Although she chatted to me between the contractions it still seemed like an eternity of pain.

'How much longer?' I whined to the senior midwife the next time she checked my heart rate.

'We can't answer that,' she said matter-of-factly.

Whether she took my question to mean that I couldn't cope, I don't know, but at some point she walked in with a tray and gave me an injection.

I had no idea what it was but soon after I began to feel very sleepy and docile. I found out later that this was a sedative called pethidine which is administered for pain relief.

While I am sure the midwife had my best interests at heart, I didn't need the drug and I hadn't asked for it. You would never hear of a labouring woman being given it unsolicited these days but in the 70s that's what they did and you didn't argue.

After five hours, I began to feel the pressure of the baby's head. It felt like I was going to burst in two but I was so drugged up that the memory is hazy.

'Come on now, push,' the midwife instructed as I gripped Mark's hand.

Just after 4pm I finally squeezed my baby out into the midwife's hands. As I flopped back on the bed, I heard a lusty cry and lifted my head to see my baby.

'It's a boy,' the midwife said as my heart soared. 'He's eight pounds two ounces.'

'What are you going to call him?' the student midwife asked, smiling.

'Matthew,' I said, sharing the name I'd had picked out since the age of 14.

My face fell as the senior midwife walked off with my son, placing him in a glass box cot by the wall – ten feet from me.

'Please bring him close to me,' I asked.

When she ignored me and walked out the room, I turned to the student midwife with pleading eyes.

She hesitated before walking to the cot and wheeling it over to the bed.

'Just a minute, mind,' she whispered. 'We need to get you both to the ward.'

As everything and everyone else vanished from my consciousness, I lay on my side, eyes transfixed to Matthew's face who was wrapped up tight in a sheet. He was mostly bald with blond wispy hair and had a brown birth mark on his foot. Every part of my body ached to hold him. Straining from the bed I leant over and stroked his face.

My cooing was interrupted by a dishy male doctor who'd come to give me some stitches. My legs were put in stirrups and, to my acute embarrassment, he set to work on me.

'Do you sew at home?' I quipped, trying to cover up my embarrassment with chatter as I always do. Finally he'd finished the job and I got back to gazing at Matthew, as the student midwife watched on smiling.

Many years later I bumped into her in Tesco and we chatted about my labour.

'I never forgot you,' she said. 'I always remember how calm and happy you were. You are the only mum I've known to be laughing and getting excited between contractions.'

With the stitching completed, it was time for me to be taken off to the postnatal ward. As they wheeled me along the corridor I felt completely euphoric.

'Look what I've done!' I wanted to shout. It felt like I was the only woman in the world clever enough to have done something so amazing. It probably had a lot to do with my surge of post-birth hormones!

I was quickly settled into the postnatal ward while Matthew was taken off to the nursery.

'When do I get to see my baby again?' I asked a passing midwife.

'Tomorrow morning,' she said firmly.

I was awake all night listening to the sounds of the babies crying in the nursery and wondering if it were my son. Finally at 6am, after being woken from a light sleep with a cup of tea, I heard the distant rumble of all the cots being wheeled into the ward by the midwives as they pushed one in front and one behind and, after checking the name cards, delivered the babies to the new mothers.

All the mums on the ward were sat up in bed in collective torture as they awaited the telltale sound of a cot heading their way.

Finally Matthew was placed in my arms – perfect and beautiful just as I remembered from the night before.

This was my first chance to breastfeed Matthew, almost 14 hours after his birth, and it only occurred to me years later that my baby must have been given formula milk overnight without my permission. It's no wonder that breastfeeding took such a nosedive at that time.

With Matthew in my arms, I bared my breast and sat patiently while a midwife held his head and pushed his lips against my nipple. It took a bit of coaxing but eventually he latched on. I was ecstatic!

I was to spend a total of ten days in hospital, with every moment of my post-baby recovery following a strict protocol.

'Put that baby down in the cot, you'll spoil it,' a midwife barked at me whenever I was caught cradling Matthew for too long.

Any visitors, including Mark, were instructed to queue at the nursery door to peer through the glass at Matthew, and the first time his father held him was on the way home in the car.

As I sat in the back next to my little family while my dad drove and my mum sat in the front gazing back at all three of us, I felt so proud.

I loved motherhood and found Matthew to be a good, easy baby. He was a contented, happy little soul who slept for hours and put on weight easily.

Nineteen seventy-six was one of the hottest years on record and Matthew grew into a responsive, happy, chubby-cheeked fat baby. He was very low-maintenance and I could easily leave him outside in the shade on a blanket with his toys. Sweetly, he was too scared of the grass to crawl off the blanket so if I popped inside for five minutes I'd return to find him exactly where I'd left him – sitting on his blanket playing contently.

I didn't have a car so I used to walk everywhere with Matthew in his big navy pram. Mostly I would go to Mum and Dad's or visit friends I'd met at mother and baby classes who'd had babies around the same time.

Sadly, although I loved being a mum, it turned out that I wasn't so keen on being a wife and, from the moment Matthew was born, he got my sole attention. Mark never showed any jealousy but I think that after a while the novelty of having a baby began to wear off for him. He was only young himself after all. As inevitably happens with many teenagers who think their first love will last forever, I was growing out of my relationship and when Matthew was one year old I realised that I just wasn't in love with his father anymore. It may have been irresponsible of me as a wife to walk away so easily but it was a normal reaction for a teenager. All around me my friends the same age were falling in and out of love. Granted they weren't married with a baby, but my mind was made up.

All I wanted was to be on my own with my baby and, as my interest flagged, Mark started spending more time with his friends, drinking and partying. Eventually he moved out, leaving me content to be at home with my baby. It wasn't long before I heard he'd met someone else, which made me feel a bit less guilty at pushing him out. I always knew deep down that I had forced his hand and that he'd really loved me and had been hurt by my actions.

As a single mother I made ends meet by working evenings in a pub and employed a gaggle of local teenagers to babysit while I was at work.

We spent a lot of time with my two nieces Karen and Diane, who were now ten and eight, and they fussed over Matthew the way I had fussed over them when they were little.

We'd go for days out to the funfair or the beach, and then they'd come back to mine and bicker over who got to pick Matthew up, dress him or help me bath him.

I never felt like I was missing out on a normal teenage life as it was all I had ever wanted and most of my friends were young mums, too. I was in my element being a mum to my growing son and kept busy doting on him throughout the day and working at night while he was asleep in his cot watched over by a babysitter.

Every night I'd return home to gaze at my beautiful son lying peacefully in his cot and making little contented sighs as he slept. Motherhood and the miracle of babies never failed to enthral me.

Chapter Two

'Do you need to be somewhere?' my friend Carol asked, with an amused look on her face. 'Only you keep looking at the clock when I'm talking to you!'

'Oh God, sorry!' I replied, shamefaced. 'It's weird, but I think I might be having contractions.'

I was 39 weeks and three days pregnant with my second child but, despite feeling a familiar sensation throughout my body that I would definitely associate with contractions, there was no physical pain to speak of. As a midwife I now know that painless contractions, while rare, are entirely possible.

'Virginia!' Carol scolded, her eyes wide. 'Do you want to give birth on the kitchen floor? You need to call the hospital.'

'OK,' I agreed, leafing through my address book and picking up the phone to dial the number of the labour ward.

'Come in and let us look,' instructed the woman on the end of the line after I'd explained my strange predicament.

Pacified that I was doing the right thing, Carol got up to leave, just as Dave, my partner, walked in the door.

I'd got to know Dave, a handsome regular at the pub I worked in, as he'd wooed me across the bar inviting me for expensive dinners and driving me around in his shiny Jaguar car.

He moved in with me towards the end of 1978 and, although he embraced being a stepdad to Matthew, he'd been keen to have a child of his own. I'd duly stopped taking the pill and in April 1979 my pregnancy was confirmed.

But now, as a strange, painless sensation came and went, I wasn't entirely convinced my labour had started. Despite the conversation I'd had with the midwife, I didn't want to seem silly, so, stalling going to hospital, I went upstairs and tidied Matthew's bedroom and then did some vacuuming. Finally, Dave and I headed over to my mum's to drop Matthew off.

While we were there, I continued to faff around making Dave a toasted sandwich and then reluctantly said goodbye to Matthew.

'I suppose we'd better go,' I said.

I arrived at the hospital at 7.20pm, walking through the swing doors of the maternity ward to be met by an anxious-looking, mumsy midwife in her early 50s.

'Where have you been?' she chastised gently. 'We've been ringing you at home. Can you come with me, please, so we can get you checked over. The waiting room is over there,' she indicated to Dave.

Lying on my back in an examination room, I stared at the ceiling as the midwife poked around.

'You're well on your way,' she said, continuing to move her hand around inside me.

Whatever she was doing felt very uncomfortable. There was a sensation of something popping and warm water trickled between my legs.

'There you go, dear, I've just broken your waters,' she said.

She hadn't told me what she was going to do or asked permission, and I didn't question her judgment!

'You go and have a bath and then I'll take you to a room,' she said.

Getting off the bed, I waddled into the adjoining bathroom where the water had already been running and the tub was almost three-quarters full. With the midwife's help, I climbed in and lay in the warm water.

'I'll be back in a bit,' she said. 'The cord's here if you need it.'

Lying in the bath I couldn't get comfortable and as the pressure built in my pelvis I had a massive urge to go to the loo. After a few minutes, I couldn't stand it any longer so I gingerly heaved myself out of the tub and plonked down on the toilet next to the bath.

'Stupid woman!' I suddenly thought. 'I don't need the loo, the baby's coming!'

Panicked, I pulled the emergency cord. Why had that bloody midwife left me on my own?

'Everything OK, Virginia?' the midwife asked, peering around the door.

'It's happening!' I said, gripping on to the safety rails next to the toilet.

'Right, let's get you into bed,' she said, helping me up.

Grimacing in pain, I followed her down the corridor to the birthing room. It was small and pokey just like when I'd had Matthew. Inside Dave was waiting for me.

'OK, love?' he asked.

Helping me on to the bed, the midwife handed me a mask attached to a cylinder.

'Here's the gas,' she said. 'I won't be long.'

Before I could protest, she was walking across the room and I moaned as a horrendous pain tore across my lower abdomen and I felt the urge to push. I tugged on the cord.

The look of irritation as the midwife did an about turn at the door was remarkable.

'I want to push!' I gasped. By now it was just past 8pm.

Seeing as I'd only had a few contractions since she'd broken my water I could tell she wasn't convinced.

'No, don't push,' she said examining me. 'You're not ready.'

I tried very hard not to push but my body was not letting me stop. Everything was happening involuntarily.

'Oh my God, what's that smell?' I heard Dave ask as my baby's head began to crown. Despite being very preoccupied with the pain, I knew exactly what he was talking about. I was mortified. Like so many women who give birth, the contents of my bowels had been forced out as the baby's head pushed its way through me. Now I know it is a perfectly normal function, but at the time I felt humiliated.

For that reason I now make it my mission to joke about it with my expectant mums so they don't feel embarrassed. 'Midwives get excited when they see a bit of poo,' I tell them. 'It means the baby will be here soon.'

Sure enough, within 15 minutes I'd pushed out a beautiful baby boy – just one hour after casually strolling into hospital convinced I was making a fuss over nothing.

He was 7lb 11oz and the perfect birthday present three weeks before my 21st birthday.

'I can't believe it, I have a son!' Dave said, as he studied our baby, his eyes watery with emotion. 'I've got to get down the pub and tell everyone!'

'OK,' I agreed, secretly disappointed that he didn't want to stay with us a little longer. That night Dave certainly wet the baby's head – even knocking on our neighbour's door to share the news at 3am.

With Dave gone, I sat up in bed while a midwife sat beside me giving my baby a bottle of formula milk.

'It will keep his blood sugar up then you can have a good sleep,' she explained. Once again, the Virginia of today would have told her in no uncertain terms to stop what she was doing and hand the baby over but, not knowing any different, I just accepted it.

I got to hold my baby for a few minutes before he was put back in his cot and we were both moved to the ward. This time, I was relieved to find that babies were allowed to stay with their mothers. When, four hours later, he was hungry again I was finally able to breastfeed him for the first time, before settling him down all floppy and content in the cot next to my bed. I was thrilled to have him by my side to pick up and cuddle at any point in the night. It was so different to three-and-a-half years earlier when Matthew had spent his first night away from me in the hospital nursery due to the strict routine then.

I was in hospital for five days but during that time our little boy remained nameless. Prior to the birth I'd been convinced that I was having a little girl and had picked out a long list of names for a daughter. So when my little boy arrived unexpectedly I had no idea what to call him.

Matthew, however, now three-and-a-half, had a very clear idea.

'It's going to be a brother called Andrew!' he'd exclaimed to my bump weeks before. His enthusiasm had prompted Dave and I to exchange amused smiles. Andrew was Matthew's little friend from down the road that he adored playing with.

When Dave brought Matthew in to see me the following day, he was a toddler on a mission. Dashing on to the ward in his little tartan coat with a fur collar, he ignored me and ran straight up to the cot. Putting his hands on the side and pulling himself up, he peered in.

'Hello, Andrew!' he exclaimed.

Two weeks later and now back home, our baby still had no official name.

'What are we going to call him?' I asked Dave.

'He's called Andrew!' Matthew interrupted, staring at the two of us with a confused look because we still weren't catching on.

'OK!' I laughed, looking at Dave as he shrugged in agreement. So Andrew it was.

We settled into family life but while Dave was a good dad who absolutely adored his son, he still wanted his busy social life. For a good while I tried to keep up, playing the role of hostess with the mostess as we held raucous dinner parties for our friends until the early hours of the morning. I always dreaded the thought of leaving the dishes until the next day when I'd have two boys under four demanding my attention. So, as Dave snored, I'd start to tackle the washing up, sometimes finishing up around 6am – just as Andrew was waking up for a feed.

While I loved Dave, our relationship was beginning to become volatile and to add even more stress to it, I was worried sick about my father. After a difficult few years suffering and overcoming a series of minor heart attacks and bypass surgery, he had just suffered another huge heart attack.

When I'd taken the boys to see him in hospital most recently, I'd been cheered to see him laughing and joking and seemingly his old self. Halving a peach for the boys to share, he beckoned them over to the bed.

'You see this?' he said, holding the stone of the peach in his hand. 'They're going to use it to replace Grandad's broken heart.'

As Matthew scrunched up his face in disbelief we'd all laughed. It was great to see him more cheerful, and we were all looking forward to the day he would be home again.

When we left I was so preoccupied with turning around to wave goodbye that instead of walking into the corridor I walked into a cupboard. Red-faced and smiling, I gave a last wave, my heart warmed by the sight of Dad, Mum and my brother all crying with laughter.

The last thing I'd expected was to get a call at 2am that same night from Mum.

'Your father is bad, come quickly,' she urged me.

Panicked I turned to wake Dave but he was not in bed next to me. When I rang the pub to ask him to come home he was not happy but hearing my explanation he agreed to come straight back. I then had to beg my brother to collect me on his way to the hospital as I had no way of getting there.

We arrived to find that it was too late. The doctors had been unable to revive Dad after another massive heart attack. He was only 52.

Dave eventually arrived at the hospital having called his parents to babysit but when we returned home in the early hours of the morning he fell into a deep sleep.

Feeling bereft and truly alone, I sat up and wrote a poem dedicated to my dad. As I watched the sun come up I knew that nothing would ever be the same again but his death also made me strong where Dave was concerned.

Four months later, I asked him to leave.

Being a single mum of two was challenging but, determined to be resourceful, I started a business with a fellow young single mum, my friend Cheryl, and soon we were raking in the cash – as kissograms!

It was hardly conventional but the craze was just taking off in America and Cheryl, being slim with dark hair and olive skin thanks to her Anglo-Indian heritage, was the opposite of my more voluptuous figure, blonde hair and green eyes. We were sure we had something to attract all tastes.

Before I got the business up and running, I'd been claiming benefits as I couldn't cover the mortgage by myself. I knew that working as a kissogram would mean an end to my £42-a-week payout which was a bit worrying, given I had two little boys relying on me. But then I heard about a Government grant which meant that I could apply for an 'enterprise allowance' which was a cash incentive for people to come off benefits and start up a business. All I needed was £1,000 in the bank and a good idea and I'd get £40 a week for the next year – that was only a little less than I was getting in benefits.

So I borrowed £1,000 from my mum and went along to a group meeting at the local DHSS where everyone who wanted to apply sat together to talk through ideas with the view that we could support each other.

Everyone was sitting in a circle like at Alcoholics Anonymous and reeling off their business plans. After we'd heard about a pine furniture shop, a window-cleaning business and a cake-baking venture it was my turn to speak.

'Hello, my name is Virginia,' I began. 'I have a thousand pounds, I've opened a bank account and I want to be a kissogram!'

Everyone howled with laughter.

'Well, you fit the criteria,' agreed the man from the DHSS and soon I was using the first instalment of my allowance to splash out on tight corsets, basques, stockings, garters and sexy high heels.

Initially we'd created another side to our business dressing up as furry characters like Kermit the frog and Fozzie bear for kids' parties and it was at one such party at a local hospice that we got talking to a local journalist.

Thinking that we were talking 'off the record' we told her all about our kissogram business and the grant we had so cleverly secured.

I went home thinking no more about it but that night at around 10pm I got a frantic call from Cheryl.

'The *Sun* newspaper just called – we're going to be in tomorrow's paper,' she said. 'On the front page!'

I immediately rushed up to Cheryl's house and we cried together. What had we done? After a feverish night's sleep I got up the next morning to find Cheryl on my doorstep clutching a copy of the *Sun*.

'*Strippers get Government Money*' screamed the headline.

'You are kidding me,' I said, hands shaking as I read the wildly suggestive story that, reading between the lines, made us sound like hookers.

We were mortified and worried about what everyone would say but then the phone started ringing off the hook and we were inundated with clients. We couldn't have asked for better publicity!

Getting paid to dress up and surprise people like Jeremy Beadle did on *Beadle's About* was lots of fun and when the story was followed up locally people realised exactly what it was we were really doing and we had the last laugh.

Seeing as the business brought in plenty of cash and I could work flexible hours it meant I could really enjoy time with my boys, who were now six and two. I'd often pop in to see Mum who lived nearby after dropping Matthew off at 'big school' which was within spitting distance of our home.

I loved being a mum and seeing my boys grow and develop. Matthew was my little laid-back dreamer, who was very well-behaved and happy and loved reading his *Mr Men* books. Meanwhile 'Andy Pandy', as we called him, was a good little boy who wouldn't go anywhere without the blue blanket he'd had from birth. The rag of a thing was always stuffed in his mouth or dragging on the floor as he ambled around. On the odd occasion he got distracted, I'd quickly grab it and wash it but I hoped he'd eventually grow out of wanting it. Andrew did indeed part ways with 'blue blanket' when he was three and even placed it in the dustbin himself.

'My blue blanket gone now,' he announced as we both watched from the window as the dustbin men took it away.

'Yes, it's gone,' I agreed, my heart in my mouth.

Although we had a couple of teary moments, he seemed to understand that was the last he'd see of it.

'Dustbin men got my blue blanket,' he told me forlornly a few days later.

Thankfully, by the time he started going to nursery near Mum's house, the blue blanket was long forgotten.

As the boys grew older they became good friends, playing nicely together and being very affectionate towards each other. I was proud of them and loved dressing them in matching red baseball jackets.

After my own stuffy school experiences I was keen not to put too much pressure on them when it came to their education so instead I encouraged them to be free spirits. But that's not to say I was a pushover – and Matthew still remembers the strife he got into when he was brought home by a policeman aged seven!

That afternoon Matthew had asked if he could go out to play but, before he could hurtle out the door, I'd stopped him.

'Put a jumper on,' I instructed, wrestling a thick woolly sweater over his head as he pulled a face.

Within a few hours he was back standing shamefaced on the doorstep as the constable filled me in on his misdemeanour.

After kicking a ball around for a while it transpired that Matthew and his friends had crept under the wire fence of a nearby dairy determined to steal the bottles of chocolate milk they'd spotted sitting in a crate ready to be loaded on to a milk float. But as they carried out their crime with whoops of excitement, the dairy security guard had spotted them.

'Oi, you lot!' he'd bellowed.

The boys had immediately scarpered but Matthew, being the youngest and smallest, was bringing up the rear and, as he scrabbled under the fence, his jumper caught on the wire, leaving him flailing like a fish out of water until the security guard hauled him out and handed him over to the local bobby.

I was very angry about it and made him stay in for a week as punishment but, to this day, it has remained an amusing family story – particularly given Matthew's cheeky complaint at the time: 'It's your fault, Mum! You made me wear a jumper!'

Within a couple of years, Cheryl had opted out of the kissograms but I continued to run the business by myself, employing six other staff, including a plus-size lady and three Tarzan men to cater for all different tastes. Sometimes I'd leave the boys sleeping in the back of the car, run in, flash my lingerie, sing happy birthday and then dash back to the car.

Mum used to come for dinner on a Sunday and spend time with us all or sometimes she'd come with me to a kissogram job, laughing at whatever silly routine I was pulling off and defending me to the hilt should someone dare to say something derogatory.

'Oh, it's just a bit of harmless fun,' she'd say.

When Dad had died I'd been very worried about her but, about a year later, Mum got talking to a man of a similar age at the graveyard; he was tending to the grave of his wife right next door to where Dad had been buried. The man introduced himself as Rudi and offered Mum a lift home. From that point on they were inseparable, going to meals and the pub together. It was touching to see her having a new lease of life after she'd been so sad. My whole family were very fond of Rudi and if ever I got stuck with the job, he and Mum would drive the kissograms around for me.

It was a fun time for me and, comically, my business afforded me and the other kissograms a bit of a celebrity status locally – including free entry to nightclubs.

'Are you the kissogram girls?' the bouncer would ask, unclipping the rope on the door and ushering us past the queue of envious-looking revellers.

One such night in August 1984, with the kids in the safe hands of a trusty babysitter, Cheryl and I headed to a nightclub in Gillingham, Kent. I was having a great time dancing to 'When Doves Cry' by Prince in my tight leather trousers and glittery boob tube when I noticed a guy who was dark and good-looking chatting to Cheryl.

She beckoned me over to the bar.

'Hi, I'm Barry,' the guy introduced himself. 'And this is my friend Ron.'

'Hi,' I said, smiling at Ron, who was aged around 30, tall and blonde. He had a tooth missing in the front of his teeth but it didn't deter from his good looks.

He didn't say very much but smiled and offered me a drink. The four of us propped up the bar for a while before heading back to Cheryl's place as a group to carry on the party.

I'd thought Ron was pretty aloof and uninterested but at 4am as I made to leave he surprised me by asking for my phone number. In actual fact, he was just a bit shy and when we went out as a foursome a few nights later I decided that I liked him.

Things were soon serious and after a few months Ron moved in. It was not a huge love affair at first, with hearts and flowers, but after the turbulent time I'd had with Dave it felt calm and relaxed. Ron was quite content for me to be the boss in the relationship and there were no rows.

Within a year we started to discuss getting married and Ron was eager to spend the money he had saved in the bank on a beautiful opal engagement ring surrounded by diamonds.

'Nice going, Liz Taylor!' my brother Stephen joked as we planned the wedding for 4 August 1985 – my own parent's wedding anniversary.

I was determined that this time I'd found 'the one'. I was going to make this one work if it killed me. I was a hopeless romantic and, in truth, I just wanted what my parents had achieved – 35 years of loving and passionate marriage. My mother had confided to me that the week before my dad died they'd made love in the car in a country lane. I wanted to look back when I was older and say I'd achieved that sort of love.

Thanks to my decent wage from the kissogram agency I was able to afford a lovely wedding with all the trimmings. My bridal gown was a beautiful dress of pale pink satin covered in a white see-through lace that shimmered as I walked and all the men wore top hats and tails, as did Matthew and Andrew who were my page boys.

Before the ceremony, Mum came to the house to help me get ready.

'You've obviously had a word with the boys,' she said laughing. 'They're sitting down there on the sofa in their top hats and tails like statues!'

The day turned out to be comical in so many ways. First of all, we battled through the rain, and then, after my brother had walked me down the aisle flanked by my two nieces, who were my bridesmaids, the vicar accidentally splattered me with saliva as he addressed the church animatedly during the ceremony. Finally, as we posed for photos around a gorgeous Tudor house, the calamity was completed as Ron picked me up and hit my head on a beam.

We were happy and, keen to add to our happy family, I fell pregnant within three months of the wedding. But, this time, my pregnancy was far from easy . . .

I was 24 weeks pregnant when I started to bleed. Panicking, I immediately called up the hospital who asked me to go straight in. Once there, I was taken to a ward and put into bed.

'We need to put you on bed rest,' the midwife told me. 'We'll organise a scan for you to make sure the placenta is not detached.'

I lay there terrified, wondering if I was about to go into premature labour. What I didn't know then is that this happens to a lot of women who go on to have perfectly healthy babies.

Although the scan revealed that all was well, I was to go through this worry four times in total before everything began to settle down finally at 35 weeks pregnant. I eventually went into labour after once again having my waters broken manually.

Third time around my baby was lying back-to-back and the positioning caused me even more agony than the eye-watering contractions did.

'Mum, it is so painful,' I winced to my mother who was supporting me through the contractions.

'Why don't I give you some pethidine?' the midwife suggested. 'It will help you relax.'

'No,' I said, as I continued to cry out in pain. 'I want to do it without.'

Having experienced labour both with and without painkillers I knew that I did not want pethidine again. While the pain was acute, I knew that pethidine would quickly make me feel docile and out of it. Six years had passed since I'd given birth to Andrew but I still loved the fact that his birth was so clear in my mind. I could recall sitting up afterwards feeling completely awake and alert – whereas with Matthew there were times when it was all a bit of a haze.

As I continued to wince in pain, I caught my midwife looking at a colleague who'd just come into the room to assist.

'Are you sure you won't have some pethidine, Virginia?' she said softly. 'It would make it a lot easier for you.'

As I shook my head Ron grabbed my hand. 'Maybe you should listen, Virginia,' he said. 'They do know best.'

This was by far the worst thing my husband could have said to me during my labour. Women in the midst of giving birth need to feel supported and when Ron sided with the midwives over me I didn't have the strength to stand my ground.

'OK, give me the bloody pethidine, then,' I snapped, now too weary to fight. Instead I watched, dismayed, as the midwife sunk a needle into my thigh and injected the strong relaxant drug. Before long, I started to feel very sleepy and my memories after that are clouded and sketchy.

Later, when I had trained as a midwife, my outrage at being bamboozled into taking that painkiller was only strengthened. I began to understand the way positioning during the labour can both ease and aid the mother without the need for intervention – what those midwives actually needed to do was get my backside off the bed. By being upright or leaning forward, I could have relieved the pain and encouraged my baby into the anterior position ready for birth. Unfortunately this was still a time when midwives had been taught that lying on your back was the accepted way to give birth so I wasn't given the choice.

In the end, my labour was quick and five hours after it all began I gave the final push and my baby slipped from my body. The room was eerily silent.

'It must be a boy,' I thought. Ron and my mum knew that I'd been aching for a little girl and were probably scared to disappoint me. But as I gingerly lifted my head I was alarmed to see my baby, the little girl I wanted, looking limp and pale. She wasn't breathing. After quickly cutting the cord, they whisked her out of the room.

Looking back now, I strongly believe that the pethidine played a part in my baby's poor condition. It is well documented that pethidine can cause breathing problems after birth because of its depressive effect on the baby's respiratory centre and the risk of this only increases the nearer to birth the injection is given. In short, I should not have been injected with it just two hours before my baby's birth.

Thankfully, as I heard a shrill cry, I knew everything was going to be fine. Soon a smiling midwife returned holding out my crying daughter to me.

'Give her to Mum,' I said, watching contentedly as Mum carefully took my baby in her arms and gazed in wonder at her newest grandchild.

'Aren't you beautiful,' she cooed.

After a short cuddle, Mum leant down to pass my daughter to me.

'Hello, Sophie,' I whispered softly as I held her close for the very first time.

As the pethidine began to wear off, a real euphoria set in. I loved my sons dearly but having a baby girl after two boys was a dream come true.

That night I sat alone in the hospital nursery staring at her as she fed from my breast and admiring every detail; her masses of dark hair and the prettiest face imaginable. As the radio played softly in the background, I cried tears of joy as the words of love in 'Lady In Red' by Chris De Burgh summed up my feelings for Sophie.

* * *

Ron was a very good father who loved spending time with his daughter, giving her baths or helping to spoon-feed her when she started to eat solids, and Matthew and Andrew, who were now aged ten and six, also loved their little sister. Seeing as they were a bit older, I could leave them to dress themselves and play nicely while I fed Sophie or changed her nappy. Matthew was adorable fussing over his baby sister and keeping her amused with toys or pulling funny faces. Matthew had always loved little children and whenever we went on holiday he'd end up being the Pied Piper with the kids trailing behind him. He always thought of new and entertaining ways to make his sister laugh and when he was 12 he often took two-year-old Sophie on short bus rides around the estate and back again for 10p.

With kissograms more popular than ever, I was doing a roaring trade. I'd snapped back into shape after breastfeeding so was doing kissograms myself at weekends, as well as having plenty of employees to send out. It was easy money and with more disposable income than ever before, I decided to buy a horse called Mouse, a six-year-old mare with a short-cropped mane that was prickly on my hands.

I arranged to keep her at a local stable run by a girl called Melanie and her parents. Melanie was 24, five years younger than me, and as my riding instructor she really encouraged me, even persuading me to enter a competition or two.

I loved spending my free time at the weekends riding Mouse while Ron put Sophie in a child seat on his bike and took her cycling with the two boys. Unfortunately, Mouse, being young, was skittish and, after suffering a couple of long walks back to the riding school having being thrown off, I decided to sell her and buy a more ploddy horse called Bob. He was better schooled and calmer.

Looking after a horse took a lot of effort, especially with three kids, so I made an arrangement with a girl called Caroline, who was 29 and worked as a hairdresser locally, to do half the work of mucking out and feeding Bob in return for riding him.

It was during my time at the stables that I got talking to Melanie's parents.

'I know you!' her dad immediately told me, his brow furrowed as he tried to place me.

There were giggles all round as we made the connection and he pulled out a photo of his retirement party a few years earlier. There I was dressed in my lingerie and sat on his knee!

Somehow we got round to talking about how Melanie's parents were selling their home along with some land. Ron and I had been talking about building a new house with some money we had saved and it seemed like the perfect spot.

'There's plenty of room,' I said to him. 'Maybe we could build two houses and sell the other one for a profit?'

So after getting a loan from the bank and a large amount of help as always from my mum we sold our house, and moved into a caravan on the site in 1989. We demolished the old house on the land and the building work started.

We had such fun living in that caravan and watching the houses go up. The boys used to push Sophie around in a wheelbarrow and they all played in the mud.

Because I was always working weekend nights, we got into the habit of going out for breakfast the next morning and we would visit as posh a place as we could find, driving to hotels all over the area for sumptuous feasts on Sunday mornings.

By now the boys, aged 13 and 9, were growing taller by the day and Sophie was a beautiful little girl with angelic blonde hair and a gentle and calm disposition. I used to love dressing her in beautiful clothes and she would proudly walk along beside me, well aware of the admiring glances and 'Ooh's and 'Aahh's that came her way.

It was around this time that I sent her photo to a child modelling agency. They snapped her up and Sophie appeared in TV commercials, magazines, on the front of board games and even in a party political broadcast for the Conservative party up until the age of eight.

All three of my children were easy and well behaved, and I was very proud of my family and how I had brought them up.

In 1990 I found myself back in hospital when another baby was born – but this time it didn't belong to me.

While pregnant with Sophie and for many years after, I'd been plagued by haemorrhoids. I'd rank the pain as even worse than childbirth – and that's really saying something!

Eventually when Sophie was four I could take it no more and I was admitted to hospital to have them removed. Following the surgery, I had five days recovery in hospital.

As my discharge day approached and I lay in bed feeling increasingly bored, I got a call on the ward. I hobbled over to the nurse station wondering who it would be.

'Virginia!' a voice I immediately recognised as my friend Melanie from the riding stables filtered down the line. 'I'm in labour! Can you come and see me in the maternity unit?'

'Of course!' I agreed. 'I'll be there in a minute.'

'I'm going to visit my friend,' I told the nurse as I wandered off in my nightie. 'I won't be long.'

Ever since Melanie had fallen pregnant with her first child she'd been keenly firing questions at me and I was touched she wanted me to visit her now.

Arriving at the labour suite, I found Mel sat in a rocking chair with beads of sweat on her forehead tucking into a meat pie dinner! She had always loved her food and I almost laughed at the sight of her eating away in between her contractions. How times had changed since the days when I'd been starved!

'Can you stay for a bit?' she asked.

'Of course,' I agreed.

Although she seemed relieved to have me there, as her contractions got stronger Mel also wanted complete silence.

'Shhh!' she'd hiss, throwing her boyfriend, John, and me a look if we as much as whispered to each other.

At one point the heart monitor made a cracking noise as her baby moved. 'Shut up!' she snapped as John and I shared a sideways look of amusement, biting our lips as we tried not to laugh.

Observing Mel's noise irritation was a good insight when I went on to become a midwife. During births I'd always be sure to ask women if they were comforted by silence or preferred gentle conversation in the background. This is also one of the reasons I find two midwives at a birth counterproductive – they chatter.

Being careful to be as quiet as possible, I pulled up a chair next to Mel and gave her my hand to squeeze while I mopped her brow with a flannel. Soon I, too, was grimacing in pain as a writhing Mel kneaded my fingers with an iron-like grip as she endured each contraction.

Although the atmosphere was intense, I didn't feel pressurised or nervous. I enjoyed supporting my friend and felt like I was meant to be there.

After about six hours rocking in the chair, Mel's discomfort was visibly increasing.

'Why don't you try on your knees?' the young midwife suggested. 'The gravity will help bring the baby down.'

I watched intrigued as she helped Mel off the rocking chair and into this new position.

Sure to the midwife's word, Mel immediately appeared to be coping much better and in no time at all we were all watching as a small head began to appear in between her legs. Crouching down, the midwife braced herself to catch the baby. When I think about it now, it was very forward-thinking of the midwife in question.

As Mel's baby slipped out into her caregiver's hands, I watched in wonder as the midwife passed the baby up to her. The look of love that came over her face was just beautiful. I stood back smiling as John moved nearer and the new little family embraced with happiness.

The midwife seemed delighted, too, until with a swing of the birth suite door, the atmosphere changed in a second. There stood in the doorway was the midwife in charge of the ward whose frown at the blood on the floor spoke volumes about what she thought.

As she left I caught the midwife's eyes and for a silent second we shared a resigned look. It was a feeling that I would come to know well myself during my own years as a student midwife. Sure as night turns to day, you can guarantee a judgemental senior midwife will walk into your birth suite when you've just overseen your messiest birth of the week.

My thoughts were interrupted as I glanced at the clock. It was now long past midnight and I'd been gone for seven hours! Oops! Heading back to the ward I was met by a bemused-looking nurse.

'We thought you'd done a runner!' she said.

As I got into bed, the warm thoughts of the amazing day I'd just experienced were fresh in my mind. Was that a familiar broody feeling stirring inside me?

'No, it's only the excitement,' I told myself. 'You've just got your freedom back!' Sophie, now three-and-a-half, had just started nursery, while Matthew, aged 14, was fast becoming a young man with ten-year-old Andrew hot on his heels.

Did I want to experience birth again? No, no, surely I didn't?

Chapter Three

I grabbed my stomach protectively as I listened to the drama unfolding behind the curtain in the bed next to mine.

Now aged 32 and 34 weeks pregnant with my fourth child, I'd been admitted to hospital on bed rest the day before after I'd noticed some blood mixed in with a watery fluid.

I'd been married to Ron for five years when I'd fallen pregnant for a fourth time. Despite my broodiness over Mel's baby there had been no discussions about having more children, but I was not on the pill and we weren't exactly being cautious so it wasn't that big a surprise when I fell pregnant just three months after being Mel's impromptu birthing partner.

By now we'd moved into our big new house with four very spacious bedrooms. Work continued on our home and on the second property we intended to sell and I was all ready to welcome my fourth baby into the world.

I'd been admitted to the nearby Maidstone Hospital on a Friday as the midwives thought my waters might have gone and were keeping me in for observation. With Ron back at home looking after the kids, having visited earlier that day, I was being kept company by my friend Caroline from the stables who had promised to look after Bob in my absence and was now visiting me. We could both hear what was going on on the other side of the curtain, where a midwife was examining a woman who had been admitted in labour. Caroline and I looked at each other and I grabbed for her hand as we heard the scrape scrape sound of the fetal heart monitor as the midwife moved the probe over my neighbour's abdomen.

'Come on!' I willed silently as the noise went on for what seemed like an eternity.

'What's wrong? Why can't you find my baby?' the woman cried out.

'I'm going to get someone else to try,' we heard the midwife say.

'No, no, don't go!' the woman cried out, in breathy pants, her voice frightened and pain filled. 'The baby. It's coming now.'

The bell sounded as the midwife called out for someone to bring a wheelchair.

'This lady needs to go to a labour room now!'

There was a flurry of activity as more midwives ran to assist.

'There's no time, quick, get a delivery pack,' another voice rang out.

Tears streamed down my cheeks as we listened to the woman screaming in pain and fear.

'My baby, my baby,' she called out.

I could hardly breathe as her child was born to an eerie silence. The curtain still shielded my eyes but as the woman howled and sobbed I knew there was no hope. Her baby was stillborn.

Hearing that poor baby die right beside me, my stomach churned with anxiety for the wellbeing of my little girl I was expecting. In early 1991, technology was changing and I'd been excited to find out the sex of my baby with a scan at 25 weeks. I knew how happy I was to be having another daughter – it was unfathomable to think that joy could be crushed in one awful minute.

Sobbing into my hands I felt like my heart was breaking too.

'Is Virginia in the bay?' I heard a voice ask. I recognised it as

Alison, a community midwife who I'd first met when I was expecting Sophie. I'd seen her the day before and had happily filled her in on my news.

'Quick, someone get her moved,' she urged.

As a healthcare assistant arrived to wheel my bed to a different bay, I tried to wipe away the tears streaming down my cheeks. Caroline walked behind me, a look of abject sorrow on her face.

'I think you should try and get some rest now,' she told me when I finally stopped crying. 'I'll give you a call tomorrow.'

But as we hugged goodbye I suddenly felt something strange.

Getting out of bed, water gushed all over the floor. Whether it was due to stress or just inevitable, there was no doubt my waters had really broken this time – six weeks before my due date. It was far from ideal.

All the next day I remained in hospital awaiting the telltale contractions but, when my body showed no desire to go into labour, I was told I should be induced.

If labour doesn't commence after the waters break there is a slightly increased risk of infection but at no point were my options explained or was I given a choice. I would have been perfectly within my rights to refuse the induction and sit it out for a few more days but, not knowing any better, I did as I was told.

So Monday morning came and Mum took over the care of the kids at home so Ron could be with me at the hospital. I was induced and my contractions began quickly but after a short while of intense drug-induced contractions I knew that something wasn't right.

Having had three babies previously, I was aware that the baby's heartbeat, which was bleeping out on the monitor next to me, sounded slow. I rang the buzzer to call a midwife.

'Her heartbeat doesn't sound right,' I told her. 'Look at the monitor.'

By now my baby's heartbeat was at 60 beats per minute when I knew it should be around 120. I stared at the monitor willing it change but it was not recovering. I began to cry.

Seeing me looking, the midwife turned me over in the bed to face the other way. Then she called over a colleague.

'I can still hear it,' I cried. 'Stop trying to hide it from me.'

So they turned the sound down and whispered in hushed voices.

'The baby is in distress,' one explained. 'We need to take you for an emergency caesarean.'

By now several midwives had rushed over to get me ready for surgery.

Fifteen minutes after my contractions began I was being hurtled down the corridor for surgery with Ron running behind. Years later, when I worked at that same hospital I often had to take women along that corridor to theatre. I'll never forget that feeling of panic and fear as I prayed that Courtney, the daughter I'd already named, would be all right.

As we arrived in the operating theatre, I turned my head to see Ron standing there helpless, his cheeks tear-stained. With no time for an epidural so I could be awake for the operation, I was instantly put to sleep.

When I awoke from the operation, which felt like just a few minutes later, I was lying on my side and the pain was unbearable. I felt like I was breaking in two but my first thought was Courtney.

'My baby,' I cried out.

'Virginia, the baby is fine,' the recovery nurse told me gently.

'How much does she weigh?' I asked in a hoarse voice.

'Four pounds eleven ounces,' she replied. I decided that wasn't bad for six weeks premature.

Years later, after seeing many unnecessary caesarean sections where babies were born in perfect condition after being diagnosed with fetal distress, I decided to write off for my notes so I could read all the details of what had happened in my case. I was shocked to see that Courtney had been in a very bad condition at birth. She'd needed to be resuscitated and had been slow to respond. After discovering this I wish I'd had the information at the time to make a choice about whether I wanted to go ahead with the induction or not. While many mothers are induced and go on to have perfectly healthy babies, there is an increased risk of the baby experiencing fetal distress. This is because the hormone drug syntocinon can cause very strong contractions over and above normal labour which in some circumstances can compromise the oxygen supply to baby and cause distress.

With Courtney having been whisked off to Special Care before I'd come round, I didn't get to see her that night. Instead, a well-meaning midwife propped a Polaroid photo of my baby up on the bedside table.

Gazing as this ugly-looking scrap brought me no comfort. I could not relate to the baby in the photo. While the intention was good, I wanted my baby in my arms or you could forget it.

The next day I got my wish and when I was wheeled to see her in her incubator I was instantly hit by a rush of love. Holding her for a minute or two she looked so tiny and it was then I noticed a little cut just under her eye. It looked like a scratch and no one mentioned it but it never healed and there is a scar there to this day. When I eventually got my medical notes I discovered it was a scalpel cut.

While I was recovering from the surgery I was put into a side room and that night, still groggy from the operation and painkillers, I fell into a deep sleep.

At some point during the night I awoke with a start. The room was still dark but someone was yelling. Blinking my eyes I could just make out a large woman stood in the doorway, the light from outside illuminated her frame making her look big and menacing. I realised with a start that it was the midwife who had started the night shift just before I drifted off.

'Will you shut up crying!' she snapped. 'You're frightening the rest of the women on the ward.' Then she turned on her heels and stomped down the corridor.

My heart racing, I lay in bed trying to work out what had just happened. I had no recollection of crying but I must have been sobbing in my sleep.

I was so embarrassed that I'd caused a commotion and also really shocked that the midwife had shouted at me. Up to that point I'd viewed all midwives as angels so to have one be so mean when I was recovering from surgery and clearly vulnerable was surprising. It still breaks my heart now to hear about mean midwives. What happens to women in labour stays with them for many years and can have a monumental effect on their future experiences of childbirth.

While Courtney remained in Special Care for another day, I was moved to the main ward where I sheepishly apologised to the other mums for scaring them in the night.

'Don't be silly!' one mum in her early 30s scoffed. 'The only thing that frightened us was that silly mare waking us up by shouting at you. We were worried we'd be in the firing line next!'

Later that morning they wheeled me to see Courtney where, once again, I gazed at her lying there with a feeding tube up her nose. They were feeding her formula but no one had asked my permission to do so! As a midwife placed her in my arms and I let her nuzzle at my breast, my heart softened and once more the feeling of utter love and devotion flooded my body.

In hindsight, I wish I'd been asked to express some milk for her. By this time expressing milk was common practice and I had even bought an expressing machine for when I came home. It should have been easy to do in hospital but in that particular hospital at that time it was viewed much simpler to give the baby formula. But the fact was I was an experienced breastfeeding mother and I could have easily provided the best milk possible for my premature daughter. Thankfully, by the time I took her home four days later, she was guzzling away on my breast greedily.

As our first week at home flew by Courtney seemed in good health but yet was always sneezing.

'Do you think she's allergic to something?' I asked Ron as I gently wiped her nose for the umpteenth time.

Finally at three weeks old Courtney did a colossal sneeze and spotting a bogey in her nose, I pulled it out. I was alarmed as she squealed in pain.

On closer inspection I saw that I'd dislodged a fingernail-size piece of sticky tape, now stiff with mucus and which must have been a remnant of the tube she'd had in her nose to help her feed in Special Care.

I was so angry. How had it been missed at the hospital? What if she'd got an infection? Didn't her tiny body have enough to cope with without someone leaving plastic in her airways?

I immediately strapped her in the car seat and drove the ten miles to the hospital. Marching to the postnatal ward I insisted they check her over.

When I told my community midwife she seemed bemused. 'It wouldn't have done her harm,' she said, clearly judging my concern as an overreaction. But I found her comment dismissive and it just added to an overall feeling that my experiences of Courtney's birth clouded any good memories I'd previously had.

However, I am positive that it also shaped the kind of midwife I became myself. Even if a woman is being what some might consider high maintenance or difficult I try not to lose my patience. You can choose to be kind or nasty and I always try to be kind.

After ten years of roaring trade, kissograms were becoming old hat. The business was slowing down and it just wasn't supporting us financially any more. In the year since Courtney's birth, we'd seen our hopes and dreams shattered when the 1992 recession hit, interest rates rocketed and we'd been unable to sell the second house we'd built. The repayments on the two houses were crippling us and I was losing sleep trying to work out the solution while Ron seemed oblivious.

Having sold my horse and cut back on any excessive spending I'd become exasperated that, despite our dire straits, Ron was not making as much of an effort as I felt he could and should to boost the family finances. With our debts spiralling by the day, we ended up selling both houses for far less than we'd expected so we could pay off our bank loan and buy a smaller house.

While our finances were now manageable once more, the kissogram business was still only limping on so I began to wonder what I should do next.

I was doing the ironing when I decided I wanted to be a midwife. As I pressed folds into Ron's trousers, my thoughts wandered to my dwindling business and the career I would have liked to pursue had I made more of a success of school.

As I wracked my brain thinking about all the things I could have done, all the different ways to make a living, I glanced at Courtney fast asleep in her cot. Even now I could still recall the special feelings, smells and the anticipation of joy for each pregnancy. It saddened me to think my own experiences of child-birth and breastfeeding were now over.

'I should have been a midwife,' I thought wistfully as I reached for one of the boys' school shirts. 'Should have been?' I suddenly corrected myself. 'What are you on about? You're still a young woman. It's not too late.'

I could still be part of the birthing process. I could help other women to have babies!

Walking into the kitchen I flicked through my address book to the page where I'd kept the number for the community midwives. I dialled Alison's number, she was the community midwife who'd helped with Sophie and I'd seen her at the hospital when I'd had Courtney. Although I hadn't spoken to her much since, she'd always been very sweet and attentive.

'I think you'd make a great midwife, Virginia,' she said. 'But I'm inclined to tell you not to bother. There just aren't any jobs once the students qualify these days.'

Funnily enough, the situation is exactly the same now 22 years later. But it didn't put me off and instead I started to make loads of phone calls to find out what I needed to do to become a midwife.

I spent the whole day calling universities, asking for application forms and bracing myself to jump through a lot of hoops before I got to where I wanted to be.

The nearest place to enrol on a direct entry programme to train to be a midwife was too far away so my only viable route to midwifery was to do a three-year nursing diploma at Canterbury Christ Church University and then try to specialise.

When I told Ron about my big plan he was neither enthusiastic nor against the idea.

'All right, do it if you want,' he shrugged.

With not a single qualification to my name, I spent six months brushing up on my Maths and English in order to sit an entrance exam before I could enrol. Every night as Matthew swotted for his GCSEs I sat down beside him and studied hard, too.

The work paid off and having passed the exam I was given a place to study for my nursing diploma starting in spring 1993. Now I just had to work out how to juggle my studies with family life. While Matthew, who at the age of 17 was a metal-music-loving teenager, and Andrew, who was 13 and loved his designer clothes and pop music, were old enough to be trusted, there was still six-year-old Sophie and two-year-old Courtney to organise. While the boys got on brilliantly, my girls were partial to fighting like cat and dog. Thank goodness for Frankie, the 21-year-old au pair from Hungary I'd employed to help Ron look after the girls.

My nursing training began in March and I was pleased to see a few other mature students as well as youngsters. I enjoyed walking along with my big pile of books feeling like I was revisiting my school days. Only now I was the class square sitting at the front answering questions and shooting my hand up.

After a few weeks at university learning the theory, we were sent out on placement to get some hands-on experience.

A few days beforehand I'd stood in front of the mirror pulling a face at my unflattering maroon nursing scrubs.

'This is the most unattractive thing I've ever had to wear,' I complained to Ron, as I examined the shapeless line of my new work outfit. Compared to the 'naughty nurse' outfit I'd worn as a kissogram a few years back, the reality was far from the fantasy.

In a stroke of luck my first placement as a nursing student was with a community midwife from All Saints' in Chatham – the hospital where I'd had my babies. I was to shadow Val, an Italian lady in her 40s, who struck me as a no-nonsense type of person – friendly and efficient – as she went on her rounds.

As I awoke on the morning of my first placement, I was dismayed to find that the head cold I'd been warding off all week had hit me with a vengeance. In usual circumstances I would have gone back to bed but, not wanting to make a bad impression, I swallowed a couple of strong antihistamines thinking they might help my symptoms and headed out the door.

As planned I met Val at the hospital and she drove me five miles to the first call of the day. The door was opened by a woman in her late 20s, who took us into the front room where her baby was asleep in a basket.

Sitting next to Val on the sofa, I listened quietly as she talked for a good 20 minutes about what the mother should expect and asked questions about the past couple of days.

The room was warm and stuffy and I found I was stifling the urge to yawn. A few more minutes passed and as my eyelids drooped I pinched my thigh as hard as I could, hoping the sensation of pain would keep me awake. It worked for a minute but then my head felt all heavy again and I'd momentarily drift off twitching in my seat and then opening my eyes wide in the hope of fake alertness.

Any hope I'd had of disguising my predicament was lost as I felt Val stiffen next to me and any further sways of fatigue were met with a sharp nudge of her elbow.

The moment we left the house and the door shut behind us she had it out with me.

'What was that?' she asked furiously after making sure we were safely out of earshot. I got the feeling she thought I was an uninterested student.

'I'm really sorry, I'm not very well,' I said. 'I didn't want to call in sick so I dosed myself up. The medication has made me drowsy.'

'Well, you'd better go home,' she said. 'You're no good to me like this.' She dropped me home en route and I headed upstairs to bed feeling shamefaced.

After two days of rest, I was feeling a lot more human and rejoined Val on her rounds travelling from house to house checking on mums and babies. It was interesting driving all over Chatham going from appointments at huge, lavish houses to small, pokey council estates and encountering families of all different nationalities.

I'd noticed that Val usually took her coat off when we entered a house but on one visit to a particularly smelly, dirty house she kept it on and seemed to be sweltering as a result.

'Why didn't you take your coat off?' I asked once we were back in the car.

'Because I don't lay down my coat in a place where you wipe your feet on the way out,' she said with a wry smile.

After a fleeting insight into life in the community, I moved to the maternity unit, working in the same ward where I'd given birth to the boys and Sophie.

This time I was shadowing a midwife called Ellie, a pretty woman in her 30s with olive skin and dark hair who was really nice and made me feel like an important part of the team.

On my first morning she called me into a birthing suite where a young African woman of about 18 was lying on her back in active labour with her first child.

'I'm just going to examine you,' Ellie said as she stood beside the bed and lifted up the young woman's hospital robe. The woman didn't reply, instead her eyes darted to her husband, who looked at least ten years older. He nodded in agreement.

As I stepped closer to observe, my eyes fell between her legs and I took in a sharp intake of breath. For a split second I registered Ellie's silent shock, too. Where the woman's clitoris and labia had once been there was dark scaring. While I'd heard of genital mutilation occurring in some cultures, I hadn't expected to see it firsthand.

'You're fully dilated, Abi,' Ellie said composing herself. 'Shouldn't be long now.'

Within minutes the woman's face crumpled in pain and she inhaled the gas in short, sharp breaths indicating another contraction was well on its way.

'Do you think you can push?' Ellie said softly, squeezing her hand.

Panting with discomfort, Abi once again looked at her husband.

'Jeez,' I thought. 'The poor woman is waiting for his permission.'

While he didn't seem overbearing, it was clear she'd been brought up to be submissive.

As the labour continued I noticed Ellie was plotting points on a graph. It looked like a maths equation.

'What's that?' I asked.

'It's a partogram,' she said. 'I use it to monitor the progress of the labour, recording the mother's pulse, her cervical dilation, the fetal heart rate and then the contractions. That way, if anything goes out of the parameters of normal we can do something to bring her back.'

At the time I thought it sounded wonderful but with the benefit of knowledge and hindsight, I no longer think it's appropriate to a normal labour. The individual progress of a woman depends on so many other factors. Some women may dilate at a certain rate only to slow down for a few hours and pick back up again. Yet the active management of birth has seen women having their waters broken to speed things, all because the partogram indicates that her cervix isn't dilating fast enough. In my view, treating every woman's labour as if it were an exact science, rather than a mixture of science and art, is counterproductive and can just cause further complications.

Watching Abi my heart went out to her as she stifled every cry of pain, eyes always on her husband, despite having no control over the contractions wrestling through her body.

Even when the baby was born she made no sound. She also passed up the chance to hold her baby boy, honouring the cultural tradition that the paternal grandfather would be the first to hold her child and conduct a prayer.

Keen to be respectful, I left the room as Ellie covered up Abi and beckoned the woman's father-in-law inside. And that was to be the only birth I'd get to see during my short placement. When it came to observing births, the student midwives on the ward always took priority over the student nurses as they had to witness a certain number of births as part of their training.

Instead I spent the rest of my placement either in antenatal or postnatal, making myself as helpful as possible by fetching and carrying, getting clean vases for flowers and offering to help new mums to change their babies' nappies.

Whenever I saw a student midwife dashing into a birth suite (in their much more flattering white dresses) I felt very envious. I longed for the day when I, too, would get to learn everything there was to know about midwifery.

In the interim I was getting on well with the other students who laughed at my humour as I pretended to be reluctant to go home to reality.

'Oh no, now I have to look after Courtney,' I'd sigh dramatically as our classes or shifts ended, causing the other students to chortle in mock shock. To be fair there was never a dull moment where my youngest was concerned. Before I had Courtney I'd been one of those mothers who secretly felt a little bit smug when I saw children throwing tantrums in the supermarket. After all, it only took a look with my three and they'd do exactly as they were told. But then my cheeky, spirited Courtney arrived and I understood that sometimes there is just nothing you can do to stop your toddler having a meltdown in the middle of Tesco!

One of her funniest moments came as all the family joined my brother Steve and his family for Sunday lunch at a nice pub.

Courtney, who was two-and-a-half at the time, was sitting at the end of the table in a high chair under my watchful eye. I'd been pleasantly surprised that she'd been well-behaved throughout the meal and had eaten her food with no fuss.

As the waitress came around and took dessert orders, the majority of the table ordered apple pie. 'Would you like that hot or cold?' the waitress asked each time.

When she got to Courtney my little treasure had decided that she wanted ice cream.

'And I want it hot,' she announced, causing a great laugh around the table.

The chatting continued until a short time later the dessert arrived, the apple pies were dished out and then Courtney was presented with her ice cream.

Suddenly there was a scream of rage as she threw her spoon down the length of the table and bawled. 'I said I want it HOT!'

I could hardly tell her off for laughing.

My nursing diploma took three long and difficult years to complete. I did not want to care for sick people and while I had great compassion and determination to do my best, it was not in my blood. I found some of my placements very harrowing and hated seeing how some of the elderly patients were forced to live.

One particular day I had been doing a placement in an old people's home when I saw an old lady with dementia being fed. Her food had been liquidised but, after three spoonfuls, she clenched her false teeth shut not wanting any more. I was horrified to see a care worker prise her mouth open and force the food in.

I drove home crying and as I walked in the door my old friend Melanie was sitting in the kitchen waiting for me.

Since having her daughter, Alicia, three years earlier, Mel was pursuing a career change, too, and training to be a physiotherapist. She'd often come round with Alicia who was all the encouragement that Courtney, a year younger and mischievous enough already, needed to run riot. One day I even found them under the table squashing chocolate cake into the carpet. Despite Courtney's regular stints in the corner on her 'naughty chair' the girls are still friends to this day.

'Virginia, what's wrong?' Mel asked as she saw my tearful face.

As I told her Ron came to the kitchen door and listened.

'Oh my God, that's awful,' Mel said.

But Ron had an altogether different reaction. 'Oh, I hate old people,' he concluded. 'They should all be put up against the wall and shot.'

I just looked at him speechless. I felt completely disgusted. Not only had he failed to comfort me, but he'd come out with a comment as odious as that!

I didn't know if he'd said it to incite me but, in truth, we had not been getting on for a while. His comment acted as a catalyst in my mind, reminding me of a host of niggling worries and doubts I'd had about my marriage in recent years. I was sick of always having to be the strong one, the breadwinner, the decision-maker. Even now while training full time, it was down to me to keep everything afloat. I still had the kissogram business with a couple of girls I sent out from time to time. It brought in pocket money that just about paid for the au pair but there was hardly any profit at all.

Couldn't he just support me for once? I recalled conversations I'd had with another older trainee nurse who told me how she'd practise her presentations in front of her kids and husband while they rallied her on. Whenever I talked to Ron about what I was doing his eyes glazed over or he'd walk away bored. He never told me he was proud of me or said, 'Well done.'

We had nine years of marriage under our belt and two daughters, but how long much longer could we limp along?

'Nah, I'd rather do this on my own,' I decided. 'I need more support.'

When I called time on our marriage a couple of weeks later, Ron was heartbroken. During our ten years together I think he saw me as a bit of a mother figure. It was always down to me to solve all our problems and he could never stand on his own two feet and take the initiative. The time had come when it was me who needed the support and I just wasn't getting it.

At the same time, I decided to wrap up the business and informed the girls there just weren't enough clients. Now I had no choice but to live on my nurse's grant and benefits while I juggled a family of four children, twelve-hour shifts and studying well into the night.

Matthew was 18 and Andrew was 14, so they were more than capable of looking after themselves in many ways, but there was still eight-year-old Sophie and three-year-old Courtney who needed full-time care. The only way to achieve this was by being very organised and thankfully I had Frankie, my amazing au pair, to help. She was proving to be a housekeeper, friend and husband all rolled into one!

On a busy college day I would get up at 6am and quickly get ready. At 7am Frankie would bring the younger girls downstairs and make everyone breakfast. The boys would grab some toast and catch the bus to school. I'd leave the house at 7.30am in order to get to college by 8.45am, running round to kiss all my children goodbye before heading out the door sighing with gratitude for calm Frankie who'd stand on the doorstep with Courtney on her hip waving me off. Sophie's taxi would pick her up at 8.30am to take her to school, then Frankie would take Courtney to playschool, tidy up the house and put the washing on. She'd pick up Courtney and Sophie would come back in a taxi at 3.30pm. The boys would amble in at 4.30pm, then I'd return at 5pm and we'd all sit down to the meal Frankie had heated up.

I spent my days off shopping and cleaning and bulk cooking shepherd's pies and chilli con carne so that there was always dinner ready when I came home. The boys also had their chores, with Matt cutting the grass and Andrew cleaning the windows.

Mum helped whenever she could and was very generous, often buying lunch or doing the shopping. I also had my niece Karen who had now returned from America. She was just ten years younger than me and had recently got divorced. She was a single mum to two daughters, four-year-old Kylie and two-year-old Kathy and we'd become good friends.

I no longer had the money for elaborate breakfasts out but we had our family meal to sit down together and chat. Money was very tight but we were happy and Frankie and I ran the household like a finely oiled machine.

I was constantly tired and constantly poor but as I ticked off every passing year of my diploma my focus grew. There could not have been a woman more determined to succeed in her desire to become a midwife . . .

Chapter Four

'Please don't forget about me!' I scribbled on the back of a Southend-on-Sea postcard.

Addressing it to a lady called Moya in the admissions department at Christ Church University I smiled as I stuck on a stamp and pushed it through the letterbox. This was all part of the charm offensive to start my midwifery training sooner rather than later.

Just a few months before, having finally completed my nurse diploma, I'd interviewed to begin my midwifery training at William Harvey, the hospital affiliated with Christ Church University.

I'd been thrilled to be awarded a place – until I heard that my training wouldn't begin until March 1997. That was a whole year away.

When I'd called the admissions department I'd spoken to Moya.

'Is there any way I can start earlier?' I asked.

'I'm afraid the September intake is full,' she said. 'But I can put you on the waiting list in case anyone drops out.'

I duly took a nursing job working on the medical ward at William Harvey but I decided there was no way I was going to let Moya and her colleagues forget about me as I lingered on the bottom of their reserve list.

So every other week I'd send Moya a postcard from somewhere or other – picking up a mix of scenic or funny cards from seaside towns, country villages or the zoo.

'This is Virginia, I want to be on that list!' I wrote cheekily, or words to that effect.

I kept this up for three months until one day in June, Moya finally called.

'Your postcards have done the trick,' she said laughing. 'Someone dropped out and you're on the list for September.'

Thanking her profusely, I put down the phone grinning from ear to ear, feeling happy and satisfied that my incessant perseverance had paid off.

It was wonderful to have everything going so perfectly. I had four beautiful children, my dream career was becoming a reality and after a long single spell I had a lovely new boyfriend.

Having spent two years and the majority of my nursing training as a single mother with just my au pair Frankie for support, I'd pretty much given up on romance.

I had enough to juggle in my life without throwing a love affair into the mix but I did go on rare nights out. Occasionally when Ron had the girls, Frankie and I would dress up and go dancing. Andrew, aged 16, and Matthew, aged 19, could more than cope at home on their own. I was 36 and still attractive so I got my fair share of male attention, and one night as I danced in a nightclub I was handed a red rose by an admirer. Seeing as I was out for fun and not to meet men, I took the flower but rejected his advances.

While all this was going on I noticed another guy giving me more than his fair share of looks and the stares were so obvious I couldn't help but keep glancing back. With his long curly hair and casual dress almost to the point of scruffy I concluded he wasn't my type.

I didn't give him another thought but as I walked out of the bathroom having reapplied my lipstick there was 'Mr long hair'.

'Did your boyfriend give you that rose?' he asked, glancing down at the bloom still in my hand.

'No,' I replied. 'I don't have a boyfriend.'

'Well, if I were your boyfriend I would give you flowers every day,' he said. 'You are beautiful.'

I smiled but walked away as I was really not interested. He kept on looking, though, and eventually came over and asked me to dance. Reluctantly I agreed to one dance and as the Gabrielle track 'Give me just a little more time' came on we headed to the dance floor.

'Can I have your number?' he asked.

'No,' I said.

'Go on, let me take you out!' he smiled.

I shook my head again but all through the dance he kept on asking to the extent that it was comical.

What woman doesn't like to know she is admired but, while it felt good to be pursued, I just couldn't see myself going out with a guy who was so unlike my usual type.

However, at the end of the evening I finally relented.

'OK, I will tell you my number,' I said. 'But only once.'

'Great, let me get a pen,' he said.

'Oh no,' I teased. 'Remember it or you luck out.' Then I quickly reeled off my home phone number and walked away to get my coat.

About 15 minutes later as I was leaving the nightclub and getting into a taxi I was gobsmacked to spot him outside reciting my number over and over while asking a friend to hurry up and get a lipstick out.

As she handed it to him he quickly wrote my phone number on her arm in red lipstick. I laughed and would have forgotten all about him but at 9.30am the following morning the phone rang.

'Hi, this is Mick.' I recognised his voice immediately. 'Can I take you to lunch?'

I had nothing to do that day and so reluctantly agreed.

Later on he picked me up in a battered old car. To my dismay I saw he was wearing scruffy jeans, trainers and a leather jacket. With his long, curly hair I was almost embarrassed to be seen with him.

'Hello, Michael,' I said. 'I don't want to call you Mick as I don't like the name.'

'You're funny,' he said. 'No one calls me Michael, not even my mum.'

We had a nice day and he was great company but, by the end of the date, I was still set in my opinion that there was just no spark.

From then on Michael pursued me and I gave him the run around, shaking my head when Frankie answered the phone to him and whispering, 'Say I am not in!'

But Michael continued to pursue me and, from time to time, I'd give in. However, I continued to give him a hard time.

'You have skin like a rhinoceros,' he told me.

Although I continued to meet up with him I made no secret of the fact I was also dating another guy called Barry who I was convinced was more my type. But then one night, as I behaved quite badly flirting with Michael's friends, he got mad with me.

'I am my own person and I will speak and flirt with who I want and when I want, OK?' I told him and with that I went home to bed.

I was tucked up in bed when I heard Frankie's voice outside my bedroom door. Looking at the clock it was 2am.

'She's asleep,' she whispered.

'Just two minutes, please,' I heard Michael say. 'I want to speak to her.'

Sitting up in bed, I called out for him to come in.

'What on earth is going on?' I said as Michael opened the door and walked in with a pained look on his face.

'I love you, Virginia,' he said. 'And you are killing me. I have never been treated like this and I can't get you out of my mind. I just can't take it anymore so I am not going to bother you any longer.'

To my horror I saw there were tears streaming down his cheeks and I suddenly felt really sorry for hurting him but the fact was I just did not want this man in my life permanently.

And I thought that would be that.

However, a few weeks later as I went on a date with Barry, who was being characteristically cold and aloof towards me, I suddenly found myself thinking about Michael and the laughs we had together.

I suddenly got up and walked away from Barry and went to the phone box. Michael answered on the first ring.

'Would you like to come and pick me up?' I said. 'No more Mrs Rhinoceros.'

When he arrived, Michael lifted me up, spinning me around until I was laughing fit to burst in full view of a crowd of people.

'Just give me a little more time, OK?' I said in the words of the Gabrielle song we'd first danced to. And so began a period of time that would be one of the happiest of my life.

Three months passed quickly and in September 1996 I bounded into the classroom at Christ Church University for the nine weeks of theory and training that would be my fascinating prelude to working on the midwifery ward. Once again the disinterest of my school days was long gone as I eagerly took notes and soaked up as much knowledge as I could.

With our class time completed I'd envisaged being thrust into the thick of it on the labour ward where the cries of women coming from the birth rooms were mixed with the rapid bleeping of the fetal heart monitors and the fast pace of the midwives, rushing from place to place.

So when I learnt that my first placement would be out in the community I was a little disappointed. Recalling my time on the road with Val I envisaged hours spent traipsing from house to house unable to do anything more than watch and listen as new mums were questioned about their babies' eating and bowel habits. As it turned out, this placement would have such an impact on me that it would entirely shape my career as a midwife.

I'd been placed with an experienced midwife by the name of Paula, a plump lady with short blonde hair who was about five years older than me and never stopped smiling. She turned out to be the most wonderful mentor.

'Come on, then,' she said, after I'd been introduced to her in the staff room. 'Let's get this show on the road.'

I warmed to Paula immediately, finding her very open and friendly and a brilliant teacher. As we moved from house to house seeing the mothers she called 'her women', I liked the way she giggled her way through most situations and always saw the funny side of life.

As she called upon me to assist with all aspects of her working day she never treated me as anything other than her equal, which in turn instilled me with much confidence. Her patience was boundless – not just with her women but also with me.

If I ever got things wrong Paula wouldn't make a big song and dance, instead she'd quietly guide me. This included the time I got myself into a real muddle as I tried to take a mother's blood pressure. Instead of instructing me to hurry up, Paula simply took off the cuff, untangled it and handed it back to me with a smile. And as I watched her work, forging beautiful relationships with her mothers, I knew she was the kind of midwife I wanted to be.

I had to watch a certain number of births before I could assist a midwife in delivering a baby and Paula was keen to get me started.

'You've seen five births now haven't you?' she asked me after I'd shadowed her for a few weeks. 'It's about time you got some hands-on experience then!'

This opportunity came at a home birth where a lady in her late 20s was labouring, standing up, in her bedroom. As the head began to crown I followed Paula's instructions and knelt down next to her.

'Watch which side the baby's face is,' she told me. 'Is it facing inner thigh of left or right thigh? You know where the back is from feeling. Check to see if you're right.'

As we watched, the baby's forehead started to come into view, next came the tiny eyebrows, the eyes, the nose and finally the mouth. The baby was pursing its lips and little bubbles of thin mucus were popping from her nose.

'Once the head crowns it's a matter of minutes,' Paula told me softly. 'Get your hands into position.'

I was scared to blink as I cupped my hands with Paula's pressed gently underneath. Holding my breath I observed the gentle jolt as the whole baby's head was born and the eyes looked at us, all dazed.

'Get ready for the body now,' Paula instructed.

I could feel my heart beating in my chest as slowly but surely out came the body, little limbs falling out into the world with each progression, until I was holding a tiny newborn girl in my hands.

Passing her to Paula so she could check her over, I felt my eyes welling up. It was such an overwhelming and magical moment. That night I went home jubilant. It was the best feeling.

Paula's wonderful relationship with her mothers meant that most were more than happy for me to be there and learn, watching amused as I used them as guinea pigs to practise the art of palpation.

When I was pregnant with my own babies, I would watch the midwife place her hands on my tummy and tell me which lumps and bumps were the head and legs. 'How does she know?' I'd think in amazement.

Eventually with Paula's expert guidance I was able to locate the round contour-filled bottom of a baby resting high, almost under the ribcage at the top of the woman's uterus. I could also locate the back of the baby – sometimes on the right and sometimes on the left – feeling very clever as I'd use terminology such as LOA or LOP which, in layman's terms, describes whether the baby is laying front or back.

Alas, as Paula nodded and asked where the head was, I'd often come a cropper. Whether I used a one-handed grip just above the pubic bone or both hands, digging my fingers into the woman's soft flesh I'd find it hard to work out whether the head was engaged or not.

'I don't know,' I'd admit sheepishly.

My eureka moment finally arrived when, during a home visit, Paula asked me to examine a heavily pregnant lady called Sarah who was lying on her front room couch.

'Yes, I can feel the back,' I told her prodding away. 'Sarah, your baby is laying on the left, here is his bottom and the legs are curled up round here.'

Hovering my hand to the right hand side of her ribcage I smiled.

'I am sure you are getting lots of kicks here, am I right?'

'Yes,' she laughed. 'He is giving me a right jabbing around there.'

Moving my hands further down, I began the frustrating dig above and down into the flesh around the pelvic bone.

As a realisation dawned on me a smile spread across my face. Yes, I knew, I really, really knew exactly where this baby's head was – or rather wasn't!!

Looking round triumphantly I smiled at Paula.

'No head!' I said. 'There is definitely no head!'

Turning back to Sarah I was alarmed to see her looking deathly white.

'I think you'd better re-phrase that,' Paula said dryly, immediately patting Sarah on the hand to reassure her.

'Oh my goodness, I am so sorry Sarah,' I said. 'I meant your baby's head is deeply engaged and I can't feel the head. It's a good thing!'

'Your baby is in a lovely position now, Sarah,' Paula added, giggling as a relieved Sarah smiled. 'He's all ready to be born and you will be pleased to know he has a very lovely head!'

A week later I was just drifting off to sleep when Paula called me at 11.30pm.

'Virginia,' she said dramatically. 'The baby with no head is on its way.'

I quietly jumped out of bed and pulled on my clothes, getting into my car to drive the few miles to meet Paula, full of excitement that, yet again, I was going to see a home birth. My fellow students were all very jealous because Paula had a very high home-birth rate – well up on the other community midwives.

Sarah ended up having her baby – a little girl with a very pretty head – just after 3am and by the time we got cleared up afterwards, the sun was up and a new day had started.

'Would you be OK with heading home for a quick shower, checking on Sarah and then fitting in one more postnatal visit before we get some sleep?' she asked.

'Of course!' I agreed brightly, determined to prove that I was the keenest student she had ever had.

Racing home, I freshened up, grabbed a banana and headed back to Sarah's a good ten minutes before the agreed time. Resting my head back on the seat and relaxing as I listened to the radio I reflected on the birth the night before.

I must have closed my eyes and drifted off as suddenly the bang of a car door awoke me abruptly.

'Oh my goodness, what time is it?' I thought. Glancing at the clock on my dashboard I was horrified to see I'd been asleep for an hour.

I jumped from the car and ran to Sarah's house. The door was opened by Paula who upon seeing my face immediately started to laugh.

'Don't worry, I saw you sleeping and wanted to leave you be,' she smiled. 'You arrived before I did and had further to come. I was most impressed. Aren't you the keen one? You can make it up to me by making the teas at clinic next time, OK? Bye, Sarah,' she called back into the house, stepping outside and still laughing at my sheepish expression.

I would realise later that Paula I went far beyond what was expected of her under her NHS job description. She had the highest home-birth rate out of all her colleagues, who did not give out their own numbers to the mothers and allow themselves to be on constant call to those women. She would talk frankly to them about the importance of normality and avoidance of medical intervention and was way ahead of her time in many ways.

Sadly as time wore on, with changes in systems and the management, Paula was eventually prevented from working in this manner. At some point the Head of Midwifery decided that Paula's way of working was causing a two-tiered system that gave her women more one-to-one care than others. Instead of implementing this wonderful care across the service, Paula was forced to stop working this way. As a consequence, Paula left the profession and expectant mothers and the midwifery service lost an excellent midwife.

Attending home births with Paula I felt like I was living the dream. Whereas a couple of months earlier I'd thought I wanted to be in the hospital in a formal uniform, strutting about the labour ward saving women and babies from near-death experiences, I'd had a complete turnaround. Instead, I loved being invited into homes or sitting in gardens bonding with pregnant women or admiring their contented babies.

During a home birth, out of courtesy and comfort, I would follow Paula's lead in always removing my shoes.

Even on the occasions Paula and I would take women into hospital to give birth, I would usually kick my shoes off and leave them in the corner of the room while I supported the women.

Being at the hospital with Paula it was soon obvious that not everyone shared her ways of working. As we rearranged the room and pushed unneeded equipment outside in order to make it all feel less medicalised, I was aware of disapproving 'tuts' from the labour ward midwives.

Often Paula would leave me supporting the women while she was outside warding off doctors and an overbearing labour ward sister she'd warned me about called Joan.

During one birth, as Paula asked me to leave the room to fetch something for her, I was only too happy to oblige. Before I'd left the room, I'd completely forgotten to put my shoes back on and, as I was trotting barefoot down the corridor in blissful ignorance, I heard a bellow from behind me.

'You! Student!'

I turned to see a small, skinny, dark-haired woman who had a nose as sharp as a stick pacing towards me with an angry look on her face. 'This is MY ward and while you are on it you will dress appropriately.'

In an instant I knew that this must be Joan, the labour ward matriarch I'd heard so much about.

'Sorry,' I mumbled, looking down at my bare feet before fleeing back to Paula.

'Oops!' she laughed, when I filled her in. 'You'll learn, Virginia, you'll learn.'

During my magical time with Paula I did learn so much – how to treat women, how to speak to them and marvel at the process of birth, while all the while empowering them to be confident in the ability of their bodies and to believe in the miracle of birth.

I watched as women stood and swayed or sat and rocked or leaned over the kitchen sink, gripping the taps till their knuckles turned white. I found myself mesmerised as women's bodies stretched and widened and lumps appeared on their lower backs as bones lifted up and out of the way to make more room for the precious passenger travelling through. I saw healthy, tiny babies inching and manoeuvring their way through their mothers' pelvises as they squatted, kneeled and leaned against supportive partners or sisters or mothers.

And I'd watched these remarkable women taking control of their own birthing destiny while eating and drinking, going for walks, taking baths when they wanted, and even, on one occasion, nipping up the garden for a calming cigarette. While this was far from something a midwife should condone, who were we to disapprove? We were here at the woman's invitation in her own home.

This was her house, her birth, her body, her baby, and her experience. And while she wanted a midwife in her home to help in case she needed assistance, the midwife had no place or right to exert her own will.

I took on the responsibilities Paula allocated me with relish, always making sure the area prepared for the approaching birth was well covered so that no mess went on the carpet or the furniture. Then I would watch Paula as she sat smiling, giving gentle words of encouragement to dispel any worries the woman and her family might have. From time to time she'd jot down something in the notes about the unfolding events going on around us but mostly the atmosphere was informal.

As the weeks went by I knew that this was how I wanted to be as a midwife; this was the way I WAS going to be a midwife.

When I reluctantly left Paula's guidance and care to further hone my skills at the hospital, I was in for a shock. I had spent so many weeks with Paula, watching women give birth at home with empowerment and minimal intervention that later, when my training took me on to the labour ward I'd once eagerly anticipated, I found it very confusing as I witnessed a deluge of interventions being pushed on to women.

'I think you are going to find it a whole lot different when you go on the labour ward,' Paula warned me when it was time to move on. 'Be careful – keep your mouth shut and your head down.'

True to her word, as I entered the second phase of my midwifery training, I soon discovered that my newly acquired ideas and dreams did not fit well with the midwives I was to encounter on the labour ward. In fact, as I learnt how to perform examinations, run tests and diagnose a plethora of birthing scenarios, I also learnt something valuable and unexpected – how I did NOT want to practise as a midwife.

Rushing into the staff room on my first day, I was aware that twenty pairs of eyes looked up at me – a mix of midwives, students, health care assistants and nursery nurses.

Still unfamiliar with the layout of the hospital, I'd taken a few wrong turns along the maze of corridors and I arrived puffing and apologetic for the morning handover meeting for all the staff on incoming and outgoing shifts.

My heart sank as Joan, the ward sister I'd had the run-in with over my shoes weeks before, deliberately paused from the monologue she was giving to rest her eyes on me.

'The shift starts at seven,' she said in a slow, cold voice.

Glancing at the clock I was horrified to see that it said 7.02am.

'Really sorry, I got lost . . .' I started to splutter.

But Joan had already recommenced her speech leaving me feeling small and embarrassed. It was a feeling that would follow me throughout my training as Joan did her best to break me into a compliant, meek cog in her intervention-led midwifery machine.

Unfortunately for her, I was determined to be anything but pliable and in return she made my life hell.

As I put my growing midwifery skills into practice I tried so hard to help women to have the births they wanted. Asking myself constantly, 'What would Paula do?' I recognised that women should be able to follow their own instincts and have choices about how and under what circumstances they gave birth.

Labour and birth is not just a physical process, it is an emotional, psychological and spiritual journey that is different for each and every woman. While to some, the practicalities of wearing a clean gown that can be laundered may be obvious, it was clear that the uniformity of it puts some women on edge. For that reason if a woman expressed a desire to choose her own clothes to give birth in then I was not going to stand in her way.

One day, a few months into my training, I was helping a labouring woman to walk to the toilet in her loose t-shirt and leggings when I heard my surname screeched from up the corridor. I didn't have to turn around to know it was Joan.

'Howes,' came the cry, 'get your woman in a gown immediately.'

As I shuddered I felt the woman tense and she looked at me with questioning eyes.

'It's OK, ignore her,' I whispered as I carried on helping her to the loo and then back to her room. She stayed in her own clothes the whole time just as she wanted. Maybe I was making life difficult for myself by disobeying my senior but, when it came to what women wanted, I could never back down. In the midwives' rules it says that women should be at the centre of a midwife's care and what harm was it really doing to empower her to remain comfortable and happy?

On another occasion, the disapproving shout came just as I was pushing a tall mirror on wheels into a birthing suite.

'Where do you think you are going with that, Howes?' Joan challenged, her chest all puffed up with self-importance.

'To room six, Sister,' I said. 'She would like to see herself giving birth.'

Personally I thought it was a splendid idea but the suggestion made Joan scoff unpleasantly.

'What does she think this place is?' she snorted. 'A beauty parlour?'

My heart sank as a group of midwives sitting at the desk next to us sniggered but, without saying a word, I carried on pushing the mirror to room six, knowing it would make the woman I was caring for happy.

At home things were going brilliantly. I'd fallen totally and completely in love with Michael and it was wonderful not to have any rows or issues. Michael, who worked as an engineer for a wheel-making company, adored the boys and doted on my girls. He was full of fun, spontaneity and love and always doing sweet things to surprise me.

By now I'd sold my house and we'd moved 26 miles from Chatham to start a new life in a house in the countryside in Ashford, which considerably cut down my commute to William Harvey Hospital. Frankie and the girls, now aged 11 and six, had moved with us and Michael had let the boys move into his house in Chatham so that Matthew, who was now 21, could continue his job as a bar man at a local hotel and Andrew, who was 17, could keep up his college studies.

That Christmas Eve when I had to work, Michael arranged with Frankie to sneak the girls on to the ward to surprise me with a special stocking, and I thanked my lucky stars for all my good fortune.

As 1997 began, I worked hard at my midwifery training but over the next few months so many things about the labour ward dismayed me and it became clear to me how a pushy midwife could easily take away a woman's choice. I also discovered that, as well as facing the wrath of Joan, I'd have to deal with her tribe of 'Bison' – as

I'd come to call them. The Bison were the other senior midwives who'd realised that to get ahead and climb the ladder they should emulate their leader. Just like Joan, they ruled their colleagues and the women they cared for with a fear-fuelled authority.

Phyllis, a senior midwife who was more misguided than nasty, liked to rave about her own epidural-assisted birth. According to Phyllis, having an epidural during her own birth had allowed her to manoeuvre from watching TV to giving birth comfortably with 'no fuss'.

While many women will champion the magic pain cure of an epidural to get them through their births, it is also fact that many women who have them are too numb to push out the baby, resulting in either an instrumental or caesarean birth.

During my theory classes we'd had it drilled into us that it is a midwife's job to give all the information available – be it good or bad – to help women to make informed choices but time after time I heard Phyllis recounting her rose-tinted account to vulnerable mothers-to-be.

'Oh it's marvellous,' I'd hear her preaching as her charges navigated the most painful part of their labour. 'It will take away the pain and make a new woman of you!'

Then, instead of offering them an alternative – such as supporting them through the pain and reassuring them that it won't last forever – she would skip out of the door to await the bell that indicated the distressed woman had succumbed to her poor advice.

Seeing as we'd been encouraged by our lecturers to question other midwives about certain aspects of their practice, this was one of the points of care that I queried. In fact, I asked many questions that were pertinent to my learning. Why did the entire ward of women give birth attached to fetal heart monitors when we knew they caused more harm than good for normal woman? It was well reported that misdiagnosis of fetal distress as a result of the constant monitoring had caused an increase in the caesarean-section rate with no decrease in stillbirth numbers since the start of their use. Why did the mothers all give birth on a bed and on their backs when we knew gravity would aid them if we just got them upright?

All too often my questions and queries were met with comments of: 'That's just the way we do things here,' or 'This is the real world not all that fancy learning in university.'

I'd seen so many women give birth at home without drama or fuss under Paula's care but on the ward the opinion often came through that continuing without intervention was just 'not safe'.

'I can appreciate that some situations are more difficult than others but how on earth has the human race survived if birth is so dangerous?' I complained to Michael as I filled him in on the daily contradictions I was experiencing between what I'd learnt and what I was being told by my more senior colleagues.

'Just keep working hard, love,' he said. 'You're going to be an amazing midwife.'

One day I was assisting an experienced midwife in caring for a mother who was scheduled to have a caesarean section later that day for a breech birth.

I'd been instructed to prepare the woman for the operation and, keen to feel a breech baby, I asked if I could palpate her tummy. As I ran my fingers over her abdomen I was immediately confused. Her baby did not feel breech at all. In fact, as far as I could tell the baby was anterior with the head facing down ready for birth.

The woman's notes indicated that a scan had been performed a week earlier confirming the baby was breech but, although it was rare for a first baby to turn at 39 weeks, it was not unfathomable. I was terrified to speak out this early in my career but the thought of this woman having unnecessary surgery was far worse than any nerves.

Finding a doctor I informed him of what I thought.

'OK,' he replied. 'We'll get the portable scanning machine and take a look.'

'Yes,' he agreed as he examined the image on the screen. 'The baby has turned very late but the baby is no longer breech.'

Seeing as the woman was just minutes away from major abdominal surgery, she was delighted. This incident gave me quite a bit of pride and confidence in my own skills of palpation.

Other happy moments came for me whenever a community midwife arrived at the hospital with one of her charges and I'd be first off the mark to offer to help. These would be the times where I'd witness and learn the art of midwifery once more. It was just like being with Paula again as I watched these different types of midwives push the beds out the way and encourage the women to relax or eat when they felt like it and then squat or kneel to give birth.

While these birthing moments were precious to me, as Paula had warned I was indeed asking too many questions. I stood out from the crowd of quiet obliging students and quickly got a name for myself as a maverick.

'What progress is your woman making?' a voice demanded, making me jump as I rummaged in the store cupboard. I turned to see Joan looming in the doorway.

'She's doing well,' I said, trying not to sound nervous. 'She's eight centimetres dilated and I think her baby will be born soon.'

'She's taking much too long,' Joan concluded. 'You need to speed her up.'

By this I knew she meant putting the mother on a drip with a synthetic hormone called syntocinon, which would make her contractions stronger.

'I think she's really keen to do things her own way,' I stammered.

'If you want your washing machine fixed, you call a washing machine repair man don't you?' she said. 'Well, what makes HER think she knows better than we do? Get her speeded up, NOW!'

I was absolutely astonished by her mean attitude towards women and birth. Did she have no belief in women and their ability to give birth without intervention? She had 25 years' experience as a midwife but I would not have wanted her looking after a loved one of mine. On this day, however, I had been assigned to the woman with a mentor who was on the same wavelength as me and I knew I had her total support.

'No,' I said, returning her stare. 'It's her body and she knows it well so I will not interfere. If you want it done, go ahead and do it yourself.'

As I walked back to the birthing room, I was aware of my hands shaking. Quietly I got on with helping the mother, all the while expecting someone to come in and interfere at any moment. But no one disturbed us. When, a few hours later, she delivered her baby safely into my hands, I breathed a sigh of relief. There was no further sign of Joan and no unwanted interventions.

While a small battle was won and the woman had the birth of her choice, I am pretty sure this was the first time a student midwife had refused to do something the almighty sister Joan had instructed.

Now my card was well and truly marked.

Chapter Five

'Can you get Sam on to the bed please, Virginia,' Monica, my mentor of the day, instructed.

Inwardly I sighed. Up until now I'd developed a great rapport with Sam, a young mother I'd been caring for all morning. Now, nearing the birth of her first baby, Sam had found that standing in the corner of the room, leaning against the wall as the contractions rocked and ripped through her body was the best position for her to cope with the pain. Yet as Monica, another one of Joan's Bison, made her entrance into the room I could smell trouble.

It was normal and correct that a qualified midwife came into the room to watch the birth when a senior student midwife was assisting a woman. But the usual practice was for the mentor to stand back unobtrusively – not to interfere unnecessarily.

'At the moment Sam feels she'd like to stand,' I replied, being careful to keep my voice light.

'Oh no, you'll tire that way!' Monica intervened, walking over to Sam's side. 'Now, let's get you on to the bed.'

I knew that arguing in front of Sam would only make her stressed so all I could do was bite my tongue and listen dismayed as Monica pulled rank and Sam conformed, climbing wearily on to the bed during a break in contractions.

As Sam began to groan there was no doubt that being in this position felt alien to her. Over the next hour it was clear to me that her pain had increased and she was struggling to push out her baby.

To my dismay, Monica soon called in Phyllis, as well as a doctor, and the three of them gathered around the bed like a cheerleading team all shouting at her 'to push'.

Those of us who have been through birth will be well aware that the last thing a woman needs is frantic cries of 'push' at this time. Quite frankly the force of nature is so powerful and overwhelming that a whole army in riot gear could not stop a woman from doing so.

As I watched, Sam slowly moved her head from side to side, a look of disorientation on her face, it was clear all the noise was doing her no good at all.

'Put your chin on your chest, hold the back of your legs, take a deep breath and push,' Phyllis trilled regardless.

This type of pushing is called the Valsalva manoeuvre, or purple pushing, and really is nothing more than a labour-ward myth of how women should give birth. In fact, research had long since shown it to have a harmful effect on the baby and on the woman – the long, sustained breath-holding reduces oxygen to the baby and you are more likely to get a compromised baby.

'Keep it coming. Keep it coming,' Monica added as Sam's face flushed red with exertion.

My heart grew heavier. Earlier in the day Sam had felt relaxed and empowered. Now her birth was being taken out of her control.

'I can't do it,' she cried dropping her head back on to the bed.

Walking over I picked up a cool, wet flannel and dabbed her sweating forehead. Catching her eye I whispered so only she could hear.

'You are a strong woman, Sam,' I said. 'Just listen to your body.

Close your mind to all around you and do what your body tells you to do.'

Then as the chorus of 'PUSH! PUSH!' reverberated around the room I kept on whispering, not knowing if Sam could hear me or not.

'Breathe,' I soothed. 'Don't hold your breath. Relax and push when you need to. You are doing good.'

I continued to whisper until soon the baby emerged, wrinkled and small from Sam's tired and spent body. Job done, the cheerleading squad left the room leaving me to tidy up.

As I tidied away the birth paraphernalia I was pleased to see Sam gazing lovestruck at her baby as the stress of the last few hours began to melt away.

'Virginia, thank you,' she said looking up. 'You are going to make an amazing midwife.'

'Yes, Sam, it was lovely wasn't it?' I replied.

I didn't mention my disappointment that her birth had been kidnapped and overthrown by my shouting colleagues but Sam must have read my mind.

'I didn't listen to them, you know,' she whispered, grabbing my hand. 'I looked into your face and I switched them off. It was you, Virginia. You helped me and gave me the confidence to do it.'

As she squeezed my fingers I had to fight the lump in my throat.

'Don't let them upset you, Virginia, we know the truth,' she added as tears escaped my eyes.

Feeling guilty that she was consoling me when she should be enjoying time with her new baby I forced a smile and left her to it, walking out to the desk to write up my notes.

As I walked along the corridor I saw Monica, Phyllis and the doctor huddled in a group clearly discussing Sam's birth – and me.

'You didn't help her very much, did you, Virginia?' said Monica, giving me a long, hard look. 'Is that why you are upset? Because you realise you didn't do well? You need to give instructions to women in order to be a good midwife, not just say nothing and hope for the best.'

The injustice of her words and the nods of agreement from our two colleagues were too much. Suddenly my tears were unstoppable.

'Yes,' I replied. 'I have learnt a lot from you three today. Thank you.'

Heading to the bathroom I wiped away my tears and splashed water on my face. 'In a month's time I'll be qualified,' I reminded myself. 'No more mentors overruling the way I assist with a birth.'

Sure enough, the month flew by. I'd passed all my assessments with flying colours and, now I was qualified, I was sure things were going to be a lot easier. Heading into work on my first day as a fully fledged midwife, I joined three other former students in the staff room eagerly waiting for my allocation of the first woman I'd be helping that day.

With the handover completed I headed to room six, wanting to skip down the corridor at the delightful prospect of a Bison-free birth.

Walking into the room with a big smile I introduced myself to Susie, a first-time mother, who had her boyfriend and mum there as birth partners. She was lying on the bed in a fair bit of discomfort.

'Did you go to antenatal classes, Susie?' I asked gently.

She nodded, her face screwed up in pain.

'Well, what was the one thing they taught you in antenatal class?' I began.

'Not to lie on my back,' she puffed. This was typical of the gap between theory and practice where the most up-to-date theory was not being carried out in the hospitals due to the reluctance of some midwives to encourage women to change from more conventional birth positions. But now that I was a qualified midwife I was determined to talk to women about all their options – especially given my own lack of choice and information at my own births.

'Right,' I agreed. 'Let's get you up, then.'

Lowering the bed I helped her to stand.

'What feels most comfortable for you?' I asked.

'Like this, I think,' she said, still standing and leaning on to the bed for support.

The gravity seemed to work and before long Susie was making the familiar grunting noises that indicated the baby was coming. Things were going so well!

However, my elation was dampened with the realisation that at this point it was customary to call in a health care assistant who would be there to help should I need it. Granted I didn't have to call a mentor but some of the health care assistants could still be Bison types. I really didn't want someone looking down their nose at my methods of care but reluctantly I pressed the buzzer.

Two minutes later in walked Yvonne, a very easygoing health care assistant that I happened to like a lot. I smiled as she positioned herself by the wall, watching unobtrusively with her hands behind her back.

'Just let me know if you need anything,' she said pleasantly.

Feeling a lot more relaxed, I crouched down behind Susie ready to catch her baby.

Just at that moment the sister-in-charge opened the door.

'Oh!' she said, taking in the scene with a shocked look. 'Virginia, get that woman on the bed.' My hackles were instantly raised. I was qualified now and she was trying to undermine my autonomy and this woman's birth.

'She wants to stand so she will remain standing, thank you. I will call you if I need further help,' I replied with a firm but dismissive voice. The shocked sister then backed out the door.

Typical, I thought. She was a midwife who I got on with considerably well but she was definitely old school and I knew she never had a woman giving birth anywhere except on her back on a bed and I also knew by the look on her face she was shocked that a newly qualified midwife on her first day was catching a baby with a woman standing. But no harm done. I was elated that no one could now change the course of a woman's labour who I was caring for. It was a defining moment for me. I had arrived. I was an autonomous midwife at long last.

I continued on, sweat pouring down my neck, thanks to the pressure of wanting my first birth as a qualified midwife to go perfectly.

Focusing intently I kept my hands in place, softly encouraging Susie as, bit by bit, her baby eased out his head. The membranes were still intact and stuck to his face, squashing his features flat like a thief with a stocking stretched tight on his head.

'Here he comes Susie,' I cried with excitement. 'He looks like an upside down burglar!' Then with a gush of warm water as the membrane eventually broke, he swivelled and plopped beautifully into my waiting hands. As he let out a loud cry I could see that he was perfect and healthy. I immediately passed him through Susie's legs and up on to the bed in front of her.

Relief flooded over me. 'Yes, I've done it!' I thought.

Then I promptly cut the cord the wrong side of the clamp causing blood to squirt out. 'Oh no!' I thought as panic rose in my chest. Reacting quickly, I grabbed the cord to stem the flow and clamped it again.

I took a sneaky glance at Yvonne. Had she seen my mistake?

Yvonne to her credit didn't say a word and, as she stood there smiling, I was grateful that I had an ally – as sometimes they felt few and far between.

*   *   *

Looking at my night shift rota I sighed.

I'd be working with a midwife called Kay who had qualified a year prior to me and I'd always found her a little snooty.

I'd first worked with Kay a year earlier, when she'd been newly qualified and I had six months left as a student. That evening, on the night shift, Kay had rung the bell indicating that I should go and assist her.

'Come in, please,' she called in her plumy Joanna Lumley voice when I knocked on the door.

'How can I help?' I'd asked washing my hands and gazing around the room to take in the situation. There was a woman on the bed about to have her baby and Kay had her delivery pack open.

The instruments were all laid out on her tray in regimental order, her plastic apron was on and everything was at the ready. The most rigid of labour ward matrons of the 1970s would have been impressed.

'I need a syringe opened, please,' said Kay, hardly glancing in my direction.

As I opened the packet, took out the syringe and held it out to her I wondered why she couldn't do it herself.

'It's not sterile now, is it?' she said.

Glancing down I saw that she had taken exception to the fact that I was holding the end of the syringe. I had to stop myself from rolling my eyes. Normal birth does not have to be such a sterile procedure and a clean pair of hands can safely touch the end of a syringe without the woman falling foul of infection. But not wanting 'Miss Uppity' to know she'd rattled me I bit my tongue and just picked up another syringe and carried out the sterile procedure of opening the packet and tipping it onto her sterile tray.

'Silly mare,' I thought as I left the room.

Now a year on I wondered what delights another night shift with her would bring. But, a few hours into my shift, as I took a tea break at the desk, I heard the telltale 'click click' of Kay's shoes as she sashayed along the corridor towards me. Swinging her slim bottom on to the desk she sat down next to me, crossing her legs.

'Hi,' I said, planning to finish my tea and move on as quickly as possible. But as Kay looked around and then leaned in conspiratorially, I wondered what she was going to say.

'Goodness me,' she whispered in her cut-glass accent. 'I just saw a doctor with his fingers so deep inside a poor woman's vagina that I'm surprised he didn't give her an orgasm.'

As I spluttered into my tea and coughed till my eyes watered, I could not believe what I had just heard.

Well, with the ice well and truly broken we went on to share a few more stories of the outrageous things we had witnessed and heard while assisting doctors who were less than woman-friendly. Then we moved on to the 'Bison'. It was reassuring to hear Kay had had her own share of run-ins with Joan.

'Your woman is making a lot of noise,' Kay mimicked as she told me how our ever-sympathetic leader had accosted her in the corridor. 'That's probably because she's having a baby,' Kay added as we both rolled our eyes.

After laughing and chatting for about half an hour I realised I'd thoroughly enjoyed our conversation and the respite from the stress of a busy working shift.

Kay was far from the stuck-up midwife I initially thought her to be. The confidence with which she dealt with the Bison astounded me and I began to do an about turn and admire her as a midwife. In fact, she was also a lot of fun. And right now I needed all the friends I could get . . .

'The thing about Virginia is she's not a very safe midwife.'

I could hardly believe my ears as I heard Monica making some rather shocking statements about me as she loitered by the desk with another midwife. The pair of them clearly had no idea I was in the office next door writing up my notes and able to hear everything.

'Have you heard how she's been caught walking women who've had an epidural?' Monica continued, clearing loving a captive audience.

As I sat seething I knew exactly what she was alluding to – and how wrong she was.

A few months earlier, before I'd qualified as a midwife, I'd had yet another dressing down by Joan.

My 'crime' had occurred after I'd found a mother sitting in a wet bed with soggy sheets all crumpled up under her.

'Do you think you could stand for a moment?' I'd asked. She'd had an epidural but was able to move her legs.

'Yes,' she'd readily agreed. So, in order to get her comfortable, I'd asked her husband and mother to help support her as I got her out of bed and replaced the sheets. Minutes later I'd helped her back into a clean and comfy bed. Gosh, how reckless of me.

On another occasion I'd had the audacity to do the same for a lady who was struggling to use a bedpan while slumped in bed. Once again, after being careful to see if she had feeling in her legs, I got her out of bed with assistance and sat her on the bedpan on the chair next to the bed. Her husband and I then left the room to give her some privacy.

Unfortunately these 'incidents' had filtered back to Joan who'd scolded me for 'breaking procedure'. Then she called me into a meeting with my college tutors and the Head of Midwifery.

I'd sat there astounded as Joan insisted that I'd 'endangered' these women in my care.

I was so upset by the unfairness of it all that I'd stomped to the car park feeling completely hard done by. But as I crossed over to my car, I spied the chief anaesthetist Dr Ralph strolling towards me. Suddenly I had an idea.

'Dr Ralph,' I said. 'Can I have a word with you please?'

'Sure,' he said.

'Great!' I continued. 'I wanted to ask if, in your opinion, it would be OK for a woman who'd had an epidural but had feeling in her legs to be mobilised for a minute or two while for example she is transferred to a chair or a sheet under her is changed?'

'Yes,' he agreed. 'If she can support herself then there is nothing wrong with that.'

Feeling vindicated, I got into my car safe in the knowledge that I had his clarification that what I'd done was perfectly OK and safe.

But now, hearing my colleagues gossiping about me just a few months later angered me. That sort of poisonous chit chat on the ward could have serious repercussions for me when I'd done nothing wrong.

So later, when I saw Monica in the corridor, I asked her to accompany me into an office. She looked bemused but duly followed me in.

'I've heard what you've been saying about me walking women who've had epidurals and that I'm unsafe,' I immediately challenged.

'I never said that,' she lied, looking indignant. 'Who told you that?'

'I heard you say it myself,' I replied, watching as her cheeks flushed red. 'By the desk. Earlier today.' Now I had her attention. 'For your information I spoke to Dr Ralph and it's perfectly safe to get a woman up if she has feeling in her legs.'

'In my day, we were told you can't do that,' Monica replied, a defensive tone in her voice. 'In my opinion we should keep women in beds.'

I rolled my eyes knowing she would never back down but as I left her standing flustered in the room, I was glad I'd stood up to her.

* * *

Aside from the snide comments from some of my colleagues, my working life on the ward was getting easier. Day to day I got on very well with the majority of midwives I worked with and I loved being in the position of empowering the women I cared for to give birth in the way they wanted. It is a shame that a few people can make life so bad for the rest of the women and staff because most midwives are wonderful caring women doing their best in a difficult situation. Many of the midwives I met then I know to this day. But much as I enjoyed my job at the hospital I had my heart set on working in the community.

I wanted to be a midwife like Paula, looking after the women in my care with love and attention and helping to facilitate the birth plans they had their hearts set on. Throughout my student years and from the first day I'd qualified I'd been very vocal that this was my dream and passion. Everyone knew I wanted to be a community midwife and I'd assumed that when an opening arose my enthusiasm would put me first on the list. The last thing I expected was for that dream to be handed to the three girls who'd qualified at the same time as me while I was overlooked.

The first I knew of it was when I went to a handover meeting on a Friday.

Suddenly there was talk of the new role my colleagues would be taking on as they sat there, clearly feeling awkward. I knew then that it had been deliberately kept hush, hush.

I found out later that the view had been expressed that if I worked in the community and didn't 'toe the line' then the GPs would complain about me – all because I'd questioned conventional practice and tried to give the women in my care lots of choices.

The irony is that within a few years all the things that I'd been vocal about, all the knowledge I'd sincerely voiced after being taught about midwifery practices that were outdated and wrong, began to be accepted. Eventually the information would seep through and be put into practice. Women were no longer kept in bed and the constant use of monitors and interventions became less prevalent.

Yet my attempt to be the best midwife I could possibly be had got me an unfair reputation as a loose cannon. Now, just over a year after qualifying, my dreams of helping women with their home births in the community were dashed and I'd hit an all-time low.

'I'm so disappointed,' I confided in my friend and colleague Kay, fighting back tears as we talked on the ward.

'It must be really upsetting,' she agreed. 'I understand why you're so down. I'd feel the same way in your position. It's discrimination.'

For the rest of the day my mind was in turmoil as I tried to work out what I should do.

Driving home in tears that evening I'd never felt so demoralised.

Reflecting on my career I couldn't believe how it had come to this. No one had made more sacrifices or worked harder to become a midwife. Had I not swotted through every bit of my theory? Given my all to the women in my care? Tried my damndest to make a difference? Yet so often I found my way obstructed and my spirit crushed.

I had made some lovely friends and got on with most of the midwives and care assistants, the ones who, like me, wanted to be the best midwives they could. But the few whose backs I had put up, the few who ruled the labour ward and certainly ruled the students and newly qualified midwives, would not let me forget what they thought of my 'different' ways, my defence of women, my rocking the boat.

It felt like they were out to get me and there was only one course of action for me now.

'I can't stay there,' I told Michael, unable to hold back the tears that evening.

'You know I will support you in whatever you want to do,' he said hugging me.

Michael had seen me come home crying so many times and knew how much I wanted a job in the community. We were interrupted by a concerned-looking Courtney, who seeing my face threw her arms around me as Sophie handed me a cup of tea.

'Don't cry, Mum,' she said.

'There are lots of jobs around,' I said. 'I'm sure I can find a new one within a month or two.'

'We'll cope,' Michael agreed. 'No job is worth this.'

So that night I typed up my resignation letter and the next morning I pushed it under the Head of Midwifery's door.

I had no clue what I was going to do or where I'd work next but anything had to be better than this.

My gamble paid off. I worked my month's notice and three weeks later in the summer of 1999, I started a new job at Maidstone Hospital – with a higher pay grade to boot.

It meant a longer commute to work but I'd be working three days a week, doing a 12-hour shift each time from 7am to 9pm. As I organised the family, Frankie as usual was on hand to look after Sophie and Courtney. My new schedule worked well and with Michael working four days on and three days off, we'd organise our shifts to have days off together where we'd do nice things like go to the beach and walk the dog.

Maidstone NHS Trust had a much more favourable attitude towards the normalisation of birth and they were the leaders in the water-birth movement with Dianne Garland, a well-known midwife writer on the subject, championing the way.

Having read Dianne's work I knew that there was good evidence that a water birth reduces the risk of intervention in childbirth and helped the mother to relax. It sounded wonderful and I was keen to get started.

'We learn on the job here,' Dianne explained when I approached her about training. 'Let me know when you find a woman who requests one and I will give you a few tips.'

Well that was it. I was on a mission.

'How about a water birth?' I asked my next woman in labour, an Asian lady called Reena.

'What would that involve?' she asked as her mother sat there looking shocked.

After I explained, Reena readily agreed and it wasn't long before I'd got her settled in the water in the peaceful lagoon room.

I was eager to do everything as per the guidelines and asked another midwife to support me as it was the first water birth I had attended as a qualified midwife, with my only other experience having been watching Paula assist a woman this way more than two years ago.

Reena was having her third baby and soon enough it was clear that her waters had broken as a cloud of straw-coloured fluid, speckled with particles of white creamy vernix from the baby's skin, floated up all around her.

It wasn't long before the baby was crowning. Peering closely I could see that the baby was a reassuring mauve colour, the chin was clear of Reena's perineum giving a good indication that there was plenty of room for the shoulders.

Then, with only a few pushes, the baby was released into the water. Reaching in I grabbed the tiny baby boy and brought him to the surface to meet his mummy. We all watched awestruck as he blinked, squeaked and spluttered his way to a big breath before emitting a comforting, loud wail.

That night I went home proud as anything. It felt so exciting to be entering this new phase in my career in a new place with new midwives and birthing methods. I loved it.

After that I always offered the lagoon room to mothers in labour.

One morning on an early shift I was given the handover for a lady called Petra who'd requested an epidural.

'Petra, why don't you get off that bed and get in a tub for your pain?' I asked.

Groaning in considerable discomfort, Petra wasn't in a hurry to go anywhere, but with some encouragement I got her up and into the water pool. Once there she seemed amazed by how much pain relief it gave her. She didn't ask for the epidural again and I didn't suggest it. Before long she'd given birth to a healthy baby boy.

Afterwards I got her settled in bed with her baby, and she looked up at me and smiled.

'Thank you for not letting me have an epidural,' she said.

Although Petra was glad I'd given her an alternative, when I've looked back at that situation I've thought long and hard about whether I was guilty of cajoling her into it a little. But I can honestly say that if Petra had insisted I would have given her an epidural. What Petra actually wanted was pain relief and although at first an epidural seemed like the only option for her, I'd offered an alternative that she was happy with.

A year into my new job I found myself reflecting on how things were going. There was no doubt that day-to-day I was loving my new job. My colleagues were nice and supportive and I loved being able to practise the kind of midwifery care that had been an uphill struggle at my last hospital.

There was just one thing that would make my happiness complete – the chance to be a community midwife. I still had my heart set on attending home births and really getting to know the women in my care. The minimum wait to become a community midwife at Maidstone was two years. Could I really wait that long?

'I love my new job but I'm still no closer to being out in the community,' I confided to Kay when she came to dinner in November 1999. 'I've been thinking about doing independent work but I don't think I'm brave enough to do it on my own.'

Over the past few weeks I'd been reading up about independent midwives who worked outside the NHS and were hired by mothers to give continuity of care from the day of booking until up to six weeks after the baby was born. Independent midwives assisted their clients every step of the way, supporting them wholeheartedly as they gave birth at home – or wherever and however they wanted.

'Why don't you give Sharon a call?' Kay suggested. Sharon was a midwifery lecturer at Christ Church University who also worked as an independent midwife.

Taking Kay's advice I did indeed call Sharon who invited me to a meeting of independent midwives later that week which was being held at The Royal College of Midwives in London.

From the minute I walked into the room I felt such a buzz. There were all these women just like me talking about the medicalisation of childbirth. It was amazing listening to a group of women who really wanted to make changes.

'I feel really inspired,' I told Sharon at the end of the meeting. 'And I'm definitely going to read up more about working independently.'

All the way home my brain was racing. Being independent would mean working in a way I'd dreamt of ever since my stint in the community with Paula, but I also had a good job and it had taken me eight years to get where I was. If I went independent I'd be giving up a regular pay packet, sick pay and holiday, and I would be working unpredictable hours. As much as I'd like to go independent, I had to think about the financial implications, not to mention the effect it would have on my family life. It would mean having no set hours, call outs at all times of the day and night, and the need to abandon precious time with my children should a client go into labour.

'No, I'll stick with what I've got,' I thought. 'I can do three days a week and have a nice life with my family.' Of course I was not to know then that independent midwifery is very far from being difficult to fit around family life. I have been able to spend more time with my family and to fit the job round my life, not my life round the job. Of course there are a few sacrifices, but I don't think the paybacks in terms of free time, salary and job satisfaction can be equalled in any other way of working as a midwife.

One day before Christmas my mobile rang with a number I didn't recognize.

'Hi, I'm Jenny,' a woman said. 'Sharon gave me your number. She said you're thinking about being an independent midwife and all you need is a push. Can I be your push?'

Taking in her unexpected request I laughed. Sharon had referred Jenny on to me as Jenny lived too far out of her South London patch.

Up until now I'd been unsure about giving up a secure and enjoyable position at Maidstone. Was it better to bide my time and hold out for a community job? But as Jenny dangled this carrot of opportunity in front of me, I could tell that I was already half sold.

'What's your address?' I asked. 'Can I come and see you?'

A few days later, on my day off, I travelled to New Romney. Arriving at the small terraced cottage where Jenny lived with her husband Graham and two-year-old daughter Mia, I knocked on the door.

Jenny, a petite 31-year-old, showed me into the kitchen where we sat down to talk about Mia's birth and why she wanted an independent midwife.

'Mia was born in hospital by caesarean section,' Jenny explained. 'But this time I want to have a natural birth at home.'

'Oh God,' I thought. 'The first woman who comes to me for a home birth and she's high risk.'

This type of birth was known as a VBAC – a vaginal birth after caesarean – and although these days the medical profession will support them – 14 years ago they were considered to be more hazardous because of the risk of scar rupture.

My heart went out to Jenny, whose dream of a home birth had been met with a blank no by her local NHS Trust. If she had her heart set on having her second child at home I wasn't about to turn her away.

'Let me do some research,' I said. 'We'll take it from there.'

Back at home I had a lot to think about and quickly filled Michael in.

'I will support you in whatever you want to do,' he said. 'Do you think you can make a go of this?'

'Yes,' I said. 'I've done the research and there is a gap in the market for an independent midwife in Kent. It's just a case of getting the word out there and finding the women.'

With Michael behind me, I called Kay, who was now a community midwife at William Harvey, to discuss my thoughts with her.

'It sounds like you've pretty much made your mind up,' she said.

'I guess I have,' I agreed. 'But I have to ask you something. If I do this, will you be my backup midwife? Will you come along to the births if I pay you some of the fee? At least until I get my confidence up?'

'All right,' Kay said after she'd paused to consider my request. 'It might be tricky sometimes if I'm working but we will make it work somehow.'

Swotting up over the next few days I began to look into Jenny's situation.

I was pleased to discover that VBAC births weren't as high risk as the medical profession seemed to be making out. In fact the risk of a caesarean scar rupturing was actually only 0.3–0.5 per cent – that left a 99.7 per cent chance of a normal birth.

Taking a deep breath, I dialled Jenny's number.

'So I've thought long and hard about it, Jenny,' I said. 'And I'd love to be your independent midwife.'

'Oh, Virginia, I'm so pleased!' she said. 'I can't thank you enough!'

Smiling, I put the phone down. Now I'd committed, a familiar excitement was tingling through my body.

Looking back now it is clear that I went into independent midwifery quite blind but I was also determined. There were no guarantees this career move would work out for me but I felt positive that I could make a decent living if I put the work in.

It was a huge leap of faith but Sharon and the other independent midwives were busy and had promised to send any potential clients my way.

'You need to talk at local antenatal yoga classes and antenatal groups,' Sharon advised. 'It's word of mouth.'

When it came to engaging with people, I'd always had the gift of the gab and I remembered my dad's words from years before: 'Virginia could sell glasses to a blind man and humps to a camel.'

There was no doubt I'd inherited my dad's gregarious nature and sense of humour, and I knew I had the personality to sell myself to women who were considering independent midwifery.

There was only one thing left to do now – hand in my notice!

Typing up my resignation letter I gave my manager three months' notice and started to put the word out just as I'd discussed with Sharon.

As 1999 came to an end I was filled with excitement about the future but there was one more surprise for me before I welcomed in the new millennium.

On Christmas morning after the girls had opened their stockings, Michael handed me a small jewellery box.

'What's this?' I asked smiling.

Opening it up, I saw a small gold ring with a solitaire diamond.

'Which finger should I put it on?' I asked, my eyebrows raised.

'Put it on whatever finger you like,' he smiled, as I slipped it on to my left-hand ring finger. We didn't have an immediate plan to get married but after almost four years together it was the perfect commitment to a lifetime together.

Chapter Six

'Virginia, I'm in labour!'

As Jenny's voice filtered down the line my heart sank. At 35 weeks this was far from ideal.

'Graham is in Paris!' she added, sounding tearful. 'I can't believe this is happening to me.' Poor Jenny, although Graham worked away a lot, the plan had been for him to be closer to home near the potential time of birth. The last thing she expected was to be doing it alone.

'Try not to panic, Jenny,' I soothed, keeping my voice calm. 'I'll drive over now.'

Hanging up the phone, I dialled another number.

'Kay? Are you free?' I asked as my friend answered quickly. 'Jenny is in labour. Can you meet me there?'

Getting into the car, I took a deep breath. With Kay as my backup I could handle this. Everything would be fine.

With Kay arriving within minutes of me, the two of us gave Jenny the once over. My first action was to listen to the baby using my Pinard, a trumpet-like instrument that allows me to hear the heart beating, to ensure all was well. I then palpated the baby to feel for its position in the uterus. When I examined her further, I was dismayed to find she was already six centimetres dilated.

Seeing that she was definitely in labour we went into the kitchen to discuss the plan.

'She's too premature for a home birth,' I said as Kay nodded. 'The best advice is for her to go to hospital to have the baby.'

The likelihood was that at 35 weeks the baby would be well but in case it experienced breathing problems the best place for the birth to take place would be a hospital.

With Kay in agreement, we broke the news to Jenny who, while disappointed, consented to calling an ambulance. Meanwhile, a neighbour stepped in to look after Mia.

As the ambulance pulled into the grounds of William Harvey Hospital I almost laughed.

'Didn't think I'd be back here any time soon,' I thought, the memory of having left William Harvey Hospital 18 months earlier still fresh in my mind.

As an independent midwife I wouldn't be allowed to deliver Jenny's baby at the hospital. Instead I would be in the awkward position of watching as my formal colleagues took charge.

'Here we go,' I thought as Jenny was taken into a birth suite and helped on to her back on a bed by a former colleague of mine called Emily.

'I just need to put this line into your arm,' she said.

'Why?' Jenny asked.

'In case we have to take you for a caesarean,' she answered. Jenny pulled a face.

'If there is a problem I will have it, but right now there isn't,' she reasoned. 'I don't want to be stuck on this bed unless I need to be.'

I watched staying quiet as Emily got the same response to her attempt to put Jenny on a monitor or carry out a vaginal examination.

'I don't see why I need it,' Jenny said, her voice irritated. 'Virginia has told you everything you need to know.'

Although Emily didn't push it any further, I could see from her face that she was worried about getting into trouble. When I stepped outside for a moment she followed me.

'You should be trying to talk her round,' she said. 'She listens to you!'

'No,' I replied. 'I'm here to support Jenny's choices. She's done lots of research. This is her experience and her birth.'

I was relieved when Emily didn't push it any further and returned to the room.

Back by Jenny's side, I did my best to get her comfortable and relaxed. Her labour had slowed down considerably in the six hours since we'd arrived at the hospital but all that changed with the arrival of Graham who'd grabbed the first flight from Paris. Whether she knew it or not Jenny appeared to have been holding out for his arrival.

'Oh thank goodness,' she said, breathing deeply as he walked through the door. 'I can get on with it. Now get over here and let me lean on you.'

Within half an hour of her husband arriving, Jenny's contractions grew more intense and together we helped her manoeuvre herself around to her desired birthing position.

While Emily never refused to help Jenny or objected to what was going on, I sensed that she was uncomfortable supporting Jenny without the usual interventions for a woman having a VBAC. But performing her duty well she adapted to Jenny's needs crouching down ready to catch the baby.

As Jenny remained squatting down with Graham supporting her, I watched as she pushed out a baby boy into Emily's hands. The hard work done at last, Graham and I helped her up back on to the bed. As Emily handed her their tiny but perfectly formed son she looked so jubilant.

'Thanks, Virginia,' she said, with tears in her eyes. 'I couldn't have done it without you.'

At this point Emily, sensing the bond between us, kindly left the room to give us all a moment.

With mum and baby settled in, I strolled out of the birthing suite smiling at Emily who managed to flash me a smile from the desk.

While my first independent birth hadn't exactly gone to plan, I could feel it was the start of good things to come.

Since I'd made the decision to go independent I'd started to pick up more clients by speaking at pregnancy groups and prenatal yoga classes and via adverts I'd placed in the local National Childbirth Trust newsletters.

My next birth was due to be a mum called Harriet who'd first asked me to come and see her at 18 weeks pregnant.

Harriet, a second-time mum in her late 20s, lived in a lovely old house in the countryside not far from the seaside town of Sandwich and was married to a solicitor called Tom.

From our earlier chat on the phone I knew that Harriet had been left traumatised by the birth of her first son three years earlier.

I'd barely sat down at the table for our first appointment when she started to slide a cheque across the table. It was made out to me and was for my full fee at that time – two thousand pounds.

I got the immediate sense that she was petrified and wanted to buy a better birth. Smiling, I shook my head and pushed the cheque back across the table.

'I can't take this yet,' I said. 'You need to get to know me first. Let's talk and you can think about it.'

So as we drank tea Harriet opened up about the circumstances of her last labour.

'I wanted a natural water birth,' she said. 'But, while I was in labour, Tom was upset by how much agony I was in so he asked for pain relief on my behalf.'

Consequently Harriet had been given an injection of pethidine that she didn't want and then the hospital staff wouldn't allow her into the pool because the medicine made her groggy.

'The midwives just didn't listen to what I wanted,' she said. 'I felt it was all out of my control.'

Instead of having her planned water birth Harriet endured a 12-hour labour lying down and pushing for a very long time. To make matters worse, when Joshua was born she experienced an agonising third-degree tear that extended from her perineum to the anus. The whole experience left her feeling very low and she suffered from postnatal depression.

'It was awful and I had to see a counsellor,' she said. 'I'm scared. I can't do it again and I won't go back to that hospital.'

'Harriet,' I said, when she'd finished speaking. 'Your body didn't let you down, your caregivers did. There is absolutely no reason why you can't have a positive experience this time round. Why don't you tell me how you'd like it be?'

We chatted for a while with Harriet describing her ideal scenario – having her baby at home, while feeling safe and supported.

'OK,' I said. 'I'd love to support you. Now why don't you chat to Tom and give me a call in a few days?'

'I'm not changing my mind; I do want you,' she said, trying to hand me the cheque again.

'I'm not a sales person,' I replied, laughing. 'I don't have to seal the deal today. Have a chat with Tom.'

That night I'd filled Michael in on my day's work.

'You big softy,' he teased as I'd told him about refusing Harriet's money. 'You're not going to make it as a businesswoman if you refuse the cheques!'

But Harriet did call the next day. And with her husband in agreement, she became my next client.

Having no prior experience of caring for a woman who had a previous third-degree tear, I took my time to ask around, questioning more experienced midwives about what they would do to assist the birth.

I was shocked when most of them said they would do an elective episiotomy. Doing my utmost to read as much research on the subject as possible, I discovered that there was no evidence that this course of action would prevent Harriet tearing again. In fact, an episiotomy was more likely to extend to a bad tear. Instead it would be better to let nature take its course and encourage Harriet into an upright position for birth while encouraging her to take her time to breathe her baby out slowly.

By the time Harriet went into labour, six weeks after Jenny's baby had been born in hospital, I felt as prepared as I'd ever be.

The call came at 3.35am, waking me from a deep sleep. Momentarily confused, I fumbled for my phone. Then seeing Harriet's name I was instantly awake.

'The contractions are coming every couple of minutes, Virginia, can you come over please?' she asked.

'OK, Harriet, I am on my way,' I replied, excitement coursing through my veins. At last, my first home birth as an independent midwife was about to happen.

Although Michael stirred at the sound of the phone, he went straight back to sleep. Having discussed what would happen in this situation, I knew he would give me a call when he woke up. I'd also had a chat with Sophie, who was now 14, and she had agreed to see Courtney off to school. If I found myself out all day and night, I knew Michael would take over the evening meal.

While cleaning my teeth, I called Kay asking her to set off, too, and then pulling on some clothes I left home nervously hoping that everything would go to plan.

Arriving at 4.18am I found Harriet, who was three days overdue, coping well with the labour. She was pacing the house and seemed relaxed and excited, albeit in the normal pains of labour.

With some time to go I encouraged Harriet to get into the bath to help with the pain. Meanwhile, Kay had arrived and was sitting outside the bathroom within earshot should I need her. She was there as my support, an extra pair of hands to assist me in an emergency or for me to ask advice if needed.

'Do you think I can do this at home?' Harriet asked me. 'I won't have to go to hospital?'

'You're doing everything right,' I reassured her with a smile. 'No harm is going to come to you.'

As the morning ended Harriet's labour was progressing well and when I did a vaginal examination at 12pm I found she was already nine centimetres dilated.

I was expecting Harriet to give birth in the next hour or two but by 4pm there was still no sign of the baby and her contractions weren't coming as rapidly. Beckoning Kay I lead her into the hallway.

'I think the contractions have slowed down because she's scared,' I said quietly once we were out of Harriet's earshot. 'It's because of what happened last time. She is scared of the second stage. She doesn't want to push.'

We both knew that if Harriet had taken this amount of time in hospital and showed no sign of progress then the likelihood is she would have had some sort of intervention, whether that was having her waters broken, forceps or a vacuum birth.

'We need to try and reassure her,' Kay said. 'Or find a way to take her mind off it.'

Nodding I wandered nonchalantly into the kitchen where Harriet was sitting at the table with her head in her arms.

'Right,' I said brightly. 'How about some fresh air?'

Leading her out the back door in her dressing gown, we began to walk together around the garden.

'There's no rush,' I told her. 'When you're ready you'll have your baby.'

Later, back inside, Harriet continued to walk naked up and down the landing.

Just after 5pm her pacing took her into her bedroom.

'Virginia!' she cried. 'I think I need to push!'

As I rushed to her side, Harriet crouched down on all fours right next to her built-in wardrobe. While we'd spread a plastic sheet across the floor to protect her bedroom carpet she was crouched down right at the edge of it.

Quickly I examined the lack of space – it was going to be hard to get near her. So pulling the plastic sheet across the floor and sliding open the door I kicked a few shoes out the way and knelt down half in the cupboard. Immediately I could see the baby's head.

'Almost there, Harriet,' I said. 'Trust your body. You're getting there.'

I watched as a mop of fair hair appeared and the baby's head began to turn. Then out came the body and a little boy dropped into my hands.

I have caught babies in many ways and positions since then but Harriet's baby was the only one I have climbed in the cupboard for!

As Kay quickly helped Harriet up on to a sofa in her bedroom, I checked the baby over and recorded the time of birth as 6.10pm.

'He's eight pounds,' I said, handing him gently to Harriet.

The look on her face was just ecstatic. She had been so scared but now she looked like the proudest woman in the world.

'Hello, Alfie,' she said, admiring her son's face for the very first time. 'I can't believe you're here!'

With the placenta delivered and mother and baby doing well, and best of all NO perineal tears, Kay bid me farewell and I settled Harriet and her baby into bed.

Inwardly I was as ecstatic as she was. I was so happy that after careful thought and consideration I'd left Harriet well alone during her labour only for her to give birth without so much as a graze. Seeing her so happy and empowered by her birth was the best feeling in the world. At last I was becoming the midwife I wanted to be and with Kay by my side to support me I was ready to conquer the world.

For three years Kay was to come to births and watch me work, sitting on toilet lids as babies were born in the bath, or on the tops of stairs as women laboured on the landing. She was a steady pair of hands, both reassuring and calm. And Kay got to see what it was like to be an independent midwife herself and grew to fall in love with it.

A couple of days after the birth a pink envelope addressed to me arrived in the post. It was a handwritten letter from Harriet thanking me. 'You changed what could have been a frightening situation into a very happy one,' she wrote. I still cherish that letter to this day.

Walking across the crunchy, frost-covered undergrowth on a crisp winter's day towards the end of 2000, I knocked on the side door of an old vestry.

My latest clients, Jo and David, lived in a converted church in an idyllic setting in the middle of a wood. Even in late November the surroundings were pretty as the low sun glistened off the icy branches of the bare trees, leaving everything white and shiny.

As the door opened I was greeted by Jo, a heavily pregnant woman in her mid 20s of average build with long, dark hair, wearing a baggy top and leggings with thick socks.

'Come in,' she said, guiding me into the kitchen that immediately struck me as very homely with wooden furniture and lots of plants everywhere.

As I studied her array of vegetables and herbs, Jo noted my interest.

'We're pagans, which is funny seeing as we live in an old church,' she said, smiling. 'We're pretty much self-sufficient. We grow our own vegetables and live off the land. Apart from the odd vital supply from one of the independent stores we have everything we need right here.'

'Would you like a tea?' she added, beckoning to me to sit down at the kitchen table.

'Peppermint would be lovely,' I agreed.

She passed me a mug of tea made from fresh mint just as a man with short receding hair came into the room.

'This is my husband, David,' she said.

As we sipped our tea Jo explained how she'd wanted to book me from the beginning of her pregnancy but with money tight she and David had initially opted to use the local midwifery services provided by the NHS. A decision they'd begun to think twice about.

'Every time a midwife comes round it's someone new,' Jo said. 'I have to repeat our plans every time.'

Jo wanted a water birth at home, which shouldn't have been a big thing to ask for but, back in 2001, the local NHS treated it as a privilege rather than a right. It is now written in European law that a woman has the right to choose where and under what circumstances she gives birth. But 13 years ago a woman was merely entitled to a 'midwifery service'.

That meant that as soon as there were any issues around staffing a local trust could (and often would) withdraw its home birth service, informing women they would have to give birth in hospital instead.

'That happened to a couple of women I know,' Jo said, stroking her swollen belly as she spoke. 'I just had this bad feeling that it would happen to me, too.'

The final nail in the coffin came when the community midwife, who was also pregnant, arrived one day to give them 'home birth information' and outlined in great detail all the things that could go wrong around the time of birth. They'd found her abrupt and unsympathetic. She told Jo that she had already handpicked her caesarean team – how could Jo trust this midwife to give her a natural birth when she didn't even trust her own body?

'I told her there are just as many risks with hospital births and why weren't those pointed out to women?' Jo said, clearly getting rattled at the memory. 'Then she pulled out this form and asked me to sign it. I had to sign my life away to say that I understood all the risks of a home birth. So I told her to leave and we called you!'

'We'll be upfront with you,' David added. 'We really want you but we don't have much money.'

Sympathising with their plight I negotiated a price that they could afford.

Just two weeks after our initial meeting, the call came from David late on a Saturday night to say that Jo was in labour.

Driving through the winding woodland road to the couple's home at midnight was a very different experience to the beautiful jaunt it had been during the day. As the forest loomed in and my headlights created strange shapes and shadows, I kept my eyes firmly fixed to the road and pushed all thoughts of horror movies and axe murderers out of my mind.

Eventually the welcome sight of bright lights from the stained glass windows of the old church came into view and, after parking up, I dashed to the door keen to get inside.

This time David lead me through the kitchen into the front room of their home which had the high ceilings of the old church with an open-plan staircase that went up to the couple's bedroom.

The large old door of the church had been sealed up and the room was filled with comfy furnishings and tables and shelves displaying unusual ornaments, flags and keepsakes from their travels.

I found Jo sitting and calmly chatting with her friend and birth partner, Helen. Like an increasing number of expectant mothers, Jo felt that she would benefit from having a close female friend there to encourage her through her labour. Before the medicalisation of childbirth it would have been very normal to have a mother or a sister there for support and love while a woman gave birth. It was something I always encouraged, as feeling safe and loved relaxes a woman in labour, allowing the hormone oxytocin to work its magic and assist labour.

However, Jo was looking so relaxed that I instantly knew this was far too early for me to be there, but seeing as she had requested I come I was happy to support her.

After a while, I was aware of a pungent smell.

'What is that?' I asked curiously.

'Some herbs to relieve the pain,' David said.

But within ten minutes of drinking it Jo heaved herself up from the sofa and waddled as fast as she could to the bathroom to be sick. I suspected that the strong concoction was the culprit of the vomiting but said nothing. Until Jo took another dose and the same thing happened . . .

'Jo,' I said gently. 'Do you think it might be the herbs making you sick?'

'Yes, I think it could be,' she agreed. 'I don't think I'll have any more.'

The long night wore on vomit-free but, as we all grew weary, I suggested that it would be a good idea for everyone to try to get some sleep.

Helping Jo and David to get comfortable on a futon mattress on the floor in their bedroom, I piled cushions and pillows around Jo so David could access her back for a soothing massage. As they settled down to rest, I retired to one spare room and Helen went in the other.

I didn't bother texting home as my family knew how long a birth could take. I fell asleep feeling lucky that I had such a supportive family – Michael and Sophie were on hand to look after Courtney, and the girls also now had twenty-year-old Andrew at home. He had finished college six months earlier and had moved back to secure a job as an estate agent.

It wasn't long before I was in a deep sleep.

Waking early I checked on Jo while David readied the birth pool.

From the feel of her stomach I was able to establish that the baby was in a good position for birth – very low in her pelvis with its back towards its mother's front and head well flexed. Jo's constant bending over to tend the vegetable garden and pick wild mushrooms in the woods over the last few weeks of her pregnancy had clearly worked wonders.

Getting into the pool, Jo seemed very relaxed floating serenely in the warm water and gazing up at a photograph of a beautiful secluded beach in a small blue frame with a fixed concentration as each contraction washed over her. I also found myself staring at the photo and wondering what part of the world it could possibly be. I imagined it to be some exotic place, maybe Asia or the Caribbean.

'It's an island in the Hebrides,' Jo said. 'It's only three miles long and one and a half miles wide so you can explore it in a day. It's our special place. If we have a girl we're going to name her after the island.'

In between her contractions, David handed Jo cool drinks of fruit juice and refreshing sponge wipes as Helen read out loud from a book about relaxation techniques. Jo continued to float, gaze and smile, breathing deeply though contractions then falling into a few minutes of deep restoring sleep once they had passed.

Sensing that Jo was near to giving birth, I called Kay, who arrived around midday, breezing in smelling fresh and perfumed.

She couldn't have timed it better as within 20 minutes Jo began to show signs of being fully dilated. She was now on her knees in the birth pool with her arms over the edge and her chest pressing against its supporting walls. Her eyes were closed and her fringe wet from perspiration. Occasionally she'd let out a grunt or low moan that alerted us to the fact that something different was going on – something powerful was building.

'Wow, that was intense,' she muttered, opening her eyes as the pool water clouded leaving me in no doubt that her waters had broken.

The next contraction brought with it an even more powerful urge to push and I remained silent as Jo threw her head back to get force behind the directions her own body was giving her.

For the next 40 minutes Jo's contractions picked up speed. Gently easing my mirror into the water I angled it behind Jo where I could just see the top of a mass of dark silky hair on the baby's head.

Turning her face slightly Jo saw what I was doing and reached for the mirror to see the baby for herself.

'I see it! I see it!' she called out in excitement and then dropped the mirror in the pool as another contraction demanded her concentration.

As I retrieved it from the depths, Kay reached over the pool to use her underwater listening device, a sonic aid, to check the baby's heartbeat.

'Perfect,' she confirmed. 'It's averaging 126 beats per minute.'

Then uttering her first high-pitched sound of the day, Jo jerked her body forward from the hips and we all saw the baby's head emerge under the water.

'The head is completely out now, Jo,' I whispered. 'Fantastic work, keep your bottom low in the water and wait for the next contraction and your baby will be born.'

Two short minutes later, after another long, sustained push, the baby was ejected into the water and Jo reached down and slowly brought it up to the surface.

As David let out a cry of excitement, Jo pulled the baby, a little girl, to her chest and closed her eyes in absolute ecstasy.

'My beautiful baby Iona,' she whispered.

Kay and I smiled at each other in mutual relief but were quickly distracted by the sight of David whipping off his boxer shorts and clambering naked into the pool with his wife and new daughter! Kay and I glanced at each other in amused shock and immediately busied ourselves with clearing and tidying, both of us doing our best to suppress the need to burst out into school-girl laughter.

Just when we thought things couldn't get any less conventional I spied Helen also removing her clothes to join her friends in the pool. All three were hugging and cooing over the new baby.

As billowy clouds of bright red blood floated up to indicate Jo was about to deliver the placenta, she passed Iona to David and grabbed on to the sides of the pool, closing her eyes in concentrated effort for one last gentle push.

'There you go,' she said.

I readied myself to take it from her but instead of passing it to me she brought it to her mouth and, as Kay and I watched astonished, she took an almighty bite. But by now nothing Jo or David did surprised me, and I figured that the health benefits of such an action for a vegan would probably be positive.

With the cord cut and little Iona happily feeding on her mother's breast, we sat around for a couple of hours eating pasta prepared by Helen. Then, leaving them in their bubble of baby bliss, I headed home to bed.

The following day when I arrived to the smell of meat cooking, I was left in no doubt whatsoever what they had done with the rest of the placenta.

'Would you like some?' David asked, initially causing my stomach to lurch.

Did I try it? Did I take the only opportunity I may ever have to eat placenta? Well I guess that's for me to know and you to speculate about . . .

Chapter Seven

Pulling to a stop in Goudhurst, a quaint village in Kent, I arrived at the door of a tiny roadside cottage.

As Tonia, a tall woman in her late 20s with soft eyes and a big smile, opened the door, I had no idea that she would turn out to be one of my best and most-loved clients.

Although she was due to be a first-time mother, Tonia had more experience than most, considering that she'd been a nanny to a well-to-do family before beginning her own married life. Her former employer had used an independent midwife and had found it to be a very personal experience and now Tonia wanted to do the same.

As Tonia and I sat and chatted in the homely two-bedroomed cottage that her carpenter husband Jason was continually working on, he also came into the room to join us. While Tonia talked, Jason, a quiet, gentle man, sat smiling and listening. I thought his love for Tonia shined very brightly and I immediately warmed to them both.

Unfortunately that first tiny life that Tonia was carrying was not meant to be and a few weeks later I received a letter from her telling me that on this occasion she had miscarried. She added that she hoped to be back in touch in the future.

Thankfully it was not too long a wait and five months later Tonia called to say she was once again pregnant.

As I visited her on numerous occasions, checking her blood pressure and that the baby was growing OK, it was clear that Tonia was very sure of how she was going to do everything.

'I'm not going to breastfeed,' she told me in a 'no arguments' voice.

'I've got my bottle-feeding routine down to a tee and I don't see why it should be any different this time. My baby will be on formula milk straight away.'

Being a big advocate of breastfeeding, I tried to suggest some reading material to change her mind but she was dead set. Her baby would be bottle fed and that was that.

Apart from the usual ailments such as tiredness and puffy ankles, Tonia's pregnancy continued perfectly. Then, a week past her estimated due date, in October 2001, I received an early morning call from Jason.

'Tonia's contractions have started,' he said, sounding nervous as I asked him various questions.

'OK, Jason, it sounds like it'll be a while yet,' I said, hoping to reassure him. 'I've got some visits to do out your way but I'll be over as soon as that's done. Let me know if anything changes.'

True to my word and with my visits done at 3pm, I headed over to their cottage.

I found Tonia in the kitchen leaning on the worktop. Her contractions were coming every five minutes but were only lasting 45 seconds each time. Knowing that for a first baby that would usually indicate the birth was a good way off, I rallied myself for a long afternoon and night.

Although not much changed between then and 10.30pm I remained at the house chatting to Tonia when she felt like talking and accepting endless cups of tea from a clearly anxious Jason.

Tonia was coping well, smiling as each wave passed and moving around the house and up and down the stairs. Like many women she found that being upright and mobile helped with the pain and gravity, in turn, would aid the descent of the baby.

By 10.30pm the contractions were getting much stronger and Tonia spent time sitting on the toilet, rocking to ease the pain as she felt the strange, all-consuming pressure a woman feels in her bottom as the heavy head of the baby slowly inches its way through the pelvis and puts pressure on the back passage in its wake.

An hour later Tonia made herself comfortable on the sofa in the living room after agreeing that I could perform a vaginal examination to assess the labour progress.

As Jason kept himself scarce, heading to the kitchen to make another round of tea, I headed to the bathroom to wash my hands.

'Keep Tonia safe,' I whispered to the birth angels in a little private ritual I'd come to do for each birth. 'Please let her have a healthy baby at home.' Heading back into the living room, I snapped on a pair of gloves and crouched down between her legs.

'Now relax,' I instructed, squeezing my fingers in gently. 'Let's see how far you have to go.'

'You're eight centimetres dilated,' I confirmed, feeling her cervix. 'Only two more and we'll be good to go.'

Giving Tonia the once over, I recorded that her blood pressure, pulse and temperature were all normal and the baby's heartbeat was strong and regular.

'All good,' I smiled as Tonia manoeuvred herself off the sofa.

For the next two hours it was clear Tonia's contractions were getting tougher and more painful as the clenching and squeezing of her uterus caused tears to course silently down her cheeks.

Yet Tonia remained stoic, keeping her energy up with a banana and walking around the kitchen. An hour later she began to doze and sleep between contractions while leaning over the back of the sofa. Every two minutes the silence of her sleep was penetrated by deep intakes of breath culminating in a cry of pain until the contraction began to wear off again and she returned to her exhausted slumber. Jason, meanwhile, was dozing on the other sofa.

Sitting next to Tonia I closed my eyes and rested my head on the soft cushions during her short periods of rest. I longed to drift into the sleep my body craved but would not be allowed for many hours yet. Whereas an NHS midwife could expect her shift to end at any point during the labour, as an independent midwife I would only rest once the woman was tucked up in bed with her baby. So, instead of drifting off, I stayed awake to support Tonia. As each torturous spasm hit, I lay my hand on her arm or stroked her hair. Despite her tightly closed eyes, she had the reassurance someone was there, all was well and it would end soon.

Sometime after 3am, Tonia opened her eyes in surprise as she felt a pop deep within her body and the warm, clear waters which indicate birth will be soon, cascaded down her legs.

No longer feeling tired or sleepy, Tonia was suddenly very alert and wide awake as her contractions increased in intensity. As she moved positions over and over in an effort to find one that worked well, Jason and I worked together handing her milk to drink and wiping her sweating face with a cool, wet cloth.

Eventually Tonia found the position that best suited her – down on one knee in the middle of her small sitting room.

Jason and I sat down next to her and it was not long before we both spied the crumpled skin on the top of the emerging baby's head as it inched slowly with each push towards us.

As a little boy flopped safely into my waiting hands he was totally tangled up in his long, blue, pulsating cord and the three of us laughed as I untangled him and passed him to his waiting mother.

After a short wait, Jason followed my instructions to cut the cord and the two new parents sat together on the sofa admiring the new son they'd called Kerrec.

'That's a name I've never heard before,' I commented.

'It was inspired by a man we met on our honeymoon in the Seychelles,' Tonia smiled. 'Kerrec was the concierge who did everything for us, so we told him if we ever had a boy we would name our son after him.'

After a brief cuddle with her baby, I was surprised when Tonia lifted Kerrec towards me.

'Can you take him?' she said. 'I want to have a shower.'

Lifting the baby out of her arms I wrapped him in a warm blanket and laid him down safely on the sofa in his Moses basket. Then I helped Tonia upstairs and got the shower going for her.

Fifteen minutes later Tonia came downstairs looking tired but refreshed in her dressing gown. I'd expected her to return immediately to her newborn son but instead of picking him up from the sofa she walked to another chair and sat down.

'You feed him, Virginia,' she said, pointing to the bottle of formula that Jason had just prepared.

I was surprised as normally a new mother cannot wait to hold and feed her baby, but assuming she was too shattered I picked up the warm bottle. Holding Kerrec in my arms, I watched as he eagerly pulled at the teat, milk dribbling down his chin as he filled his belly with his very first feed.

Then I left the new parents and headed home for a long bath and some much-needed sleep.

Arriving at Tonia's the next morning it all seemed a bit *Groundhog Day*. As Jason beckoned me through the door I found Tonia sitting in the same place as I'd left her the day before with Kerrec in the basket on the same sofa where I'd left him.

'How are you feeling?' I asked.

'Alright,' she said. Judging by the flat tone in her voice I wasn't entirely convinced.

Kerrec meanwhile was feeding well and Tonia certainly had no physical ailments other than the usual soreness to be expected post birth. Yet I couldn't shake the feeling that something was amiss.

I was used to seeing new mums gazing completely besotted at their babies but Tonia just didn't have that initial glow of new motherhood about her.

'It's not unusual for women to feel detached and numb the first day,' I told myself. 'I'll keep an eye on her.'

Returning the next day I found Tonia doing the ironing with Kerrec lying in his basket. While he seemed contented, it was now two days since his birth and I had not once seen him in his mother's arms.

'How was the night?' I enquired.

'Alright,' Tonia said, shrugging her shoulders.

'What's it like having your own baby?' I added.

'Just the same, really,' she replied.

Normally I'd visit a new mother for the first three days then decrease that to every two but feeling increasingly worried about Tonia I decided to keep up the daily visits.

Over the course of a week not much changed. Tonia didn't smile or speak with love about her new baby. There was no laughter or good-natured despairing over the constant nappy changes or winding. Instead, she described Kerrec's progress in a bizarrely clinical fashion.

Did she not love her baby, I wondered.

By day eight I had developed real worries about Tonia and had decided that if she was no different I would speak to her doctor. I now suspected she might be developing postnatal depression and felt out of my depth.

'What could have triggered it?' I thought. Tonia had no history of mental health problems, had experienced a lovely pregnancy and an empowering birth – everything just the way she wanted it.

Arriving at her house at 8am that day I found Tonia showered and dressed. This was surprising in itself given that most new mothers have trouble getting themselves fed and dressed by mid afternoon when they have a new baby. As I followed her into a spotless kitchen it was obvious that Tonia had been vacuuming and cleaning as well.

'Jason went back to work today,' she said, as she opened the fridge. 'He's done all the feeding up until now.'

As she stood with her back to me, staring at a shelf full of made-up bottles of formula milk, I saw her shoulders sag and start to shake. I realised she was crying. Turning from the open fridge she looked at me with pain in her eyes and tears escaped down her cheeks. It was unlike Tonia to show emotion and it was a surprise to see her looking so vulnerable.

'What is it, Tonia? Please tell me what's wrong,' I said, rushing to her side and leading her to a chair to sit down.

As she wiped away her tears with a sodden tissue I crouched down to meet her eye.

'How can I help you?' I said.

'In the night Jason got up and went downstairs to get Kerrec his bottle,' she said, her voice wobbling. 'While he was gone Kerrec was crying so I picked him up and he tried to suck at my breast.'

Putting her head on the table she sobbed into her arms.

'Oh, Tonia,' I said. 'That's OK, that's just his instinct. If it upsets you that much then why don't you go down and get the bottle and let Jason comfort him?'

'No,' she said, her voice muffled and sheepish. 'I . . . I liked it.'

'Tonia!' I said, almost laughing in relief at the sudden realisation of what the issue was. 'Do you want to breastfeed your baby?'

'Yes,' she cried with a long and drawn-out wail. 'Yes I do but that wasn't the plan!'

'Tonia,' I said, softly. 'I know you're an organised woman but what you didn't account for is the overwhelming feelings of love that come with your own baby, did you?'

'No,' she whispered.

'OK,' I said smiling. 'I will help you. It might be hard work because your breasts have likely got the message that the milk is not needed. You will have to sit, rest, eat, drink and breastfeed constantly in order to build up your supply, maybe even use a pump as well. But come on, let's start now . . .'

As it happened, it didn't take very long. Tonia tried various different positions including leaning over her son and we started off using plastic nipple shields as Kerrec was used to a bottle. But within a few days we'd got him happily suckling without. Meanwhile, I watched Tonia completely and utterly change. With every feed she blossomed with motherly love.

'There you go, Kez,' she'd say, placing him gently on to her lap after a feed.

Safe in the knowledge that all was well with Tonia's little family I bid her goodbye.

Although Tonia went on to get Kerrec into a strict routine, she also learnt something invaluable from her first child – all the supernanny skills in the world can't suppress a mother's instinct to nurture her newborn child.

A year into my career as an independent midwife I'd never felt happier. I loved being my own boss and running my own diary and giving the women in my care the time and dedication they needed and wanted. Everything was going so well. I had the job, the family and man of my dreams.

As 2001 came to an end, Sophie, who was now 15, and Courtney, who was 10, were looking forward to their school holidays. Andrew loved his new job and Matthew, who was still busy with his catering position, had plans to come home for Christmas dinner.

As we enjoyed Christmas Day and I watched Michael playing with Courtney, a nagging feeling hit me. While he was his usual attentive self with the kids, I sensed that something was not quite right. When I'd tried to kiss him under the mistletoe he'd pulled away from me. He seemed to be avoiding physical contact.

Michael, my kind, thoughtful boyfriend, had always lavished me with love and attention but suddenly he seemed distant and distracted – what was going on?

I kept asking him what was wrong and he couldn't tell me. The New Year celebrations came and went and things still seemed strange between us. So one night while he was asleep after a night shift, I looked at the most recent number he'd called. It was listed as 'Wayne' but when I dialled the number a woman answered.

'Hello, Mick,' she said. Recoiling at the familiarity in her voice, I replaced the receiver without saying anything. I sat and stared at the wall feeling sick to the stomach.

'Maybe it was Wayne's wife,' I reasoned.

So, picking up the house phone, I withheld the number and dialled again.

'Can I speak to Wayne?' I asked when the same woman answered.

'Sorry,' she replied. 'You have the wrong number. This is Sharon's number.'

Putting the phone down I walked upstairs slowly to where Michael was sleeping.

'Who is Sharon?' I asked, shaking him awake. He sat up looking bleary-eyed and shocked but didn't even attempt to lie.

'A woman I have been seeing,' he said.

Crushed and destroyed I agonised over what I should do. Eventually I decided I loved him and was willing to forgive him. But to my devastation Michael didn't want my forgiveness. He just wanted to leave. Within a day he'd left behind a broken woman, two heartbroken girls and a very angry Andrew who couldn't believe that the man he considered a friend would hurt his mother so badly.

Unable to fathom my loss, I could hardly get out of bed. Mum had to come and look after the girls and a worried Kay arrived to check on me.

'I feel like my life is over,' I sobbed as she sat by my bed stroking my arm. 'I just can't stop crying.'

'Don't worry about anything,' she told me. 'I'll look after your appointments. You just get better.'

Thankfully with just a bunch of antenatal appointments to attend in January I was able to take a few weeks off while I cried, got angry and suffered a breakdown prompting my concerned family to even consider hospitalising me at one point.

After a month of being fussed over by Mum I asked her to leave.

'Mum, you have to go,' I said. 'I have to get back to my life.'

Duly I returned to my appointments but for a long time my loss felt like the rawest grief.

Although I did my best to claw my way back to normality, the pain followed me from winter to spring and on into the summer. Although I'd been through break-ups before, I'd never been blind-sided like this. I'd envisaged spending the rest of my life with Michael and the heartbreak was like nothing I'd experienced before.

'How will I ever get over it?' I wondered. Every day I worked caused me pain. As I watched couples in love gazing at each other as they welcomed their babies into the world, my heart would shatter all over again.

Not knowing how to heal myself, I carried on and hid my pain. I smiled on the outside but inside I felt like an empty shell.

Life went on and, despite my sorrow, I was happy to hear from Tonia again in the spring of 2002.

'Will you be my midwife again?' she asked, revealing that she'd fallen pregnant three months after Kerrec's birth.

'Of course I will,' I agreed.

'I've got something else to ask you, too,' she added. 'Jason and I would like you be Kerrec's godmother. We're having a christening in a few weeks.'

It was such an honour but with a heavy heart I had to decline.

'I'm an atheist!' I said by way of explanation. 'It would be very hypocritical of me to say yes.'

Although I'd previously got married in a church, I'd started to question organised religion during my nurse training. If I was truthful with myself, I realised that I'd never really believed in it. Praying to my own 'birth angels' to look after the mothers and their babies in my care was enough for me and I didn't want to be involved in any other worship.

But far from being offended Tonia did something very special. She planned the service so that I could play a special non-religious part in the ceremony of naming. Instead of being a godmother I became Kerrec's 'life supporter', which I found very touching.

Tonia's second pregnancy flew by easily and as I carried out each antenatal check it was fun seeing Kerrec grow from a baby crawling along to a toddler taking his first steps. During our time together I often told Tonia stories about the water births I'd attended and this time she wanted to try it for herself.

Tonia went into labour on a cold October morning, awaking me at 1am to say that her waters had gone.

'How exciting,' I said, sitting up in bed, suddenly feeling very awake. 'That's normal when baby is on its way. Are you getting any contractions?'

'No, just water pouring out,' she answered. 'I didn't get this with Kerrec. It feels really strange like I am wetting myself but have no control over it. Will the baby be all right?'

Telling her not to worry, I went through all my check questions: Is the baby moving? Do you feel well? Was the water clear with no bad odour or colour to it? When she responded with positive answers to each one I knew the likelihood of me sinking back into my warm bed was an ever-increasing possibility.

While TV dramas often depict 'waters going' with babies being born imminently there is rarely need for a mad panic. In fact, it can take hours or days for real labour to commence for many women.

'The best thing you can do right now is go back to sleep,' I advised Tonia. 'Give me a call once the contractions have started.'

Whispering goodbye I hung up and immediately drifted back to sleep.

I'd managed to get in another three hours when the call came from Jason to say that Tonia's labour had started with a vengeance.

'The contractions are coming every three to four minutes,' he said with panic in his voice. 'Tonia has asked you to hurry.' In the background there was no mistaking the deep, low moans of a woman in the midst of labour.

A midwife never waits around for a second baby as it is often the fastest to arrive. From the sound of things, Tonia's situation had dramatically changed – there was now no time to waste.

Jumping out of bed, I quickly pulled on my clothes thinking not for the first time how it would make for comical viewing to have a night-vision camera capturing the scene in a home-birth midwife's bedroom as she is called out in the middle of the night. There I was toothbrush in one hand, hopping around trying not to fall over as I attempted to get my leg into my knickers and then my trousers, while desperately trying to be both speedy and quiet so as not to wake Sophie, Courtney or Andrew.

Knowing that Sophie, who was a wonderful support throughout her teenage years, would look after Courtney, I scribbled a note and dashed out the door jumping into my trusty Citroën heading off on what would be a 45-minute journey to the little cottage in the country.

As my phone started to ring again, flashing with Tonia's number, my stomach churned as it always does when I am called en route to a birth.

'Oh no, please don't do this to me,' I pleaded silently as I grabbed the phone, knowing that I was still a good 20 minutes away.

'She wants to push,' Jason informed me fearfully.

'What is she doing Jason?' I asked, keeping my voice calm. 'Where is she? What position is she in?'

'She is in the pool, Virginia, what shall I do?' he said.

I suddenly felt sorry for Jason who was not a modern man who took birth in his stride. I knew from Kerrec's arrival that he'd found the whole thing unnerving and fretted and worried at the best of times.

'Listen carefully, Jason,' I instructed, adopting an exaggerated calmness to my voice. 'Babies that come this quick usually do not need assistance from midwives, they help themselves and baby will be fine. But, nevertheless, it is important you remain calm. I want you to tell Tonia to get out the pool now.'

I knew that disturbing Tonia or any woman's labour can have the effect of provoking a surge of adrenaline which suppresses oxytocin, the hormone driving the labour forward. As I listened to the muffled sound of Jason repeating my instruction to Tonia, I pleaded with the birth angels to allow my emergency delaying tactic to work.

Knowing that the baby could arrive any minute I contemplated telling Jason to call an ambulance. It seemed pointless, though, since with just minutes of the drive left to go, I was clearly going to get there first.

'Jason, listen,' I instructed instead. 'Tell Tonia to get down on all fours, put her head on the floor and bottom in the air. The baby may still come but keep the phone in your hand and make sure the door is on the latch. You need to keep your eyes glued to Tonia and if you see the head call me back immediately.'

'OK,' he squealed, his voice sounding a lot higher pitched than usual. As I put down the phone I could hear him urging: 'Bum in the air, Tonia! Bum in the air!'

Finally I turned the corner into the village and jerked to a stop in the pub car park opposite Tonia's house. Grabbing my equipment bag from the back seat, I rushed inside to find Tonia on the floor in the kitchen next to the birth pool and a very pale-looking Jason. I was pleased to see there was no baby – yet.

Keen to get Tonia's plan of a calm water birth back on track, I helped her off the floor and up the one very short step she needed to get back into the deep water of the pool. Submerging into the water, Tonia quickly adopted the same down on one knee position she'd had with Kerrec's birth. We only had to wait a few minutes until the contractions came back with a vengeance and Tonia looked up at me with a look that I would come to know well.

While some women let out toe-curling, ear-piercing screams during the final stage of labour, Tonia was a silent birther, her pain indicated by no more than the odd tear trickling silently down her cheeks.

'The baby's coming,' she said, instead looking up at me and scrunching her face, as out came the baby's head, swiftly followed by its body.

Reaching down with a look of wide-eyed wonder, Jason pulled the baby up out of the water.

'It's a girl,' he said as he placed her into Tonia's arms.

'Hello, Aerojen,' she said, revealing the unusual name that had been inspired by the author of a book she had read while pregnant.

Placing the baby to her breast, her daughter latched on easily and began to feed.

Smiling, I bid her and Jason goodbye, knowing that this time round there would be no reasons at all for concern. As Tonia's eyes remained glued to her breastfeeding daughter, she couldn't have looked happier.

Chapter Eight

'He's never out my thoughts. Ridiculous, isn't it?' I told Kay as I took a sip of my gin and tonic and smiled half-heartedly.

'Don't worry, you'll find someone else!' she said with good intention. I resisted the urge to roll my eyes. Kay had been happily married for many years, what did she know about being single?

But whether I cared to admit it or not, when Kay dragged me out for a drink I usually had fun – and that was exactly what I needed.

As the year anniversary of Michael's betrayal beckoned, I'd found myself moping around, unable to shake off the feeling of melancholy.

It was not like me to feel so defeated. I'd always picked myself up and brushed myself off before. Why was this time so different? Why couldn't I get past the sorrow? Little did I know that I was about to face the most emotional birth of my career to date . . .

Linda was quite straightforward in a physical sense. Having previously had a caesarean section, she now wanted a birth at home. After two years as an independent midwife I was well used to this request and felt confident that I had the experience to deal with it.

Linda lived in a charming cottage in a small town by the sea. It was only when I arrived at the house to meet the young mum and her cute, blonde, curly-haired daughter, Gilly, three, that I heard the full sad circumstances of their situation.

Tragically, just a few months earlier Linda's husband Max had died from injuries sustained in a car accident, leaving her widowed with a young daughter and another baby on the way. Max had lost his fight in the very hospital Linda was expected to give birth in and the same hospital where she'd had Gilly.

'I can't go back there,' she told me, her eyes filled with sadness.

As we talked, Linda, who was already 32 weeks pregnant, explained how she'd come up against a lot of pressure to conform to medical advice – to have the baby in hospital. While her community midwife was supportive, she hadn't fought Linda's case for her or set up a plan of care. Instead she'd suggested a more reckless plan.

'If you stay at home for most of your labour you can call a midwife when it's too late for you to go to hospital,' she'd said.

This was not the first time I'd heard this advice imparted to a woman who wanted to have a home birth after a caesarean and I thoroughly disagreed with it. Women in this situation need a midwife present more than ever to detect any early signs of problems and to arrange a speedy transfer if necessary. The only benefit I could see from this suggestion was to protect the NHS trust against being sued should a problem arise.

'I'm glad you called me,' I said.

With Linda booked in, she introduced me to her sister Anita who would be her birth partner on the day and we all got to know each well over the next few weeks. Despite grieving for her husband, Linda appeared to be coping well and the day-to-day care of her small daughter and the prospect of a new baby were a welcome distraction.

With her labour commencing one January morning, it all began in a rather stop-start fashion. Linda had called at the crack of dawn after having contractions all night. Yet when I arrived at her home expecting to find her well underway she did not look like a woman in labour.

'It all stopped when Gilly woke up,' she said, looking sheepish. I immediately knew what had created this weird phenomenon.

'Yup that happens a lot,' I explained with a smile. 'When a woman goes into labour she needs to feel safe and free to labour – but that's not going to happen if she's busy with her other child.'

Sure enough as Anita packed Gilly off to playschool Linda's contractions started up again with gusto.

'I want to push,' she announced not too long afterwards.

Knowing that Linda wanted the room to be as quiet and low key as possible, Anita and I remained silent, allowing Linda the peace to focus as she stood leaning on the mantelpiece pushing her baby out.

Crouching behind her I held out my hands watching as her new baby daughter slipped out into the world. I had braced myself for tears of sorrow and heartbreak for her lost husband at this point but to my surprise Linda acted just like any other new mother. It was lovely to see her face filled with elation as I handed her the baby. Then there were her laughs of joy as Gilly arrived home from playgroup to meet her new sister Rosie.

Confident that everything was fine I headed home.

I was just settling down to watch TV that evening when my phone bleeped. I frowned as I realised it was a message from Linda.

'I'm worried the baby isn't feeding properly,' it said.

Seeing as it was still only 9pm, I drove the short distance to see if I could help and, as arranged, opened the unlocked door, calling out to Linda as I climbed the stairs. The house seemed very quiet with Gilly asleep in bed and Anita gone.

Walking into Linda's bedroom I was dismayed to see her slumped in bed holding her baby. Her face was red and blotchy from crying.

Meanwhile, Rosie was feeding well on her breast so that clearly wasn't the problem at hand.

'Oh, Linda,' I said. 'Are you all alone?'

'It's my fault,' she said, her voice high with emotion. 'I told Anita and the rest of my family I was fine and they should all go home.'

She paused for a moment, biting her lip to try to hide her grief but instead let out big, chest-shaking sobs.

'I miss him so much, Virginia,' she cried. 'I don't know how I am going to bear it – watching my babies grow up without their daddy.'

As her face crumpled and she sobbed the pain was so obvious.

Taking a sleepy Rosie from her arms I lay her in the crib beside the bed and then, slipping off my shoes, I climbed on to the bed and threw my arms around Linda.

I'd wanted to comfort her but seeing her in so much pain triggered my own heartache and before I knew it my own eyes were welling up.

'I know, I know,' I said, squeezing her tight and trying to wipe away my own tears.

Some might say I should have been more professional, but when a woman is opening her heart to you like that how can you hold back? How many of my tears were for Linda and her pain and how many were for me I couldn't tell you. But I do know that moment brought us both comfort.

After a good cry we talked for a long time and I made us both a cup of tea. Linda told me all about the life she'd had with her husband.

'He was so happy that we were having another baby,' she told me with a sad smile.

'You know, Linda, you have something very special,' I said. 'You have the knowledge that he died loving you.'

In my head I couldn't help thinking that she was lucky – I felt like I was grieving in the same way yet I was expected to just get over it. The person Linda loved most in the world had died loving her but I had the shame of knowing the man I loved in the same way chose to leave. He was still out there living his life, which in my mind just magnified the pain.

With Linda exhausted but clearly feeling a lot better after a good cry and a chat, I told her I'd leave her to get some rest.

'Thank you,' she said, taking my hand as she walked me to the door. 'I will never forget what you have done for me, Virginia, and tonight is part of that thank you.'

It was funny but the unexpected emotions of the evening had sparked something in me, too.

If Linda was brave enough to carry on then so could I. It was time to stop grieving and start living again . . .

Ever since we'd bonded on the maternity ward six years earlier, Kay had been my ally. So nothing lifted my spirits more than when, after three years as my backup, Kay decided to quit the NHS and set up practice with me in 2003.

'I've sat on so many toilet seats watching you work,' she'd told me. 'I want to be an independent midwife, too.'

'It won't be very sterile,' I'd teased, referring to our old hospital days.

She raised her eyebrows knowing full well that in normal family homes with cats, dogs and children she'd be swapping 'sterile' expectations for 'clean'.

Toasting our new venture with gin and tonics, we agreed that we'd call our business Kent Midwifery Practice.

As our business got off the ground, it was wonderful to get another call from Tonia who had fallen pregnant again three months after Aerojen's birth. Baby number three was expected in the autumn of 2003.

Sure enough, in early October Kerrec and Aerojen's pretty younger sister Anzonia (inspired by the name of a grand house in America) was born in a water pool at home. Although she was not in as much of a rush as her big sister, her birth was also quick and she was born a few hours after Tonia went into labour.

And keeping up with her habit of popping babies out annually, it was really no surprise when Tonia was pregnant again in 2004.

The family now lived in a 1960s semi-detached house a short distance away from my own home in Ashford where they'd squeezed into three bedrooms, a lounge, a dining room and a kitchen. The plan was for Jason to build an extension and add on rooms to accommodate the growing family.

I'd smiled as Tonia greeted me at the door with baby Anzi on her hip, a growing baby bump and blue-eyed Kerrec hanging on to her legs. The bashful toddler I'd known was developing into a bossy little boy and it was cute to see how shy little Aerojen constantly followed him around.

With Tonia well I bid her goodbye, telling her to stay in touch.

As part of my ongoing happiness project, in the summer of 2004 I decided to treat my whole family to a trip to Turkey. Being very reasonably priced I was able to hire a huge villa and we had the best holiday for years with so many laughs. While I was there I spotted an apartment for sale and decided to buy it, thinking that it would give me something exciting to focus on. Matthew chipped in with some of the money until I could afford to pay him back. It was purchased from plans and I'd be able to pick up the keys the following May.

As October arrived so did Tonia's labour. I received a call from her at 8.30am to say her contractions had started but there was 'no need to rush'. That all changed half an hour later when she called back to say she wanted to push!

'I'm on my way,' I said, grabbing my bag and dashing out the door, grateful in the knowledge Tonia now lived just 20 minutes from my home.

I arrived to find her already in her birthing pool in the dining room.

'I'm so glad to see you!' she said. 'Now I feel safe.' Despite her vast experience as a nanny and her clear ability to have children with ease, Tonia remained strangely nervous at every birth I attended. Not one birth went by without her telling me she was scared in the last few moments before her baby was born. Jason also remained nervous, with the offers of tea clearly in sync with his growing anxiety.

With Tonia in the pool and a history of speedy deliveries, I assumed Tonia's next child would arrive shortly. However at 11.30am she still had not given me her telltale look or uttered her usual verbal confirmation, 'The baby's coming,' to indicate the baby was on its way.

'Do you mind if I take a look?' I asked.

With Tonia out of the pool I was surprised to find her only six centimetres dilated and yet still feeling the urge to push. I suspected that the baby was trying to turn to get into the optimal position for birth.

'Let's try moving you around a bit,' I suggested.

For the next two hours I walked her around the house before getting her back into the pool.

As she adopted her usual position down on one knee, she looked me in the eye.

'The baby's coming,' she whispered at last.

Her new arrival was introduced as Ennieco – named after an Italian children's shoemaker.

'Born on October fourth. One day after Anzonia's birthday and two days after Kerrec's!' I confirmed, writing down Ennieco's birth date in my records. 'October's going to be an expensive month!'

As usual, the couple's other children were being cared for by Tonia's family during the birth, giving them the rare luxury of a day and night to acquaint themselves with their newborn son. However, when I returned the next day to check on Tonia and her baby, normal service had clearly resumed.

'Look at my brother!' Kerrec yelled proudly as he tugged on my dress.

As usual, Tonia was excelling at multitasking – juggling four children under four with an impressive amount of calm and order.

'I'm done now,' she smiled, as I discharged her from my care a week later. 'I've got my four. Two boys, two girls.'

'Same as me,' I smiled.

Although I didn't say anything, I had a sneaking suspicion that Ennieco would not be the end for Tonia. And, as April neared the following year, I did wonder if I'd get my usual spring call to reveal she was expecting.

But April gave way to May, then June to July with no word from Tonia. It seemed that contrary to my hunch her family was complete.

One Sunday in May 2005, fifteen-year-old Courtney was over at a friend's while I spent the afternoon pottering round a local garden centre with Sophie, now 19. We were just picking out some plants when I was interrupted by a phone call from Kay.

'Virginia,' she said. 'Denise is in labour and it looks like it's happening really fast. I am on my way now but I think you might be nearer. Can you meet me there?'

Although she was calm, I could hear the urgency in her voice – and with good reason. Denise was pregnant with twins and had been due to give birth a week from now.

Denise, a bubbly woman in her late 20s with short, blonde hair, had already had one home birth with her first baby while under the care of the NHS. She'd been all set to take this route again when, during their first scan, she and her husband, Rob, had discovered she was expecting twins.

They'd been delighted by the news until their midwife dropped the bombshell that a labour involving twins was deemed 'high risk' and therefore their local hospital would not support a home birth.

But neither the prospect of an early caesarean or giving birth surrounded by a huddle of medics in the cold clinical surroundings of a large, brightly lit hospital theatre appealed to Denise.

Like all women who are deemed high risk Denise had the right to an informed choice of birth, and when she did her research she discovered many stories of women having twins quite normally without intervention. And while there was a slightly higher chance of a problem with two babies, the most likely outcome was absolutely normal.

While making their decision, Denise and Rob had talked in depth to Kay and I. While we had limited experience of twins, we spoke at length to colleagues and did lots of reading on the subject.

It was agreed that over the following months Denise would have all her routine screening and visits with an NHS obstetrician but the birth plan was for Kay and I to deliver her twins at home.

Kay and I had last visited her two days earlier when both babies had seemed healthy and well with strong heartbeats. Now mentally plotting my route I worked out that it would take me a little under 45 minutes to drive the 40 miles on the motorway to her home in South London.

'Sorry, Sophie, but you'll have to come to this birth with me,' I said. 'Kay is bringing Alex, too.' Alex, who was also 19, was Kay's eldest daughter. Her son William, who was 12, was out elsewhere with his friends.

'OK,' Sophie agreed, looking excited. Thankfully both Sophie and Alex were well used to their mothers being called out at a moment's notice.

As I spoke to Kay on the hands'-free telephone en route to get an update, it was obvious it was going to be a race between us as to who was going to arrive first. It was good to know that we'd both be supporting Denise together and, not for the first time, I was grateful to have such a good friend and colleague in Kay.

The times we really worked together closely were on complicated cases like Denise's and I always appreciated Kay's cool, calm take on things.

Arriving at Denise and Rob's home, a terraced house in the town of Erith, I pulled up quickly alongside the broken-down car on the driveway that Rob was fixing up. I was relieved to see that Kay's car was already parked.

Jumping out the car I grabbed my bag.

'Sophie, grab the other bag and bring it in, please,' I called over my shoulder. I didn't know what equipment Kay had with her so I was not taking any chances that something of mine might be needed.

Running into the house through the already open door I took in the scene.

Denise was lying in the birth pool with a baby in her arms while Kay was standing over her and palpating her tummy to ascertain the way baby number two was laying.

'OK, Denise,' she said. 'The baby is in the breech position so, as we planned, we would prefer you to get out of the pool to birth baby.'

As she and Rob made to help Denise out it was clear the second twin was already coming.

'I need to push,' she said. Despite how quickly everything was happening she seemed calm and confident.

Putting my bag down, I joined the huddle at the pool as Kay clamped and cut the cord, then took the baby from Denise's arms, wrapped him in a towel and passed him to me.

Thinking fast, I knew that I needed to help Denise and Kay. So in a continuous movement I turned and passed the baby to Sophie who had just come through the door and placed my second equipment bag on a chair.

'Hold baby and go sit in the other room, Sophie,' I said.

Together Kay and I helped Denise out of the water on to the small area that Rob had prepared with plastic sheets and towels next to the pool. She immediately lowered herself to her knees and I could already see the tiny buttocks of a breech baby starting to emerge.

'Wow, that was fast,' I thought as I watched Kay sink down to the floor in readiness to catch the second baby. My heart was beating fast, more from the physical exertion of rushing in with heavy bags than with the excitement, but I was really pleased that all was going well.

But as Kay prepared to catch the second baby, two little legs dropped down and I knew immediately that something was wrong. As Kay glanced up at me I could read the concern in her eyes. The baby was a mottled colour, a mix of mauve and white but his skin was peeling off in sheets from his body. As the rest of his torso appeared in much the same condition, it became more and more obvious this was not going to be a good outcome.

'Oh God,' Rob cried out covering his hand with his mouth and I saw Denise looking at him with panicked confusion. Someone had to prepare them. I sank to my knees and put my arm across Denise's shoulder.

'Denise, something is not quite right with baby,' I said gently. Immediately she started to howl.

'Get him out, get him out,' she screamed.

'Virginia, take over please,' Kay said moving out of the way. Returning to the baby I saw that it appeared to have stopped descending and the head was not delivered.

Placing my hand on to the hanging baby, I traced my finger up into Denise's vagina until I reached the back of the baby's head. From the feel of its head, I now knew that hope was dwindling. When a baby dies in the womb it loses all tone and the head drops back on its shoulders causing it to get stuck on the public bone. Gently pushing the head down to flex it I did my best to make it easier to be born.

As a sobbing Denise pushed the baby into my hands he flopped out lifeless. Laying him on a towel I grabbed my emergency resuscitation equipment and put the oxygen mask over his face. At the same time I put my hand on his chest feeling for a heart rate. The urgency to save this little boy's life was my only thought as I began cardiac compressions in the hope of restarting his heart.

Somewhere in my mind in those frantic few seconds I was aware of his sunken chest and soft bones. I knew my attempts were to no avail but yet I could not stop until Kay placed her hands on mine and stilled their activity.

'It's no good, Virginia, please don't,' she said softly.

Stopping I sat back on my heels.

'I am so sorry, Denise, Rob, but your baby is dead,' I said.

All Kay and I could do was sit silently as Denise let out a low howl and Rob wrapped her in his arms and rocked her, tears trickling down his cheeks.

'Oh my God, oh my God, I am scared to look at him,' she cried.

'He is lovely, Denise, look,' I said. While the baby's body showed signs that he had died around 24 hours previously, his face was untouched and he looked serene and beautiful.

I watched, my own heart aching, as Denise looked at her baby, her face crumpling with stark despair. 'We were going to call him Trey,' she said, her voice shaking.

'I will dress him for you while Kay delivers the placenta,' I whispered.

Once this third stage of labour was complete, Kay guided Denise slowly upstairs to the bathroom and Rob walked outside with his head in his hands I looked down at the dear little boy in my arms.

'Your family is going to miss you,' I whispered to him.

I was interrupted by a cry from the other room and with a jolt of concern, remembered who was holding Trey's brother Zane.

Laying Trey on a chair I went into the other room where I knew immediately that my daughter Sophie had heard every moment of the tragic outcome unfolding.

As she sat silently, gently rocking the baby, there were tears rolling down her cheeks and I exploded with love for my own child. Easing baby Zane out of her tight grip I laid him on a chair then I wrapped my arms around MY baby and pulled her to her feet.

'I'm so sorry you heard all that,' I said hugging and rocking her. Then I gently led her outside to where Kay's daughter Alex was still waiting in Kay's car.

Wiping away her tears and kissing her cheeks, I asked Alex to look after her, glad that Kay's husband was on the way to pick them both up and take them home.

This was not the first time Sophie had been at a birth with me – previously, after she'd expressed an interest, a client of mine had invited her to see her birth. On that occasion Sophie had stood behind mesmerised, while I'd knelt in front of the standing mother, as a tiny scrunched baby came into sight.

'It looked blue!' she said afterwards. 'It seemed strange and I was worried!'

I'd laughed, explaining that babies always look a bit blue until they take their first breath. But this time round Sophie really had experienced a tragedy and I felt terrible.

I spent some time afterwards worried that she would be traumatised but we were able to have a good chat about it.

'That was very rare, Sophie,' I told her. 'Even I haven't seen many babies die and I attend births all the time.'

Although it was a sad thing for her to witness, it didn't discourage Sophie and three years later she went on to begin training to become a midwife herself.

Walking back into the house I dressed the lifeless baby and watched as Kay scooped up Zane from the chair and handed him to Denise, who was now sat on the sofa next to Rob.

Gently picking up Trey I passed him to Rob to hold, knowing that Kay would have prepared Denise for how important it was for them both to hold him and say goodbye. As Rob wrapped an arm around his wife and the two of them sat and cried, Kay and I went into the kitchen to give them some privacy.

Once there we held each other tight, still shocked and devastated at how fast the events had unfolded. It is impossible not to get emotionally involved when you work as a midwife. The reward of handing a mother her newly born child is amazing, so when you have to face the opposite scenario it is just devastating.

The Baby's Coming

With no choice but to stay strong and press on with her mothering duties to a healthy and hungry Zane, a shell-shocked Denise managed to breastfeed while Kay and I made the arrangements to take baby Trey to the chapel of rest at the local undertakers. As Kay drove and I sat with Trey's tiny body wrapped in a blanket snuggled in my arms, I will never forget that journey.

Searching hands on soft stretched skin
The beating heart heard deep within
My patient ears hear mother's woes
It's such hard work how well I know

Each one special yet just the same
Another day though sure the aim
A sweet soft cry when work is done
Another life, another one.

This is how it's meant to be
A work of love for you, for me
How we suffer when it's not so
Who do you hold, where do I go?

It's not the way to end my part
Empty arms and a broken heart
Not for this sorrow did I learn
A mother's pain a mother's yearn

Do I go on the journey's way?
Another mother, another day
Will the one I see for time to come
Be the eyes of pain, the other one?

This wasn't how it was meant to be
Not for you and not for me.

There was no inquest as the baby was stillborn and Denise declined an autopsy. She and Rob reflected long and hard about how they would proceed with the situation but placed no blame on anyone, including herself, for Trey's death. She and Rob knew that even if she had made it to a hospital in time, the outcome would have been just the same as the baby's appearance indicated that it had been dead for around 24 hours. Denise had made her choices of care and never for one moment regretted her home birth.

Afterwards Denise kept in touch and wrote to both of us to say she felt that she'd had a very positive birth despite the circumstances and she was glad it had happened at home with midwives she knew and trusted. Two years later she went on to give birth to a healthy baby boy at home, helped every step of the way by Kay.

For a long time Trey's death weighed heavily on our hearts but I am just grateful that we had each other during one of the lowest moments of our careers. Kay will always remain my colleague, supporter and advocate, and most of all an amazing, true friend.

Chapter Nine

Seeing Tonia's number on my phone I smiled to myself.

It was August 2005 and, despite her vow ten months earlier that her family was complete, I suspected she had some happy news for me.

'You're pregnant again aren't you?' I said.

'Yes,' she laughed. 'Twelve weeks.'

On a lovely sunny morning a few days later, I arrived at Tonia's home where she greeted me with a smile and I followed her inside, eager to see how much her brood had grown.

By now Ennieco was toddling and, while Aerojen was still shy and quiet, Anzonia was pushing herself forward to be the centre of attention. Then there was Kerrec, a handsome boy who knew his own mind.

'I thought Ennieco was going to be the last one,' I said, as we sat on the sofa in the living room. 'And when I didn't get the usual call in April I thought that really was it.'

'We always wanted another one,' Tonia confessed. 'But I just couldn't face being heavily pregnant in the summer.'

'Well, it's good to be able to help you again,' I smiled.

After getting her wish of bypassing a long hot summer to endure the more uncomfortable months of her labour in the heart of winter, Tonia went into labour with her fifth child on a cold

February night. And, once again, she gave birth in the pool, down on one knee, this time to her largest baby yet.

'Wow, this one's pretty ugly, I think!' she commented as I wrapped her chubby little girl in a towel.

'No,' I laughed as I laid the baby on the sofa. 'She is just fat and scrunched up. Now let's get you out of that pool.'

With the placenta delivered, Tonia snuggled up on the sofa with baby Orlena – named after a Russian gymnast at the Commonwealth Games.

'Here you go,' I said, handing her a hot water bottle to keep the two of them warm.

Once I could see that baby was breastfeeding contently, I left them to it.

Somehow I didn't think that cuddly Orlena would be the last winter baby for Tonia.

Not long after, as I shimmied into a room that was as small as an aeroplane toilet to kneel down in front of another client, Jackie, I was to experience one of the more comical births of my career.

Jackie, a tall woman who had put on a considerable amount of weight during her pregnancy, was sat on the loo in the final stages of labour, blocking off all access to her rapidly approaching baby.

'Jackie,' I said, my mouth twitching with amusement. 'I am not in the mood for fishing. Can we manoeuvre you up just enough so I can catch baby?'

'Oh my G-G-God,' came the answering cry in a contraction-fuelled warble. 'I. CAN'T. MOOOVE. OFF. THIS. BLOODY. TOILEEEET!'

I'd first met Jackie, a nurse in her late 20s, a couple of years previously when I'd been a midwife for her Filipino sister-in-law. Bituin spoke very little English but, knowing her well, Jackie had been there throughout her labour and birth to help me communicate with her.

During our regular meetings Jackie had confided in me about the birth of her own son, Tristan, now four, which had happened under very stressful circumstances via caesarean section.

'I don't want to have my next baby in hospital,' she admitted to me. 'But I am deemed high risk now, aren't I, Virginia? I suppose I won't be allowed to have a home birth.'

Women often talk about 'being allowed' and it never ceases to amaze me how some very well-educated and empowered women still believe that such decisions are not theirs to make.

While you will always get doctors and midwives who state, 'You will have to do this . . .' or 'We can't allow you to do that . . .', the fact is that the professional is merely there to give advice in regards to safe evidence-based care. Whether or not the woman takes that advice is completely up to her. This matter has been tested by law and I always tell pregnant women: 'It's your body, your baby and your right to the birth you want!'

Sadly Jackie had not made informed choices when it came to the end of her first pregnancy and had been induced because she was a few days over her estimated due date. The resulting cascade of intervention had lead to a caesarean section.

Of course, once a woman has had a caesarean section then the scar on her uterus puts her into a whole new category and she will be forever more regarded by the medical profession as 'high risk'.

So there was Jackie thinking she would need to have a repeat caesarean – until she met me and we had a discussion about risk and informed choice. Once I was assured it was a decision made based on evidence and information then I was happy to support her wish to have a home birth.

Her decision to step outside the NHS for her own care meant risking critical comments from her hospital colleagues but, once Jackie knew she could have a home birth, she had made up her mind.

As the due date for Jackie's second baby approached, I noticed she was getting a little nervous. But it wasn't fears about giving birth that were plaguing Jackie, rather she was worrying herself sick with concerns about what might happen should complications arise. Still haunted by memories of being left alone in pain in a cold, clinical hospital bathroom for hours on end, the thought of returning to hospital was her worst nightmare.

So when Jackie went into labour she was determined to ignore it for as long as possible. In her mind, the less time she admitted to being in labour the less opportunity there was for a transfer to hospital.

The first I knew about it was when her husband, Lance, called to say that Jackie had been having contractions for a while but had busied herself playing Scrabble as she believed she had 'hours to go yet'.

However, when she found herself going so cross-eyed with the pain that she could no longer differentiate between the 'b's and the 'p's in her Scrabble letters, she had relented and allowed Lance to summon me.

As I set off at 11.20pm on that cold winter night, I was alarmed to see the first few flakes of a snow storm swirling across my windscreen.

'Please let the weather hold out until I get there,' I prayed to the birth angels. 'And please let Lance have a hot cup of tea for me,' I added for good measure.

I arrived to find the back door had been opened for me but otherwise the house was quiet. Creeping inside, I followed a creaking noise from upstairs where I found Jackie pacing the landing.

'Oh, Virginia, I told him it's far too early!' Jackie said. 'It's all stopped now.'

'Don't listen to her, Virginia,' Lance interrupted, walking out of the bedroom. 'She's been having pains all day long, stronger this evening, but we were playing Scrabble and she just didn't want me to win.'

'But I'm fine now!' Jackie insisted.

'Don't worry, I believe you,' I laughed. 'But shall we have a little listen to baby anyway then you can get on with everything else in your own time.'

Getting out my sonic aid I sloshed some contact gel on the end and pressed it to Jackie's lower tummy to hear the baby as she held on to the upstairs banister and closed her eyes.

As we both counted a slow steady beat of 90 to 100 rather than the expected variable beat of 110–160 Jackie's eyes sprung open with concern.

'Wow, is that OK?' she said.

'Well, it really depends how far along you are with the labour,' I answered. 'I think it best if I examine you, is that OK?'

Jackie agreed and after I'd helped her to lie down on the landing I turned to Lance.

'I think you had better call an ambulance as a precaution,' I said, as I pulled on my gloves. His face turned ashen as he dashed off to call 999.

As I peered between Jackie's legs to examine her cervix it was my turn for a shock.

'Jackie,' I said. 'You're about to have your baby!'

I was flabbergasted. I had not seen Jackie have a single contraction since I'd been at the house but yet she was on the verge of giving birth. The lack of contractions were probably due to what midwives call the 'rest and be thankful' stage often seen at the end of the first stage of labour when there is no longer any cervix for the head to press against to release the oxytocin which in turn causes the contractions. And I could only assume that the slow heartbeat was due to the baby coming down through the pelvis and having his head squashed.

'Get me up, get me up,' Jackie suddenly cried out as the 'rest' stage came to an abrupt end and lying on her back proved to be far too painful.

'Oh good, the contractions have come back,' I thought, helping her to her feet.

'The ambulance is on its way,' Lance said, running up the stairs.

'I'm not going in no ambulance,' Jackie barked. 'I will be a laughing stock going through A&E! "Oh look," they will say, "It's Jackie and her big ideas about her home birth",' she whined, mimicking her work colleagues and then pulling a face as yet another contraction rippled through her body ending on a huge bearing down grunt.

'Oh my goodness, it feels like I'm going to shit myself,' she cried, staggering past me to sit on the loo in the upstairs toilet.

Jackie and Lance had recently moved into an older property where, little by little, they were making structural and decorative changes to their home. Of course, paying for an independent midwife had meant putting some of the home improvements on hold and this included knocking down the wall between the upstairs bathroom and the toilet.

As it stood, the lavatory bowl was almost as wide as the tiny room that contained it and you were lucky if, when sitting on it, your knees did not touch either side of the wall. Due to the lack of space, I quickly set up my birth equipment at the top of the stairs on the landing as Jackie started to push in earnest, going red in the face with all the effort.

Although many a baby has been born on a toilet with ease and comfort for the mother, my big concern was there was absolutely no space between Jackie's legs for me to put my hands in order to catch the baby before it landed in the pan.

'Can you move?' I asked.

Jackie looked down to where her tummy was rested on the tops of her legs, her vagina nowhere to be seen beneath but clearly positioned to deposit her baby directly down the pan.

'Oh bloody hell!' she bellowed, grabbing on to my arm with a vicelike grip. 'It's going down the loo if I don't get my arse off this seat!'

'Quick, Jackie, stand up a bit so I can get my hands under you before the next contraction comes,' I instructed. 'It's only a small move forward.'

Still grabbing my arm and her legs shaking, Jackie attempted to shuffle forward, her face panic-stricken.

'Don't worry, baby won't go down the loo,' I said, remembering that this was her first vaginal birth. 'The head will come first, then it will stop, then the body will come with the following contraction.'

'The paramedics are here,' Lance said hovering by the door.

'Can you tell them to wait downstairs?' I said loudly without turning my head.

As the next contraction started to build and I angled myself to see if I could spot the approaching downy head, Jackie managed to heave her heavy body up off the toilet to a half-standing, half-crouching position. Forget my 'the head comes first, then the body' reassurance, quick as a flash, the whole baby spiralled out of her and in a clap catch that would make a cricket coach proud I clasped him to my chest.

Unbelievably the placenta came flying out behind the baby, making me jump out of my skin as it splatted into my lap and then slid with a sloppy 'Plop!' on to the linoleum floor next to my knees.

As my eyes fell on the floppy, not-breathing baby in my arms, adrenaline coursed through my body. Glancing over my shoulder, I saw my equipment approximately 12 feet away on the landing. It had all happened so quickly I had neither a towel to stimulate the baby or scissors to cut the cord to hand. Trying to pick up the placenta as well as hold on to the baby was like attempting to carry a bag of snakes and so with the baby flopping over one arm I had to hold the cord by the end nearest to the placenta and drag it across the floor still attached to the baby to reach my equipment. The problem with his lack of breathing was due to the placenta becoming detached so quickly, but thankfully with a few puffs of air to expand his lungs Jackie's son was just fine.

Panic over I helped Jackie into her bedroom and asked Lance to send the ambulance crew away. As I placed baby boy Conor into Jackie's arms a smile crept across her face.

'We weren't expecting you to arrive so fast,' she cooed. 'You were in a real hurry!'

With little Conor no worse for wear after his dramatic entrance, I left them to it, returning the next day when we both had a good laugh about it.

'You should have seen how much you jumped when the placenta flew out,' she giggled. 'Your face was a picture.'

To this day Jackie's 'flash in the pan' birth will be up there as one of my funniest midwifery moments.

As spring was beginning to creep into sight, I took on a new client called Danielle.

One of the many things I love about life as an independent midwife is setting off to meet a mum-to-be on a fine day never knowing what beauty awaits me as I follow my trusty satnav through the countryside.

However, when I keyed in an address for Danielle and her husband Mark that took me into the busy urban town of Orpington I wasn't expecting much scenery en route. Having anticipated quite a boring drive along the M25 I was delighted when I found myself veering off along the only country lane for a 20-mile radius winding through acres of fields.

As it happened, Danielle and Mark had rented a small bungalow five miles from Orpington where, if it wasn't for the distant rumble of delivery lorries heading around the busiest motorway in England, you would have no clue of its proximity to the town and roads.

As Danielle, wearing not a scrap of make-up and dressed in loose clothing with her long, dark hair flowing, showed me around her large garden it was clear she had a real affinity for nature.

Having grown up in the New Zealand countryside, Danielle had put her green-fingered skills to good use growing an impressive harvest of home-grown fruits and vegetables.

It was no surprise to hear that she wanted her birth to be as natural as possible as well and that was why she was opting out of the NHS.

'The local hospital has a birth pool but there was no guarantee I'll get it on the day,' she told me. 'It all depends on whether the midwife I'm allocated to is trained to attend a water birth!'

With Danielle also wanting the guarantee of a midwife she knew and trusted, she and Mark had decided to Google independent midwives in the area and had shortlisted several for interview. So, over the course of an hour, we talked about my experience and philosophy on birth.

I never knew why Danielle and Mark chose me until several weeks after the baby was born and Danielle revealed she had liked the testimonials on my website and how one mother had said that I had stood up for her like a lion when the need had arisen to defend the client. 'It was good to know that, if necessary, you would fight my corner if we go to hospital,' she said.

I, in turn, was pleased they'd chosen me and found Danielle a delight to care for. With her laid-back and healthy attitude to life I never had any doubt about her ability to avoid intervention and have the normal water birth at home she so wanted.

During the weeks leading up to her labour, Danielle asked me endless questions while introducing me to her passion for healthy cooking and organic foods. Many a day I would walk in the house to the mouth-watering aroma of Danielle's homemade cakes and light fluffy pastries only for her to smile and hand me a paper bag of goodies to take home.

Danielle showed her first signs that baby was on his way with a 'bloody show' on a busy Friday morning. This can occur towards the end of pregnancy when the cervix begins to move and shorten causing the mucus plug that had sealed its entrance to be released. This can happen up to a week or more before active labour commences but if the mucus has fresh blood mixed in it, then labour may well be imminent.

We kept in touch for the next 48 hours as Danielle experienced irregular contractions and I found myself sleeping fitfully as I awoke regularly to glance at my clock and wonder how Danielle was doing.

At 7am on Monday morning the wait was over and Danielle called to ask me to head over. As I rushed out the door, I kissed 20-year-old Sophie goodbye as she was busy putting her make-up on in the bathroom ready to go to work in a call-centre. Peering into Courtney's bedroom, I saw that she was just stirring but I resisted switching the light on because of the inevitable shouts of protest.

Setting off in heavy rush-hour traffic, I made it there in good time and found Danielle in great form, seeming chirpy and excited as she chatted away between contractions.

Mark was still sleeping in the bedroom, having been awake a lot in the night supporting Danielle, so the two of us talked as she leaned over her birthing ball or paced around the garden pointing out her ripening crop of fruits.

I was pleased to find all her observations were normal, the baby's heart was steady and regular at 130 beats per minute and Danielle was calm and confident. Now all we had to do was await her progress. But after an hour or so Danielle suddenly looked up at me from where she was leaning over the birth ball.

'I think you should go home, Virginia,' she said. 'I want to be alone.'

Although most mothers I've worked with have wanted me there all of the time, it was not unusual for Danielle to feel this way. Some labouring women do want to be alone and others report feeling pressurised if the midwife is there.

I am always aware that a woman needs to feel relaxed and in control in order for the hormones to flow and her labour to commence but I couldn't help worrying about being too far away.

'I'm happy to go home, Danielle,' I agreed. 'But what if you end up giving birth when I'm half-way down the motorway? Would you agree to let me examine you to get an idea of how much time we have?'

Danielle agreed and I found she was four centimetres dilated but her cervix was paper thin and stretching easily. I decided that if her need and desire was solitude, then it was probably a good idea for me to go now rather than later.

'Call me as soon as the contractions get stronger,' I instructed. Having been home for a few hours I was surprised when the afternoon passed by with no telephone calls from Danielle.

By 6pm like a worried mother hen I was unable to concentrate on anything and even called my own mobile to make sure it was still working! I was itching to pick up the phone and check everything was OK but I also didn't want to annoy Danielle. It is, after all, the woman's place to request help of a midwife and she is the one who should be in control.

By 7pm I could resist no longer and full of apologies for calling I made a silly excuse. 'I was thinking about baking a cake,' I lied. 'But if I start now will you need me there soon?'

'Virginia, I was just about to call you,' Danielle replied to my stark relief. 'The contractions are stronger and more painful now so I want to get into the pool. Can you come?'

She didn't have to ask me twice. I was out the door and on the motorway in a flash. By now the sun was going down and there was a crisp chill in the air but at least the roads were quiet. I made it back in about 40 minutes.

Quietly letting myself in the kitchen door I noticed immediately that the usual smell of baking had been replaced with the warm, sticky smell that every midwife knows means birth is imminent. In a hospital, the yeasty scent has the added antiseptic and clinical components and at home the underlying smell is just the same but laced with the sweet aroma of candle wax, lavender or incense. It always evokes such joy in me and I rank it up there with the scent of freshly cut grass, baking bread or steaming coffee.

The house was very quiet, and keen not to disturb the peace I crept into the room where I knew I would find Danielle in the pool. As I expected, Danielle was in the water with her head resting on the side of the pool and Mark was by her side. Small beads of sweat were dotted all over her face and the room was damply hot from the heat of the water. Tiptoeing in, I tried to make myself as inconspicuous as possible.

I watched silently for a while and, sure enough, the contractions were very different. By now the usually chatty Danielle was completely in the zone with her sole focus on her labour.

As each contraction came she made no noise, but took a deep breath lifting her head with a gentle sway as the muscles of her body tightened. Then when the exhausting wave subsided her head fell back to its resting place on the side of the pool and she appeared to fall into a deep sleep until the rhythm began again. I was able to tell they were coming every two minutes.

After about 15 minutes Danielle raised her head and opened her eyes to look at me.

'Hi, Virginia,' she whispered with the tiniest hint of a smile teasing from the corners of her mouth. 'You OK?'

I answered with a nod and a question of my own.

'Is it OK to listen to baby, Danielle?' I was already picking up my handheld, sonic-aid, heart-listening device in anticipation of her agreement. She nodded and moved just an inch so I could get my hand into the pool and towards her tummy to find the heartbeat.

I found it straight away, remembering the lie of the baby from an examination earlier in the day and counted the fast rhythm while watching the display window.

It was 170 – much too fast – unless the baby is moving around and responding well to labour.

'Is the baby moving, Danielle?' I asked.

'Not as far as I can tell,' she said, shaking her head.

The temperature of the pool was quite hot and so my next thought was that Danielle's core temperature was too high. I took her temperature. It was marginally raised but not enough to affect the baby.

Waiting a short while, I listened to the baby's heartbeat again. It was still too high.

'The baby's heart is a little higher than it should be,' I told her calmly, not wishing to alarm her. 'It might be because you're too hot. Can you stand up in the water to let your body cool down a bit?'

As she stood up and gave a small shiver, I listened again to the baby's heartbeat. Still 170.

'Can you get out the pool?' I asked.

After fanning her with a rolled-up paper for five minutes, I checked again. I was relieved to hear a very normal 130 and heaved a big sigh of relief.

With Danielle sat on the loo in the dark, I checked again a few minutes later. Now it had shot up to 180. My heart fell knowing that I could no longer ignore it. I would need to suggest taking action, even though it would deeply disappoint Danielle and Mark who totally and utterly believed in normality of birth.

'Can I examine you again please, Danielle?' I asked. With her consent I gently explored her cervix while explaining my concerns in a hushed voice.

'It might be a good idea to go to hospital to make sure everything is OK,' I said. 'You're six centimetres dilated so it would be advisable to go now. We can get you hooked up to a fetal monitor to check the baby and if everything is fine we can always come back home.'

I could see Danielle's mind digesting the information. When I had finished examining her she turned on to all fours and rocked her hips from side to side.

'But what if it's not OK?' she said staring intently at me during a break between contractions.

'Then we will be in the correct place for the safest birth, won't we?' I whispered softly.

With Danielle in agreement, I stood up and gathered a few things I would need for the journey to the hospital, then helped Danielle to her feet. My heart was like a stone. I knew how much Danielle wanted a natural birth and I knew they had little faith in the system of maternity care in the hospital so it would be stressful for them to go. I wanted it for them as much as they did but, while home birth is safe, I also knew to turn to medical backup when it was needed.

The hospital was not far away but when we arrived we found the maternity ward heaving. We had to wait about 15 minutes for them to prepare a room while all the while Danielle was on her knees breathing through the contractions and clinging on to the only empty chair in the waiting room. As a few expectant fathers looked on anxiously, I could tell they were worried they might see a woman other than their wife give birth that night.

To everyone's relief we were eventually shown to a hospital room and, before the midwife assigned to Danielle could even introduce herself, I grabbed for a sonic aid to listen to the baby. The heartbeat was 160.

Danielle sat on the bed as the midwife hooked her up to a monitor looking like a frightened deer caught in the headlights. Almost immediately the motor on the fetal heart machine started pushing the paper out for all to see. As the graph paper emerged spiking up and down like a small mountain range, a smile spread across my face. I turned to Danielle who was puffing, panting and squirming as she tried to remain in an uncomfortable position sat on the bed.

'The baby is moving all right, Danielle, can't you feel it?' I said incredulously.

From the lines of the graph it was clear that while the baby's heart elevated to 170–180 beats per minute it also returned to 140 after each burst of activity. The only explanation was that I must have been listening to the baby every time it was moving and missed the periods in between. I suddenly felt like a bit of a fool and was embarrassed that I'd brought them to the hospital – the place they least wanted to be, with a perfectly healthy baby to boot!

So all we had to do now was go back home where the nice cosy atmosphere and warm pool awaited us. But getting out of a maternity unit on a busy night is even harder than getting admitted into it. A discharge falls right to the bottom of any priority list.

In the meantime, I tried to make the room a bit more comfortable for Danielle. The lights were on the brightest setting and the hospital radio was tuned into a talk show about heroin addiction – not exactly conducive to giving birth. I quickly turned off the radio and dimmed the lights. We waited for a while, Mark and I pacing the room like caged tigers, until eventually I went outside to speak to the midwife in charge. Her name was Babs and she'd been lovely for the short time she cared for Danielle. But hospitals have their rules and Babs was not about to break them easily.

'I can't discharge you till the doctor sees the monitor trace so he can sign it off and he's in surgery,' she said.

Clearly Danielle could have walked out of the hospital any time she wanted but the staff had been so pleasant that I wanted to be nice in return. However, when another hour had passed and Danielle's contractions were coming fast and furious, it was time to leave – with or without the discharge.

'OK,' I said, straightening my shoulders and adopting my famous 'stroppy' face. 'I will go and tell them we ARE leaving.'

But on my way out the door I almost collided with a doctor. Hardly even glancing at Danielle he walked straight up to the machine where the graph was awaiting his gaze.

'I understand you want to go home,' he said, examining the long scroll of paper in his hand.

'Yes, we were just leaving,' Mark replied quietly but with great authority. I almost giggled at the little twitch I saw at the corner of the doctor's mouth.

'Well,' he began, clearing his voice. 'I am very happy with this trace and happy for you to be discharged back into your midwife's care.'

'Thanks,' I smiled as Mark and I bundled Danielle out of the room.

Within minutes the three of us were in the long hospital corridor walking towards the lift when Danielle stopped in her tracks and leant against the wall to give one almighty, strong, body-bending push!

'Mark, run, run quickly,' I said. 'Get the car and take it to the exit door.'

As Mark took off running along the corridor I put my hand under Danielle's arm and pretty much frog-marched her towards the lift – contractions or not I did not let her stop walking. We made it down in the lift in record time and, as instructed, Mark was waiting at the door with the engine running.

Danielle half climbed, half fell into the back seat of the car and as soon as the doors were shut Mark was heading out of the car park.

I gritted my teeth as Danielle let out another big groan as she fought the urge to push and I glanced sideways at Mark from where I sat next to him.

'Step on it, Mark,' I urged quietly.

'Really?' he said, his eyes widening and doing a double take at me but putting his foot down. I nodded. I didn't need to do any invasive examinations to know that Danielle was well into the second stage of labour and the baby was ready to be born.

Late on a Monday night the roads were clear but my heart was pounding fast as I prayed to the birth angels that we would make it home in time. I kept my eyes fixed on Danielle, who could not hold back from pushing as the surges rippled through her body.

As Mark pulled up at their home, I leapt up to help Danielle out the car.

'Go, Mark, open the door,' I shouted. 'Get some hot water topping up that pool.'

Once again Mark ran to do my bidding, leaving the door open for Danielle to waddle in with her knees together as quickly as she could up the garden path.

Swaying through the kitchen door she turned right into her birthing room and heaved herself over the side of the inflatable pool to sink her body into its warm, soothing depths. The look on her face was one of pure ecstasy as she breathed a sigh of relief that at last she was back where she wanted to be, safe in the comfort of her own home.

No more than ten minutes later Danielle's final expulsive effort launched her beautiful baby boy, Jack, into the world and she scooped him up into her arms.

I couldn't help smiling as the realisation hit me that Danielle must be one of the only women ever to rush AWAY from a hospital to give birth.

Chapter Ten

Flying down the motorway at 7am in my self-styled 'mess-on-wheels', my thoughts were filled with the two postnatal and antenatal visits ahead of me. As times got busier, predictably my Citroën car got messier as I found myself eating hastily bought garage sandwiches en route.

Business was going really well and I now had my holiday home in Turkey to escape to with the family whenever I needed a break.

After five years alone with just me and my kids, in 2005 I'd met a lovely guy called Sean through online dating. From the minute I met him at Frankie and Benny's I knew I wanted to continue seeing him. Not only was he much better looking than his profile picture but he was also the type of man I had always considered I needed. If I had a checklist he ticked every box. He was smart, clean and tidy, had a good job and was very responsible and sensible.

For our second date he'd invited me for dinner at his and within half an hour of me being there, I was semi-clothed and we were working up a sweat on his carpet – but not in the way you'd think.

Eager to impress me, Sean had started the evening by showing me the tricks he'd taught his pet dog. Unfortunately, as his dog jumped up, he hit my wine glass sending red wine flying all over Sean's creamy white carpet, all up his cream blinds and all over my pink jumper.

Thankfully we both saw the funny side and, after he'd apologised profusely and given me a T-shirt to wear, we both got down on our knees and attempted to scrub the carpet clean.

Sean, too, had had a bit of heartbreak in his life and so for a while we were two lost souls who needed each other. We'd both wondered if the time for exploding love had passed us by but as the months turned into years, I grew to love Sean like the roots of a mighty oak tree. It is a stable and togetherness love, which admittedly is not like the wild crazy times I spent with Michael, but there is a lot to be said for loyalty, respect and commitment, and that makes Sean the man I will spend the rest of my life with. Sean is my rock and we all love him to bits. As much as I love my job nothing makes me happier than spending time with Sean and my family. Now celebrating our ninth year together, we are firm and strong and I am still very proud to say he is my man.

As I planned in my head the best order to carry out my visits, my hands-free in-car telephone rang. It was my friend Leah and she could hardly contain her excitement.

'I'm pregnant!' she squealed.

'That's wonderful!' I replied, knowing just how much it meant for her to be pregnant with her long-awaited first baby at the age of 38.

I'd met Leah, a slim, chic blonde, through a mutual friend several years earlier when we'd both attended the same Christmas dinner bash for single women. Over the years she and I had often swapped stories of our hopes and dreams, with Leah sharing her desire to have a child of her own – and for me to be her midwife!

There had been some bleak years but now in 2006 things were looking up for both of us.

As my relationship with Sean blossomed, so had Leah's with Alan, a tall, handsome, 48-year-old airline pilot who she'd met through her job as cabin crew.

Head over heels, they'd moved in together near me in Ashford and were overjoyed when Leah soon fell pregnant.

It was no surprise when over dinner, Leah, who generally took a holistic approach to health and wellbeing, told me that she really wanted a home birth. Alan, on the other hand, being quite a conventional man, was dubious.

Like many men who can only see the practicalities and perceived safety of giving birth in hospital, it was just a case of him knowing the correct information and, after an informal chat, it did not take long for him to change his opinion.

Leah's pregnancy progressed as normal and it was fun to see my glamorous friend turn from the party girl she had been into an excited and serene expectant mother.

Leah had read up extensively on her choices for birth and always had questions for me.

'If I have my baby at home, does that mean I can't have pain relief if I need it?' she asked.

'No,' I replied. 'You can have almost everything at home that you'd have in hospital. I carry Entonox, or laughing gas as it's known, to take the edge off the pain. And there's pethidine, too. The only thing I can't give you at home is an epidural but if you want that we can go to hospital.'

'Oh no, I've read about them and I don't want an epidural,' Leah replied.

Although many women choose an epidural there are risks which Leah had discovered from her research. Epidurals can lower the mother's blood pressure and also the baby's and, as a result, the baby goes into distress. There is also the fact that not being able to feel your legs means that the expulsive feelings aren't as strong, which can result in the need for further interventions, such as forceps. Also, being strapped up to a drip and a monitor means that the mother can't change positions easily.

'That's fine, Leah,' I agreed. 'If you don't want an epidural and the pain gets too much we can try submerging you in the pool, massage, walking and standing upright. It is good you are learning about this now. Often confidence and lack of fear are the best forms of pain relief.'

With Leah feeling informed and happy, many an appointment was extended as we discussed days gone by and the raucous, late nights out we'd had on the town with the girls.

But then, at 35 weeks, Leah called me in a flap. 'Virginia, I'm in Tesco and I just had this weird feeling,' she said. 'I think my waters have gone.'

'It might be nothing,' I said, trying to reassure her. 'Lots of women have an increase in discharge at the end of a pregnancy but why don't you pop round seeing as you are near.'

But when Leah arrived, to my dismay, I confirmed her waters had broken. There was no doubt in my mind. I immediately checked her temperature and the baby's heartbeat which were both normal.

Armed with cups of tea we sat down on the sofa to discuss her options.

'Most babies would be born perfectly fine at thirty-five weeks,' I told her. 'But there is a small chance of respiratory problems for a few and so it is not advisable to have a home birth. The hospital will advise induction because of the early dates and ruptured membranes but it is always your choice, of course.'

'I need to talk to Alan,' Leah replied. 'I'll see if anything happens tonight and give you a call tomorrow.'

The following morning Leah called to tell her decision. 'I've decided I want to wait to see if the labour starts on its own,' she said. 'Maybe I'll make it to 36 weeks and then I will have a home birth.'

With her decision made, I advised her to go to the hospital to have a group B streptococcus test and a scan the following day. Both of which she did before returning home to await the results. We had already discussed the risk of Group B streptococcus, an infection which, while rare to pass on to a newborn, can be fatal. As the hours pass following the waters breaking, if a woman carries GBS the risks for the baby increase. However, they are dramatically reduced if intravenous antibiotics are administered in the hours before birth.

Over the next couple of days Leah willed her body to wait, to keep baby inside for another week or more to develop his tiny lungs.

On the third day after Leah's water had broken, I was sitting at my desk chatting to Andrew on my landline. Now 26, he was telling me, his voice full of excitement, about the house he'd just bought in Ashford. Matt, who was 30, also had his own place in Chatham. I was so proud of the way both my sons had grown into responsible, loving, young men.

'Sorry, love, I'd better go,' I told him as my mobile started to ring. The other call was from the hospital to tell me the GBS test had returned positive. My stomach sunk to my shoes. Leah was not just my client, she was my friend and I was sad and disappointed for her that her already slim chances for a home birth had just been dashed.

Phoning Leah I broke the news.

'I'm so sorry, Leah,' I told her. 'But now it's strongly advisable that we get the labour going and get you started on antibiotics.'

As I spoke I could hear the distress building as she began to cry, her voice wobbling as she tried to hold back the sobs.

'I am so scared, Virginia,' she said. 'I didn't want to go to hospital and now I have to go for all the interventions I didn't want.'

'You don't have to go, Leah,' I said. 'It is your choice. You only have to have the interventions you agree to; you always have the right to say no.'

'Yes,' she whispered. 'It is my choice and I am choosing to do this to keep my baby safe, but please don't leave me at the hospital, Virginia, I am scared.'

'I promise I'll be there all the time,' I said. 'Now let's get this done, shall we? I will meet you at the hospital, OK?'

Picking up my bag, I let out a sigh and said goodbye to Sean and the girls. In a situation such as this, who knew when I would see them again? But at 20 and 15 my daughters were old enough now to cope and they also got on well with Sean so I had no reason to worry. My support for Leah began now and would only end once she was tucked up in bed with her baby – no matter where or when that would be.

Ringing ahead to the hospital where I'd previously worked, I'd been pleased to speak to Jill, the midwife in charge and one of my old fellow students, who I had a great respect for.

As long as we were on her watch I knew we'd be fine. So when I met Leah waiting tentatively in the hospital reception, the smile I gave her was real and hid none of the trepidation I'd usually feel in this situation.

As we walked the long maze of corridors towards maternity, Leah and Alan did their best to seem upbeat, joking and laughing despite their gut-wrenching disappointment.

Arriving on the ward we were all given a welcome cup of tea as we filled out all the necessary paperwork to get Leah admitted.

The Baby's Coming

We had arrived at 8pm just as the night shift was coming on duty and Jill had assigned a willowy blonde midwife called Kara to us. She was mild-mannered and calm and turned out to be delightful to have around. Best of all, she seemed to totally understand that Leah and I were close and after carrying out her routine checks she more or less left us alone.

The induction process had been commenced with a pessary placed inside Leah near to her cervix. This would help to soften and prepare it to open up for labour.

Sometimes, if a woman is already about to labour, this part of the process can succeed in moving her quickly into labour but, more often than not, it is a long, drawn-out and painful event. Leah had not reached her due date yet but, on the plus side, she did have ruptured membranes, so I had high hopes that the induction could work quickly.

'The more you can move around the better,' I told her, enticing her out into the hallway for a walking tour along the twisting hospital corridors that, apart from the occasional nurse passing us by, were pretty much deserted.

Arriving at a staircase we trotted down the flight of stairs, before turning and doing circuits up and down a couple more times, as an elderly cleaner watched us in total confusion.

The activity worked well. By the time we returned to the maternity ward Leah was stopping to lean against the wall as an onslaught of contractions told us her labour was under way.

It was time to get the birthing room ship shape and ready for her.

Leah wanted to remain upright in labour but would also need to be able to rest and sleep between contractions. I knew from experience that the hard hospital bed in the labour suite would made it tricky for Leah to get on and off so instead Alan and I moved the bed over to the far side of the room along with any other unneeded medical equipment.

Then I set about making Leah a nest on the floor with a mattress and pillows with plenty of room for her to move about. We also turned off the harsh, bright lights as Leah preferred.

By the middle of the night Leah was contracting really well. She had IV antibiotics going at regular intervals and our lovely midwife Kara tiptoed in unobtrusively to do her checks, respecting the quiet and the dark as Alan and I sat rubbing Leah's back and crooning soft words of encouragement to her.

Meanwhile, Leah used her well-practised self-hypnosis to breathe through the ever-strengthening contractions as we all acknowledged her need for peace and quiet to aid her concentration. As I sat there observing a calm, focused Leah, I was so grateful that we'd managed to create this special home-from-home hospital birth.

At 6am as the light of dawn started to creep under the hospital blinds, Kara performed a gentle probing vaginal examination while Leah remained propped up against me on the floor.

'You're progressing really well!' she said with a smile.

Leah looked delighted but I knew that the birth was still a fair way off and a creeping anxiety was beginning to build in my mind. It was likely that Kara would go off duty soon and I shivered at the thought of who might come on duty. My memories of the overbearing behaviour of certain members of staff in this hospital were as fresh as they had ever been.

All too soon, Kara came in and said her goodbyes.

'Who is taking over with Leah?' I asked.

'It's Phyllis,' she replied, rolling her eyes. It occurred to me that she, too, had hoped for a more like-minded midwife to support Leah for the rest of her birth.

'It could be worse,' I told myself. Phyllis, who I'd worked with as a student, was not a bully and she wasn't even mean. But she was not warm and was unfortunately the type of old-school midwife who follows rules for rules' sake. She'd always reminded me of the old matrons who thought it was more important not to crease the bed sheets than to have a patient comfortable in them.

All too soon, she came into the room and, as I expected, she eyeballed the 'disarray' with a look of horror.

'My goodness, what on earth has been happening in here?' she said, turning on the lights causing Leah to squint in discomfort.

'Come on, get up off that floor, dearie, you will catch a cold,' she said, busying herself moving things back into their usual places.

My mouth went dry with nervous tension at I steeled myself for the uphill battle I was about to embark on.

'Hi, Phyllis, shall we just have a little chat outside?' I said.

'Phyllis,' I said, once we were in the corridor. 'Leah wanted a home birth and I am trying my hardest to help her have the active birth she desperately wants. The night has been wonderful, please don't mess it up for her, leave her alone on the floor. It doesn't matter that the furniture is in the wrong place.'

Phyllis looked flustered but was not about to back down. 'I can't deliver a baby on the floor. No way,' she said. 'Anyway, it's time she was examined.' Given that Leah was still a far way from giving birth, I suspected her primary motive was to get Leah into a position she preferred. But before I could argue she'd flounced back into the room.

'I need to examine you now, Mrs Carter,' she said. 'Can you pop on to the bed for me, dear, please?' I bristled at the infuriatingly honey-like voice she was using to disguise her true intention. She wanted to shift the power and be in control.

Sighing, Leah nodded wearily. Taking her time as the contractions slowed her movements, she eventually climbed on to the bed.

As she attempted to lie down, I saw her face grimace in uncontrollable pain for the first time since her labour had began.

'No!' she cried. 'I can't lie down, it hurts more. Please get me up. Get me up!'

'I need to examine your tummy, dear, please,' Phyllis insisted.

'Oh my God,' screamed Leah. 'Just hurry up, will you please.' She lay back down gripping her tummy with one hand and squeezing Alan's hand with the other.

Once on the bed, it was very easy for Phyllis to release the brake and slide the easy-glide bed back into the usual position in centre of the room. I looked at the ceiling in exacerbation at this futile and pointless action. Phyllis then proceeded to palpate Leah's tummy, digging her fingers deep into the pubic arch area and wrinkling her brow into a worried frown.

'This baby is breech I think,' she said, as Leah jerked like a bee had suddenly stung her.

'Oh no!' cried Leah. 'Please don't say that, he wasn't breech yesterday.'

The panic on her face was heart-breaking and she started to cry, her sobs getting louder as the contractions continued to come one after another. I could feel the anger rising in my chest. Leah's concentration on her labour, her hypnotic state and her calm ability to cope were being annihilated by Phyllis with every passing minute.

'Phyllis,' I said as calmly as I could. 'Leah has had me and another midwife caring for her and feeling her tummy regularly. She has had vaginal examinations overnight and a scan yesterday, all of which said the baby was head down. I really don't think this baby is breech, maybe you just can't locate the head because it is so low now?'

'I am going to get the doctor,' Phyllis replied marching out the room. She returned almost instantly with a tall, gentle-looking man who gave Leah a warm smile and also acknowledged both Alan and me.

After asking permission, he gently felt Leah's tummy, also digging deep above the pubic arch, prodding and searching with his expert fingers to find the presenting part of the baby. He stopped every time Leah had a contraction and waited patiently for the spasm to pass. Then asking her if it was OK to continue, he drew his hands to the top of her uterus and back down either side. Then looking bemused he picked up Leah's notes.

'I think the baby is deeply engaged, Phyllis,' he said. 'And from the notes it appears your colleagues have actually felt the head during vaginal examinations.'

As he leafed through the notes I caught sight of the scan report dated the previous day and slid it into his hand. He glanced at me and stopped just short of raising his eyebrows.

'I will run the scan over you, Leah. Just in case,' he said, now duty-bound to double-check. He walked from the room to get the scanner himself, returning a minute later with the portable machine. Then he splashed the cold contact gel on to Leah's tummy. Sure enough, there was the tiny baby deeply engaged into his mother's pelvis and squirming around as if to say, 'Hold on, I am coming soon.'

With this evidence the kindly obstetrician made his apologies and left the room.

'That was a waste of time and distress for that woman wasn't it?' I heard him say to Phyllis on his way out. 'Don't you respect your colleague's findings?'

I must admit it gave me a childish jolt of satisfaction.

By now, Leah was in very strong labour and was rolling around on the bed in absolute distress. The glare of the lighting, the arguing, voices and being made to lie flat on her back, were all contributing to this labour becoming out of her previous control.

'Please, Virginia, get me an epidural,' she begged, tears coursing down her cheeks. I wanted to cry at the injustice of what I could see, in all likelihood, was going to happen. The events had rocked Leah's confidence off its axis and now scared and disempowered, her labour was spiralling out of her own control. I had to help her get it back together.

From our lengthy discussions throughout her pregnancy I knew an epidural was not what Leah wanted but, as she begged me now, I knew Phyllis would have the anaesthetist in the room in an instant.

Leaning over Leah, I looked into her panic-stricken, pain-filled eyes. 'Leah, think about everything you've read,' I said. 'You made the choice not to have one, remember? It's not long now and you will have baby in your arms. He is well, he is strong and so are you. Come on, dig deep and find that confidence to carry on you had just a short while ago.'

As her latest contraction subsided for a moment Leah smiled to acknowledge she'd heard my words.

'It really hurts though, Virginia,' she whispered. 'I think I am going to need something soon. It's killing me.'

'How about you try some gas and air?' I replied, offering the mouthpiece as another contraction rocked her body. I watched as Leah took a long breath from it, gripping the nozzle tightly between her teeth.

To my relief I saw Leah visibly relax as the contraction ended. Putting a glass of water to her lips to relieve the parching effects of the gas, I stroked her brow as she swallowed. Leah then sank her head back on to the pillow.

'OK,' she whispered. 'I can do this, I can do this. Give me a minute and I will get up off this bed.'

'That's it, Leah,' I responded, wanting to punch the air. 'You are a strong woman and you CAN do this.'

I was now going to help her to go back to her original plan, to get back to the lovely place we were in before Phyllis came on duty and ruined it. It was my job, after all, the job of a midwife, to support Leah through labour, through the pain and the difficult parts of the journey of birth, not to relieve her of it, to take all the pain away along with all her hopes, dreams and choices.

My rallying call was interrupted at that moment by the opening of the door and Phyllis came bustling into the room talking about the vaginal examination Leah needed and which, according to her, was long overdue from its four-hourly regime.

Leah let out a long cry. 'Noooooo, please just leave me alone,' she said. 'I don't want you to examine me.'

But Phyllis was not about to have the routine of her shift disrupted. 'Sorry, my dear, but it's hospital policy,' she trilled. 'I have to examine you or it's my job on the line.'

My jaw clenching with irritation I decided enough was enough. I was not about to let Leah's rollercoaster of a labour take another nosedive thanks to Phyllis.

'Phyllis, she has said no,' I said with steel in my voice. 'You can document that, which will not put your job on the line and you and I both know our rules state that we should not coerce women. You need consent or it is abuse and Leah does not consent.'

As I spoke I could see Alan working hard to control his own irritation.

'OK, fine, it's your baby's health I am trying to safeguard,' Phyllis announced sulkily as Leah looked at me through pain-filled eyes and started to breathe deeply on the gas once more. I slowly shook my head to let her know her baby's health was not at risk because she refused a vaginal examination.

My heart was beating fast as I eyeballed Phyllis, who turned her back and gave great pretence of clearing up until she could regain her composure and leave the room. As she turned into the corridor I thought I saw her chin wobble.

My heart sunk knowing that I had upset her and I was sorry it had needed to get to this point to stop her being so bossy. She was not a cruel person, it was just that she had practised this efficient, no-nonsense, 'I know best' way of midwifery all of her career and knew no other. I hoped she would relent now and Leah could get up and resume her labour in a calm manner.

A noise at the door made me look up. As I readied myself to see what Phyllis would say or do next, my stomach lurched. Instead of Phyllis, in marched Joan my old nemesis and the last person I wanted to see right now.

As my mouth instantly went dry with fear she stared me down.

'Can I have a word with you outside, please, Virginia?'

It is strange to fathom how someone can instantly create power over another. I am a strong individual and by now I had almost a decade of midwifery experience, yet I was instantly transported back to my days as a fearful student midwife.

Leaving Leah's side I followed Joan out to the corridor and braced myself.

'How dare you question one of my midwives and make her cry,' she began. 'When you come in here on my labour ward with a woman, you are not a midwife. You are nothing more than a sister or mother and you will not interfere with clinical care.'

As she continued to berate me I was aware of midwives and support staff hurrying past us pretending they couldn't hear. These were midwives I knew, who had also had their fair share of the rough side of Joan's tongue but who chose to keep their heads down for an easy life.

'We had a lovely night,' I tried to explain. 'Leah was calm and in the right frame of mind to cope with giving birth. Now she has been forced to get on to a bed . . .'

But as Joan stood with her hands on her hips glaring I could not get the right words out. So instead I turned my back on her and walked away towards the changing rooms. I certainly did not want her or anyone else to see the effect she had on me.

Standing in a changing room, I locked the door as a sense of injustice over what was happening to Leah overwhelmed me and hot tears spilled from my eyes and dripped off my chin.

After crying in the quiet solitude of the changing room for several minutes I dried my eyes and pulled myself together. My priority was to help Leah and now I had to compose myself and get back to her.

Walking in, I saw Leah still puffing on the gas and fighting her way through the contractions. But at the end of each wave of pain, I could now hear small grunts emitting from her throat. Leah had reached second stage!

'I want to get up,' she said in a desperate voice.

Sensing that the baby was coming she was suddenly alert and awake and I helped as she began to swing her legs over the side of the high bed.

On wobbly legs she pushed herself to her feet. Standing up, concern spread across her face.

'Virginia, why are you crying?' she said staring at my face. 'It's not me, is it? Nothing's wrong, is it? Is my baby OK?'

'No, Leah, of course not, everything is fine, believe me,' I said quickly. 'So come on, let's concentrate on what is happening and let's have a baby.'

'You can't lie to me, Virginia, I know you too well,' Leah insisted panting out her words as another contraction began to roll in. 'Who upset you? That silly woman?' She turned to Alan. 'Help Virginia,' she said. 'Find out why she is upset.'

'Stop fussing!' I said. 'I am fine! You need to concentrate please!'

My reassurances seemed to work as once again her mind focused on the contractions and the overbearing pressure that heralded the baby's advancement.

As Leah continued to stand, leaning on the bed, two new midwives came into the room. They didn't introduce themselves and I immediately felt awkward knowing that the only reason they had come was because of the problems with Phyllis.

However, unlike Phyllis, they weren't obstructive. I was relieved when one midwife watched quietly from the corner of the room while taking notes and the other knelt down in front of Leah.

I remained where I was, supporting Leah and whispering gentle words of encouragement into her ear.

Back in the zone, Leah remained in her standing position squeezing out her baby boy into the gloved hands of the new midwife. He cried immediately and, as the midwife passed him up to Leah, I watched as a calm, serene look came over her face.

After a sobbing Alan had embraced her and their son we both helped Leah on to a chair where she could sit and wait for the placenta.

I was so happy for them but at the same time the frustration of the last three hours was still simmering in my stomach.

It angered me immensely that Phyllis had almost changed the course of Leah's labour and in the process had caused her a lot of unnecessary distress and worry. Then there was Joan's dressing down in the corridor, which had led me to cry.

Those tears had not only worried Leah for a while but they had changed the relationship between Leah and me. For a few minutes she had become the carer and I'd been the vulnerable one. That was not right. As the urge to put right all this injustice built up inside me I felt assertive and strong. After spending a couple of hours sharing Leah and Alan's joy, I decided that the time had come to stand up for myself.

Leaving the room I went in search of Joan. Finding her I asked her to join me in one of the unused offices. I was not going to lower myself to her level and shout in a corridor of people.

'I've thought about what you said earlier and I'd like to give you my version of events,' I said, going on to explain how even the doctor had questioned Phyllis's judgement.

'Whether you like it or not, I still have a duty of care towards "my" women, even if I do not have a contract allowing me to give clinical care,' I continued. 'All I was doing was trying to help facilitate a normal birth for Leah and if Phyllis is not comfortable with a woman refusing a vaginal examination, then she should re-evaluate herself as a midwife.'

As Joan stood with her eyebrows raised and arms folded, I delivered my final parting shot.

'You said I have no more than a sister or a mother's role when I am here,' I stated. 'If that is the case then don't you EVER, EVER call me out of a room to discuss things with me again. You would not do that to a sister or mother of a pregnant woman and you will NEVER do it to me again.'

Then before she could say a word I left the room with my head held high.

Chapter Eleven

The voice on the telephone was soft but determined.

'I don't want to hire you,' Lottie, a 28-year-old single mother told me. 'But I'd like some advice on how to give birth alone.'

This wasn't the first time I'd heard of a woman wishing to have her baby by herself. The unassisted birth movement is growing worldwide with books and websites dedicated to supporting women who do not want any sort of help during childbirth.

It is a human right for a woman to give birth under any circumstances of her choice. She does not have to agree to being helped by a caregiver or seek medical help during the pregnancy or while giving birth. While I respected this right, as a midwife I could never advocate it because I know how important having care at this crucial moment of a woman's life is. I am especially saddened when I know the decision has been made due to the traumatic experiences a woman has endured in the past.

This was clearly the case for Lottie, who explained that she had come to her decision after being let down by the medical profession with her previous two births.

As we chatted on the phone Lottie confided that she had a history of feeling overpowered or abused by the people around her. An alcoholic mother and a stepfather who had sexually abused her had caused Lottie to spiral into teenage rebellion as she tried to numb the pain with drugs and alcohol.

It is a well-known and accepted phenomenon that the feelings of horror, terror and loss of control of rape experienced by abuse survivors can be relived during childbirth and the procedures surrounding it. So when an 18-year-old Lottie fell pregnant she'd asked the doctors not to touch her. But they hadn't listened. Whether or not Lottie had explained the reason why she didn't want to be examined was irrelevant, if a woman makes this choice she should be respected.

'A male doctor said that if I didn't get examined then my baby could be in danger,' she said. 'But the examination made me feel sick and I asked him to stop. I tried to close my legs and move away from him but he kept his hand inside me and prodded around. It was like being abused by my stepfather all over again and it took me screaming to make him stop.'

As I listened aghast I felt revolted as Lottie revealed how the unapologetic doctor told her, 'It would have been easier if you'd kept still.'

In the end, Lottie gave birth to a baby boy with no problems but not before having overheard the staff discussing her and how she'd 'made a fuss' outside the birthing suite door.

The next birth of her daughter, around a year later, was quite fast and straightforward but again Lottie was subjected to unwanted vaginal examinations which brought back the usual flood of unwelcome memories.

'I just felt like I was on a conveyor belt,' she said. 'That no one cared a jot about me. I was so tired after the birth and wanted to rest but a midwife shoved my toilet bag at me and told me to "hurry up and shower" as they needed the bed. Well, they got the bloody bed, because I got dressed, picked up the baby, walked out and called a taxi,' she added with a bitter laugh.

Now pregnant for a third time there was no way Lottie was giving birth in hospital.

'The baby's father isn't around so I'll do it by myself,' she said. 'Can you talk me through what I need to do?'

'Sure, where do you live?' I asked.

'Margate,' she replied with caution in her voice. 'But I'm happy just to chat over the phone.'

'Look, I am coming by your way tomorrow, Lottie,' I lied. 'Shall I just pop in for a cuppa? I actually have some maternity bits and pieces that you might want. I have been hoping to find someone who wants them and, to be honest, you would be doing me a favour by getting them out of my car . . .'

Lottie laughed. 'I can see what you are doing, Virginia,' she said. 'But, OK, I will give you my address and put the kettle on around one o'clock, then.'

Arriving at a local council basement flat in a poor area, I met Lottie, who was already 39 weeks pregnant and, while attractive, looked tired and seemed older than her 28 years. She had a distinct air of sadness about her.

'Come on in,' she said leading me through into a small, run-down but clean flat filled with her children's toys and very few creature comforts for her.

'Here you go,' I said, remembering the box full of useful but unused items that had been donated by some of my former clients.

'Thank you so much!' Lottie said taking the box and looking delighted as she surveyed the haul of incontinence pads, sanitary towels, disposable knickers and breast pads. 'Things are a bit tough so this is a real help.'

Sitting down in the sitting room, we sipped our tea and Lottie began to open up, telling me more about the heartbreaking story of her life so far and about how she lived alone with her children, ten-year-old Simon and nine-year-old Callie.

'The kids' dad went off with one of my work colleagues three years ago,' she said quietly. 'But we're doing OK without him.'

It would take a few more visits and some tears over her tea before Lottie would tell me what had happened with the new baby's father.

'I met this guy, Greg, out walking,' she said. 'He was nice and we started to make some plans. I loved him, you know?'

But a year into their relationship when Lottie fell pregnant she faced devastating news.

'He was two-timing me,' she said, her grey eyes filled with pain. 'He even had a daughter with his other girlfriend. So now it's all over. I wouldn't have him at the birth if he was the last man on earth.'

It took all my willpower not to grab her and hug her. It beggared belief how badly Lottie had been treated by people who were meant to love her or in whose hands she put herself and her trust.

First her mother and uncle, the first man she loved, her colleague, Greg and, of course, as she'd told me during our phone chat, the medical establishment.

As we talked about her pregnancy, she confirmed that she had received no antenatal care so far in this pregnancy and now wanted some tips and a quick lesson in emergency procedures.

'What do I do if the baby isn't breathing or I'm bleeding a lot?' she asked.

Of course I willingly talked to her and gave her the information she required. My reasoning was that if she was dead set on her course of action, as was her legal right to do so, then by imparting my knowledge I was helping, although in a minimal capacity, to ensure her safety.

It reminded me of a time during my nursing training, when we were instructed to design a health educational project on the subject of drugs and alcohol.

While most of the other students were hell bent on telling the public not to take drugs or to avoid alcohol I did the opposite. Knowing that human nature dictates that certain groups of people, especially the youth, are always willing to take risks even if they are aware of potential adverse effects, my approach was to write an educational leaflet about how to take a popular nightclub recreational drug safely. I got the best marks in any piece of written work I had done.

Of course as I gave Lottie all the information she needed, I was also hoping to develop a relationship with her. If I could gain her trust, maybe I could convince her to change her mind and have me present at the birth of her baby?

'Bloody baby, trust me to go and get a bloody bun in the oven,' Lottie laughed, as she scribbled down notes. 'Wait till it's born, I am going to leave it out for the bin men!'

I laughed but was determined not to leave without offering further help.

'Lottie, give me a break here,' I said. 'I am a midwife, come on, what else can I do to help you? I am not going to tell you what's what but I do want you and baby to be safe!'

'I'll tell you what you can do, then,' she said, as she swivelled on the sofa and brought her legs up to lie down. 'Have a feel of my tummy and see that the baby is in a good position for birth, if I know it's head down I will be set up just fine.'

'Small steps!' I thought and walked over to where she lay. Gently lifting her t-shirt I looked at her swollen stomach heavy with baby and lined with stretch marks from the previous two pregnancies. I ran my hands down the sides and up over the top, noting the height of the uterus and deciding the size was just about right for her gestation. Finally, I located the head and felt it, not engaged but just above the pelvis and right in the middle.

This was perfect and I was relieved that everything was normal. Many women who have had babies before find that their babies do not engage until the first early contractions of labour, but this baby was in the right place just waiting. A few contractions would make it head, excuse the pun, in the right direction. A few kicks on to my hands also told me baby was alive and well.

'Everything is fine,' I told Lottie. 'The baby seems in great condition. Now please think about what I have said and do let me know if I can help any more. There will be no charge for any care that I give you.'

As she walked me to the door I tried one more time to get her on side.

'I would be honoured to care for you and help you have the birth you want,' I added. 'Just please give me a chance to show you that you can be in complete control and have help.'

She made no comment, bit her lip, smiled a sad smile and closed the door. I drove home that day with a heavy heart, never expecting to hear from Lottie again and I whispered to the birth angels to keep Lottie and her baby safe.

Another year also heralded another winter birth for Tonia.

It was a speedy labour again but this time the contractions were spaced out to every four minutes, giving Tonia a calmness leading up to the birth.

Sticking with tradition, Tonia's sixth child and fourth daughter was born in the water with Tonia on one knee and Jason holding her hand, once he had finished filling the pool and making tea. Markeeta was one of Tonia's largest babies at ten pounds and her name was chosen as it was a variation of Tonia's mother's name – Markeeta is Margaret in Old Greek.

'She's not bad, is she?' came Tonia's verdict.

Two days later, as I was having my breakfast, my telephone rang and I saw it was Lottie's number on my caller display. My heart jolted, was she in trouble? Was she calling to say baby was born?

'Hi, Lottie, how are you?' I answered in a light-hearted, sing-song voice.

'Virginia, I have decided that you can help me, but only the way I want, OK?' she said, the words rushing out. 'I will pay you as well, I don't want any charity.'

'That's fine, Lottie,' I said. 'Let's discuss the payment after baby's safely born, eh? Now how can I help?'

'I want to pay you to be my stand-by,' she said. 'When I go into labour you can stay in the car and I'll call on you if I need you. But I don't want you asking me any questions or bringing your equipment into the house. I've got my own scissors to cut the cord as well as anything else I need.'

I readily agreed to her plan. Of course I wished I could do more to help but was just glad she was allowing me to be there in some capacity.

Unbelievably, that very same night around 7pm, as I was cooking dinner, Lottie called to say she was in labour, her contractions were coming every five minutes or so and I would be welcome to come and be outside. Remembering that Lottie was a third-time mum and her labour might be fast, I would need to set off immediately.

'I'm heading out to a birth now,' I called to Sean and the girls who were in the other room watching TV. 'Courtney, can you take over with the dinner? It'll be ready in fifteen minutes.'

Then, grabbing a banana to keep me going, I set off on the 45-minute journey to Lottie's home.

When I arrived, as per our plan, I sent her a text message to say I was outside and she replied to say she was fine. I then pulled out a magazine and started to read. Before long, I was so cold I could hardly feel my toes. I started the engine and turned on the heater and then became so hot it was unbearable. Suddenly I could understand why Lottie had insisted that she pay me some money. Sitting in a car for what may be hours on end on a winter's night was not any fun and was very uncomfortable.

This on and off with the engine went on for about an hour as I tried to distract myself by listening to an audio book. Suddenly a tap on the window caused me nearly to jump out of my skin.

I opened the steamy window to see a little girl who I presumed to be Lottie's nine-year-old daughter Callie. I had not seen her coming up the basement steps.

'Mummy says come in for a cup of tea,' she said.

Following her into the house, I sat on the sofa. There was a cup of tea already on the small table next to me that I presumed Lottie must have made. I had no idea where she was in the small flat but the little girl sat on the floor with her brother, Simon, and soon the pair of them had their heads down busy colouring in their books.

I was half-way through my tea when Lottie walked slowly into the room, leaning her head back on her shoulders and placing her hands on her hips as she swayed in that all-too-familiar way that women in labour do.

'I am sorry, Virginia, I know you are cold and I do feel bad you are out there, but really I don't want you to stay,' she said. 'Feel free to finish your tea.'

As she grabbed for the door frame I watched as a strong contraction gripped her body and made her knees buckle. Her head went down lower and lower until she was almost bent double then she slowly started to rise again and leant against the frame to rest.

The children glanced up at their mum and then turned back to the job at hand. I wondered what Lottie had said to them for them to be so nonchalant about their mum in labour and having a cold, shivery lady sitting in their front room.

'Kids, bed please,' Lottie puffed out her instruction to the children and I was shocked to see them obey her immediately. There was no whining or moaning like many would, just respectful obedience.

'Good night mummy!' they trilled, wrapping their arms around her swollen body. Lottie leaned over, kissed their heads and put her arms round both of them for a quick hug then let go as another contraction started to build.

'Go! Shoo!' she said and they both ran from the room. Not for the first time I was amazed by this remarkable woman.

Now doubled over in pain, Lottie gasped through another very powerful contraction. As she rose again, her waters broke with a very loud pop which made us both jerk our heads up and stare at each other.

'Wow,' I said. 'That's a first; I have never heard that before.'

I automatically grabbed for one of the towels that were on the floor in preparation for the coming birth and it was only as I was putting it under her that I realised Lottie had not asked for my help. I really did not want to alienate her now.

'Oops, sorry, Lottie,' I said. 'Didn't mean to interfere, it just comes naturally to me.'

'It's OK, Virginia, I know,' she said with a little laugh. 'Drink your tea, I am not going anywhere.'

I sat back to drink my tea, thinking that any minute with the next contraction, Lottie was going to want to push. Did she still want me to go back outside? If I stayed would she allow me to bring in my birth kit?

I realised that quite a few minutes had passed and no contractions had come. Lottie was still standing in the doorway holding on to the frame. She had put the towel I had passed her underneath her legs to catch any flowing water and was waiting ready for the next contraction.

But no contraction came. After 15 minutes of waiting and my tea almost drunk, I was torn, wanting desperately to say something but not wanting to overstep the mark and upset Lottie.

'Um, Lottie,' I began. 'It is very unusual for contractions to stop after this amount of time when the waters have broken and they had been so strong.'

Lottie didn't respond and instead started to walk up and down the room. She started to do squats and even did a few bunny jumps. As the time ticked on, I was beginning to get a sinking feeling in the pit of my stomach. I was putting an empty cup to my lips on regular occasions so Lottie would be fooled into thinking I was still drinking my tea. It was now 45 minutes after her waters had ruptured and the last contraction had passed. Lottie looked at me and raised her eyebrows.

'Well, this is different for sure, isn't it?' she said.

I took a deep breath.

'This is most unusual, Lottie,' I said. 'I would go as far as to say I am concerned. I know I promised not to interfere but I am worried now.'

She ignored me initially and I thought I had upset her but after another ten minutes she sat down next to me.

'I suppose you had better have a feel, to see what's happening, then,' she said.

I was shocked at Lottie's words, as I knew how difficult the contemplation of vaginal examinations was for her.

'OK,' I agreed before dashing out to my car, grabbing my equipment bag and rushing back into the flat in less than a minute. I pulled on sterile gloves and gently with relaxed and slow movements performed a vaginal examination on Lottie. At first I could not make out what it was I was feeling. What was this presenting part?

It certainly was not a hard head and neither was it the soft squidgy dented roundness of a bottom. It was not a leg or a foot, so what was it? Finally it dawned on me. It was a shoulder! A shoulder presentation. My heart sunk. There was no way this baby could be born alive vaginally. Withdrawing my hands I took a deep breath. I was fearful about what this news might do to Lottie's mental state.

'I am so sorry, Lottie, but please don't shoot the messenger,' I began. 'The only way you are going to have this baby is by caesarean section.'

I held my breath as I awaited her reaction.

'OK,' she said, with casual acceptance. 'Let's get sorted, then.'

She didn't have to ask me twice. Asking her to remain lying down, I said I'd call an ambulance.

'Virginia, I am very grateful to you,' she interrupted. 'But I need to sort out the children. And you can forget an ambulance 'cause it isn't gonna happen. I'll drive myself.'

My heart in my mouth I had no choice but to help Lottie gather some things together for her and the baby, telephone a friend to come and babysit and then follow in my own car as she drove herself to the hospital. I had no idea if the baby she was carrying was alive or dead because she would not let me listen to the heartbeat.

'He is fine,' she said. 'He is kicking me all over.'

All the way there I was consumed by the horrible thought that the cord could prolapse out, due to the space around the shoulder.

If that happened the baby would almost certainly die but I knew that I could not push Lottie. My mind also raced as I imagined how we would explain everything to the doctors and midwives we would meet. Lottie had no notes and had received no antenatal care except the minimal instruction I had given her in the last couple of days. God help us both!

When we arrived at the hospital, Lottie was shown to a birth room to await assessment and I quickly explained her chequered history and the current situation to the midwife in charge and the registrar on duty. They were dumbfounded but not unsympathetic.

'I will need to examine her,' said the registrar.

'I don't think she will allow you to and if you go in there and suggest it, she may just get up and go,' I told him.

'OK,' he agreed. 'We will start with a scan then. Is the baby OK?'

'I don't know,' I replied. 'She says he is.'

'You mean you haven't even . . .' he began, cutting himself short as he saw me grit my teeth. Had he not heard a thing I said?

'Oh yes, sorry,' he acknowledged. 'OK, let's go and see her.'

To my stark relief, Lottie agreed to a scan and it was clear that indeed the baby was wedged into her pelvis by his shoulder. The doctor was very nice to her, reiterating exactly what I had said that the baby was unable to be born without a caesarean section.

'I'll come to the theatre with you,' I said.

Throughout the procedure Lottie was very emotionally strong, even though it took a lot of tugging and pulling to free the baby that was wedged into her pelvis. As I held her hand, tears trickled down Lottie's cheeks but she didn't make a sound. From my vantage point next to her I could see he needed a little resuscitation but, not wanting to alarm her, I chose my words carefully.

'They are just giving him a couple of breaths of oxygen,' I said. 'Now he is getting nice and pink.'

As they brought the crying baby over Lottie smiled.

'Hello, James,' she said.

Lottie remained in hospital for 24 hours before she was able to take her son home to meet Simon and Callie.

Before she left, I went to see her and was touched when she thanked me for being there for her.

'Thank you for being so persistent, Virginia,' she said. 'If it hadn't been for you I probably would have gone to bed and waited for the contractions to start up again in the morning.'

I never charged her a fee and was just grateful that the birth angels brought us together and that baby James arrived safe and well into this world.

Chapter Twelve

As I flicked through a pile of photographs, I could feel my client Mary studying my face with amusement.

Coming to a photo of Mary competing in a horse show, her legs stretched, muscles bulging and six-month baby bump clearly visible as she triumphantly jumped over a fence, I had no doubt this was the picture she was anticipating a reaction to. It brought back fond memories of my riding days, a hobby I'd long since given up due to my hectic life.

'Oh my goodness, Mary, weren't you afraid you would fall?' I exclaimed. 'Most women are too afraid to run when they are pregnant let alone ride a horse!'

'No!' she scoffed. 'I have not fallen from a horse in years and I am more sure on its back than you are walking.'

By now, I covered a huge patch as a midwife, including the whole of Kent and parts of East Sussex, South Sussex and Surrey. As a rule I wouldn't travel for longer than an hour to get to a client, due to the danger of missing a quick birth, although I did once make an exception and travel to the Cotswolds to look after a client who had recently moved.

While my work took me to stunning homes that could grace the pages of *Good Housekeeping*, it is a misconception that independent midwifery is an elitist service that only the rich can afford.

In actual fact, the majority of my clients were everyday women who lived in terraced houses and small flats and who budgeted and saved. I found myself caring for all kinds of women, though, varying from those who lived in huge houses to those who struggled to make ends meet. Just like Val, the community midwife, had told me years earlier, there were places I avoided putting my coat down and where I needed to wipe my feet on the way out!

My line of work also introduced me to some real characters – and Mary, a 30-year-old vet, was definitely one of them.

Having been Mary's midwife for three months now, I knew her well enough to know she enjoyed saying or doing things to shock me.

From the minute I'd clapped eyes on Mary, a beautiful, tall, slim woman with long hair pulled back scruffily into a top knot on her head, I instinctively knew she was a woman who didn't give a stuff what anyone else thought.

Dressed in the jodhpurs and long muddy boots that confirmed her love for all things equestrian, Mary had invited me into her dusty, cramped, cobwebby cottage near her husband's family farm in Herne Bay with not a care in the world.

The door from the street took me directly into a cold, small living room where there were three old wooden armchairs, a table and not much else. Mary's husband, Tony, greeted me with a bashful smile and I sat in the chair nearest the window opposite both of them.

As Mary began to tell me why she wanted me to be her midwife, I watched in fascination as dry mud dropped from her boots on to the floor without her batting an eyelid. It was just so alien from my own home, which I obsessively kept squeaky clean.

'I need someone who is on my side, someone who is confident and strong, and I have heard you will fight a woman's corner like a tiger,' she declared. As her husband smiled and occasionally agreed by way of a nod, it was clear that Mary wore the trousers.

'I want to be in charge,' Mary said. 'My body, my pregnancy, my labour, my baby! I want to feel I have the best information available in order to form my own judgement and make my own decisions about my care, which will then be supported.'

'I can definitely help you with that,' I agreed.

The next few months saw us developing a relationship that left me in no doubt of just how formidable Mary could be. There were plenty of stories of her holding her own at male-dominated vets' conferences and, as she revelled in stories of getting up-close to wild and unpredictable stallions in her daily work, I wondered if she was silently challenging me to tell her not to put herself in danger.

I never returned to the little dusty cottage where we'd first met and from that day on I visited Mary at the family farm for her antenatal appointments, where the couple had moved in with Tony's parents. For one such visit she took me into a very dirty caravan which was used as the tea room.

The caravan was situated in the middle of the stable yard, with the smell of manure strong in the air and horse owners milling around outside and occasionally interrupting us to ask Mary a question concerning the location of hay, oats or riding crops.

When I asked to examine her I was quite horrified when Mary laid herself on the cramped, muddy, straw-littered floor of the caravan. But duly I knelt down to listen to the baby with my Pinard stethoscope, well aware that my own clothes were getting covered in all sorts of horse matter. It took me the rest of the day to rid myself of the musty aroma, but this was Mary's environment and I was the visitor.

Autumn turned to winter and when I next visited Mary in the old farmhouse belonging to Tony's elderly parents the fire was alight in the hearth. Jan and Fred obviously had lots in common with their daughter-in-law as they, too, appeared to be unconcerned with clutter but the house was always warm and welcoming.

'Here you go, Virginia, have a nice cup of tea. Go and sit down while I give Mary a call,' Jan said smiling warmly. 'You know what she's like running around all over the place as usual. We don't know what we'd do without her!'

Eventually Mary arrived, dominating the conversation with her stories and feisty personality. We all chatted for so long that I didn't notice it had got dark and I was relieved when Tony escorted me out of the house with a torch so I could avoid tripping on anything in the shadowy front yard en route to my car.

When Mary reached 38 weeks I arrived at the farmhouse to find Mary and Tony sitting in the kitchen. This visit was due to be the one where we talked about the birth itself and finalised all the arrangements but as usual Mary immediately took control.

'I am going to tell you how I am going to give birth,' she said with a serious face.

'OK,' I acknowledged, wondering what she'd say next.

Standing up, Mary started jumping up and down with one arm raised in the air, her swollen tummy bouncing all over the place as she punched the air like a cheerleader.

'This is how I am going to be,' she panted, leaving me seriously contemplating how on earth I was supposed to catch her baby in such circumstances. Thankfully, the bouncing Tigger performance was purely a metaphorical show.

'It's going to feel like a party!' she confirmed. 'I don't want calm and candles. There is to be no panic and worry. Just a party atmosphere.'

'OK,' I smiled.

Mary also had a set of rules for me. I was only allowed to come into the birthing room and help when she asked me to and I was to wait outside at other times.

'When the baby comes I don't want any interruptions,' she added. 'I don't want any help cleaning the baby up and all the weighing and measurements can wait until the next day. When I help an animal give birth I leave them alone to bond and I want the same respect and privacy for my baby.'

As I sat and nodded I was filled with admiration for her. I love women who take control and feel empowered by the process and I sincerely hoped everything would unfold just the way she had planned it. As long as women are making informed choices and their babies and they are safe then I have fulfilled my role.

Mary's 'party' began just eight days later when she went into labour late on a dark January afternoon.

'I'll call you back later when I need you,' she said with her usual blunt authority. 'But at the moment I want to be alone with my family.'

Just a few hours passed before she called again at 9pm to say that her contractions were very intense and could I head over.

By now it was pouring with rain and it took me an hour to drive to her cottage. Stumbling out into the downpour, with my birth equipment in hand, I saw Tony anxiously peering out of the window. Spotting me, he hurried out with his trusted torch to help me navigate through the ever-deepening mud.

Once inside the cottage, Tony led me upstairs to a small, sloped-roof bedroom which, as I expected, was filled with clutter and the familiar smell of birth. Mary was on her hands and knees beside the bed rocking her hips in rhythm with the waves of intense contractions. Although I found the room very cold and pulled my cardigan around me, it was clearly just fine for a hot, labouring Mary whose brow was dotted with tiny beads of sweat.

Crouching down next to her I waited till the current wave of pain passed and she was able to communicate with me.

'Do you want me to examine you?' I asked.

'Yes,' she replied. 'Then if it's early in my labour, you can go home again.'

My heart sank a little as I thought about struggling to drive through the rain and mud again. But as I carried out a vaginal examination I found Mary to be more than half-way through the cervical dilation stage.

As per Mary's birth plan to be alone to labour, I left the room and went downstairs to a very welcome, warm room where a cup of hot tea was pushed into my hands by Jan, Tony's mum. With Tony's father Fred in bed, the two of us sat and waited while the fire crackled and my cold body thawed.

'She's an independent girl,' Jan smiled.

I nodded in agreement but as Mary's moans and soft screams of labour filtered out of the bedroom I was itching to get back in the room and help.

After about 30 minutes my wish was granted as Mary summoned me back into the room. I found Tony and Mary kneeling on the floor on opposite sides of the bed but leaning across to reach over and hold hands. Mary's demeanour had changed.

'Please come in and stay,' she said her voice softer. 'I didn't realise how much it would mean to me to have you here.'

'That's OK, Mary, I am here to support you as much or as little as you need me,' I said.

Unbelievably just one short intense hour later, as Mary stood leaning over her bed I caught sight of the top of a tiny head. Before long it had expanded to the size of a fifty pence piece and then a plum.

Not wanting the baby to be born in the cold I plugged in a small fan heater and pulled it as close to Mary and me as possible to ward off the vicious cold draft that was whistling down from the loft. By now the visible part of the baby's head was the size of an orange and with a last colossal effort, Mary gave birth to a beautiful baby boy.

As I placed him into his mother's arms, there was no drama and much joy, just as Mary had prescribed for herself.

With the placenta coming a few minutes later, it was absolutely no surprise to me to see Mary getting up off the floor and putting herself to bed with the baby.

'Thanks, Virginia, for doing exactly what I wanted; it couldn't have been better,' she smiled. 'Now get yourself home and look after yourself. You need a good dinner and a good sleep.'

Respecting her wishes, I bid her and little baby Ben goodbye, smiling to myself at Mary's remarkable ability to always be in charge.

The next morning, feeling refreshed, I arrived early at Mary's cottage expecting to find her where I left her, tucked up in bed with Ben recovering from the birth. But as I was welcomed into the cottage by Jan, Mary was nowhere to be seen.

'She'll be back soon,' Jan smiled.

Sure enough within five minutes Mary had arrived with her baby in a sling under her coat, all snug and warm.

'Oh hi, Virginia,' she said as she trailed mud through the house. 'I've just taken Ben to meet the horses!' I was thrilled to see such a happy mother and a thriving beautiful baby.

One December night, as 2008 drew to an end, I found myself in a familiar situation – struggling out the door with my case and a few loose items in my hand.

Arriving at my car, I put my knee up against the door, balancing my case and the rest of my birthing paraphernalia on it as I scrabbled to unlock the door. As I fumbled with the door all of a sudden the top article, a mirror, started to slide and, although I made a grab for it, I was too late and all I could do was wince as it went smashing to the ground with shards of glass flying all over the road.

Sighing I closed my eyes in disbelief – this was the fourth mirror I'd broken in a short space of time and now I'd have to buy another one. The problem in replacing it arose because the type of mirror I needed to use to aid my vision as I accommodated women in all sorts of birthing positions, had to be just the right size and not on a stand. It also couldn't be framed in plastic as submerging it in hot water to sterilise it would just cause the plastic casing to come off. In a nutshell it was going to be a real headache to find.

That night as I was tossing and turning in bed, my post-birth brain racing as I reflected on all that had gone well and the things I could do differently another time, I had a flash of inspiration. Why didn't I invent a mirror that wouldn't break, a mirror not framed in plastic and one that was the correct size and could be angled into a shape to help midwife and mother see the approaching baby?

The next morning as I buttered my toast, I caught sight of my face reflected in our stainless steel bread bin. 'That's it!' I thought. 'I'll make it out of stainless steel!'

First of all I did a bit of research to make sure I wasn't re-inventing the wheel then I set out to find an engineer to put my idea into practice.

'You need to find a metal fabricator,' Sean advised with an amused smile as I followed him round the house talking non-stop about my big idea. He was well aware I was a woman on a mission.

Over the next few weeks I got my idea copyrighted and before long my first prototype was coming off the production line – a stainless-steel, angled birth mirror. All types of equipment have the name of the designer on them and so I named my invention 'The Howes Birth Mirror.'

Then I proudly showed it to Kay.

'Yeah, brilliant idea,' she said, turning it over in her hand. 'And it's multifunctional.'

'Multifunctional?' I asked.

'Yes,' she said, with a twinkle in her eye. 'You can also use it as a pooper scooper or a cake slice.'

'Don't think you'll be getting any of the proceeds,' I said, laughing as I snatched it back off her.

By January 2009 I was selling them all over the UK, to Australia and to other countries. Natural birth midwives and advocates bought them initially but slowly I got orders from birth centres, a few hospitals and in bulk quantities to the National Childbirth Trust for reselling. I'm not going to make my millions with them because once you have one they last a lifetime but when I heard a midwife say recently, 'Go and get me a Howes,' in the same way they'd say, 'Go and get some Spencer Wells forceps, or go and get the Hoover,' rather than a vacuum cleaner, I felt such a thrill of pride. And if one woman is saved from having to 'turn over' when she is comfortably and instinctively on all fours so that a doctor or midwife can observe the approaching baby, then I will be happy.

Spotting a familiar blonde young woman at the delicatessen counter in Sainsbury's I had to look twice.

'Charlott?' I said, turning to study her face. 'What are you doing here?'

'Virginia!' she said engulfing me in a hug. 'We've moved back!'

Charlott, a single mum of one, originally from Denmark, was the former love of my son Andrew.

We'd got to know her and watch her sweet daughter Amelia growing up when they lived next door ten years earlier with Charlott's parents.

Andrew had fallen head over heels in love with Charlott but when her family had decided to move to America their two-year romance had ended leaving Andrew heartbroken. Now seven years later she was back!

Within a very short space of time she and Andrew, now 29, had rekindled their love and were engaged.

But it was actually Matt, 33, who would wed that year – and in August 2009 I was thrilled to see him marry his girlfriend Gemma, 27, who had worked with him at the bar for some time before they got together.

Gemma always tells the story of how she flirted with Matt for ages but had to settle for them being friends because he'd been oblivious.

Finally they'd got together and Matt had proposed the year before.

At their wedding I wanted to do something special so I decided to write Gemma a poem welcoming her to our family. As I read it out there wasn't a dry eye in the room and I, too, shed a tear as I looked over at my son who was weeping with happiness.

After the wedding I had another present for them – a plaque that read 'Nana's Kitchen where memories are made and grandkids are spoiled'.

'Now, you two, I want to hang this in my kitchen!' I said. 'So please can you give it back to me one day soon?'

'Of course!' Gemma giggled. But, while Matt and Gemma were keen to start a family, it turned out that it was actually Andrew and his girlfriend Charlott who would conceive on Matt's wedding night.

Being on call 24/7 as a midwife could be gruelling so whenever I craved a much-needed break, I'd travel to the villa I'd bought a few years earlier in the Turkish village of Ovacik on the southern Mediterranean coast. Sean and various members of the family would join me at different times.

On one such occasion, in October 2009, while enjoying a break with my mum at the villa, I decided to take a day trip to Marmaris to meet an esteemed Turkish obstetrician.

Dr Hakan Çoker was very passionate about changing the medicalisation of Turkish births and had invited me to meet him after I'd emailed to express an interest in his work.

Chatting over breakfast at a lovely little restaurant, high on a cliff overlooking the harbour, Hakan, a handsome and charming middle-aged man, told me how he had obtained his basic knowledge of childbirth from his own mother in the late 50s.

'She was a midwife responsible for all the home and hospital births in my childhood town,' he explained.

Having seen from an early age how easy it could be to have a natural birth, Hakan believed passionately that the birthing culture in Turkey did not need so many medical interventions. Yet he was treated with suspicion and intrigue by his obstetric colleagues who were used to an opposite way of working.

I was staggered to hear that the caesarean section rate in Turkey was estimated to be 40 per cent of all births in

Government maternity units and as many as 90 per cent in private hospitals.

'I'm trying to get the word out that birth is normal,' he told me. 'Unfortunately, women are not very empowered in my country in general but I want to change that.'

Following our breakfast Hakan invited me to join his antenatal class.

'I thought perhaps you might like to talk about English midwifery,' he smiled.

With the class consisting of all Turkish women apart from one British and one American woman, I focused on all the good things about the NHS, midwifery and my own way of working, while Hakan translated.

They all seemed very interested and afterwards the American, a lady called Josie, who was seven-and-a-half-months pregnant, came over and introduced herself.

'My husband and I normally live in Istanbul,' she said. 'But we've come here on our yacht as Dr Çoker is the only doctor in the whole of Turkey who will support a home birth.'

As we chatted, Josie explained that she'd had her first two children in New York – one in hospital and the second at home with a midwife. She'd moved out here just a couple of years ago with her Turkish husband, Ekrem, who owned a successful clothing company.

'Do you have plans after this class?' she asked. 'I'd love you to join us for lunch.'

So heading off in her car, we took a ten-minute drive to a very plush-looking marina. I'd expected a little yacht but there wasn't a boat in sight that cost less than five million Euros.

I was astounded as Josie led me up the gangplank of a huge yacht to be greeted by her crew. I felt like Princess Diana!

'Welcome aboard!' Josie said, leading me on a grand tour of the swanky boat, which consisted of three bedrooms with en suites, a salon lounge, dining room, huge galley and sun decks.

'Would you like a glass of wine?' Josie asked, beckoning to one of her attentive staff, who speedily reappeared with a chilled Chardonnay for me.

As we stood on the deck enjoying the sunshine, Josie's waiting staff floated around us lifting cloche-covered dishes to produce sumptuous-looking canapés and then Ekrem joined us for a three-course lunch.

'There's a reason I invited you this afternoon,' Josie said. 'I'm due in six weeks and, after meeting you today, I want you to be my midwife. I wondered if I could fly you out in a month to deliver the baby?'

'Won't Hakan mind?' I asked.

'I don't think so,' she smiled. 'I've already paid him and he knows that I really want a midwife like I had in New York.'

What an exciting offer! I did a quick diary check of the dates and the only client I had to worry about at that time was Tonia who, having given birth to another little girl Anelka (named after a German mountain) in September 2008, was now pregnant with baby number eight. I wasn't overly worried as she wasn't due until four weeks after Josie and none of her children had previously been born before their due date. It can be a hard juggling act but in 14 years I have only asked Kay to attend two births in my place due to women labouring at the same time. She in turn has only ever had to call on me twice to help with a birth, so overall we have an outstanding record for continuity of care.

'Of course I will!' I agreed.

With Josie and I staying in touch by text and email we put together a birth plan. While it was perfectly fine to have a lay midwife in Turkey, both of us agreed that Hakan should still be present so there would be no legalities to worry about.

The following month I prepared to return to Marmaris on an open ticket.

'Have a good time, love,' Sean said as I wheeled my suitcase into the hall. 'I hope the baby arrives quickly so you can hurry home to me.'

'Don't work too hard,' I said to Sophie, giving her a hug as she appeared dressed in her student midwife uniform to say goodbye. Now aged 23, Sophie was almost at the end of her first year of her training. 'I've called the boys and emailed Courtney to tell them where I'll be,' I added. 'Not that Courtney will be reading her emails – she'll be having too much fun!' Courtney had recently flown to Thailand with a friend to enjoy a gap year travelling that would take her through Asia and to Australia.

Arriving in Marmaris I checked into a small hotel with wonderful views over the harbour and the Mediterranean sea that Josie had arranged for me.

I visited Josie every day at 3pm and spent time getting to know her and her two boys, Mark, eight, and Jacob, five. Josie was keen for them to be there for their sibling's birth so we also spent time preparing them with a children's book on home birth that I'd brought over with me.

Four days after I arrived I got the call at 5am. Leaping out of bed I got dressed quickly and headed downstairs, fetching the bicycle Josie had loaned me and placing my birth kit in a basket on the front of the handlebars.

As I set off cycling along a deserted promenade looking out at the moon reflecting off the sea I wanted to pinch myself.

'I'm going to a birth on a bike like an old-fashioned midwife!' I thought, wishing I could share this surreal, magical moment with Kay back home.

Within five minutes I'd arrived at the yacht where, creeping onboard, I found the pool being filled in the salon area. I met Josie in her cabin and stayed with her there until around 7am when it was obvious to me that the birth was not far off.

'Shall we get you in the pool?' I suggested.

I'd just got her into the comforting depths of the water when the sliding doors of the saloon opened and Hakan quietly crept in.

I'd never been in this situation before and, although I'd previously told Josie that I saw my role as the lead professional with Hakan there in case of emergency, I wondered whether he'd expect us to be working together or if he would try and interfere. But as he nodded his head in greeting and then adopted a low profile, standing in the corner observing and filming the birth, I knew it would be fine. He didn't say a word and there was no interference.

An hour passed as Josie showed the typical distress of a woman in labour fighting her way through the pain of each squeeze and pull of her uterus.

'It's OK, Josie, breathe, darling, it will soon be done,' Ekrem soothed as he knelt, supporting her lovingly from the side of the pool.

Josie was a silent labourer, closing her eyes and showing no verbal signs she was in pain. Having no reason to say anything other than to describe what I could see, I whispered to her quietly, updating her as her waters broke and I could start to see the head.

Opening her eyes from time to time, Josie would look to check her boys were OK before closing them once more. Meanwhile, Mark and Jacob chattered and played unperturbed by the unfolding birth.

'The baby's coming,' I told her. 'It won't be long now.'

Eventually the time came for Josie to push her baby out into the water, which she did with no problems and the placenta followed soon after.

As Josie cradled her newborn son in her arms and Ekrem brushed away a tear of joy, I was delighted to see Mark and Jacob eagerly shedding their own clothes and clambering into the pool to meet their brother Tyler who made no noise but gazed in sweet baby wonder at his family.

After a quick clean up, we all sat down for breakfast and discussed the birth.

'Thank you so much,' Josie said, her face illuminated with happiness. 'It has meant so much to me to have you as my midwife.'

'I've never seen anything like that in my life,' Hakan added. 'That was one of the most amazing births I've attended. So much confidence and calm!'

From such a respected obstetrician it was a real accolade.

Cycling back along the waterfront at lunchtime my face was fixed in a perma-grin. I felt proud as punch.

The next day, the novelty of caring for Josie continued as I did a tour of the local harbour shops to find some fish weighing scales big enough to weigh a baby on!

That evening I called Sean to let him know that the baby had already been born.

'That was quick!' he said.

'I'll be home in a couple of days but first we're having a press conference!'

'Oh, listen to you,' he laughed. 'Local celebrity!'

With Ekrem and Josie having quite the socialite status in Turkey, thanks to his business, the story of baby Tyler's midwife-led birth on a boat generated a lot of media interest and, to my astonishment, a photo of all of us after the birth appeared in the national papers.

It was a birth I'd never forget but, after staying on a week to check on Josie and baby, it was time for me to return home.

Arriving at Dalaman airport I cleared customs then followed the zigzag of people trailing across the runway and on to the plane that was destined for Istanbul. From there I'd have a short wait before boarding another plane to London. I'd just shoved my suitcase and jacket into the overhead locker when I was aware of my mobile phone ringing.

Scrambling in my bag, I pulled out my phone and flipped open the cover to see who was calling. My heart sunk immediately. Tonia would only call for one reason.

'My waters have gone,' she confirmed.

'I'm just on the plane,' I said grimacing as an air hostess loomed over me.

'Turn off your phone,' she barked. 'We're about to depart.'

'I'll ring you, I'll ring you!' I gabbled down the phone before hanging up and dropping my head back on the seat rest. Up until now Tonia had always been overdue with her babies. The one time I was out of the country she would be three weeks early. As we took off I tapped my feet anxiously, pleading with the birth angels to delay Tonia's labour.

Arriving at Istanbul in a state of nervous agitation I couldn't even bear to turn my phone on. While Tonia could call on Kay in my absence, I knew how much she wanted me there. The thought of missing her birth was gutting.

Switching on my phone the minute my second plane touched down in London I immediately called Tonia.

'Tonia, it's me. Has it started?'

'No, you're fine,' she said. 'No contractions yet!'

Smiling in relief, I grabbed my bags from the luggage carousel.

The birth angels didn't let me down and, with time on my side, I was able to go home and have a good three to four hours sleep before I woke up to deliver Tonia's baby.

Once again Tonia gave birth to a little girl, who arrived trouble free in the birthing pool.

'Hello, Carneya,' Tonia smiled, revealing yet another unusual name inspired by a South African lady she'd watched a documentary on.

With Carneya having arrived via a lovely, normal birth I had a feeling that Tonia should leave it there. She had experienced some high blood pressure this time and, while it was only borderline problematic, I suspected that another pregnancy might end her record of eight lovely and normal births.

'I think you have come to the end of perfection now,' I'd told her after checking on little Carneya a few days later. 'Any more and I think we will be facing a different journey.'

'Don't worry,' she'd said as she saw me off from the doorstep while surrounded by her gaggle of munchkins all keen to wave goodbye to the 'mifwise'. 'We can't find a car big enough now so there definitely won't be any more babies.'

In January 2010, two years after Mary had given birth to baby Ben, I was invited back to the family home. Mary and I had stayed in touch sporadically since Ben's birth, with me even calling her up to ask advice about my dog, Cherry. Over the years I'd stayed in touch with many of my clients, through sending out newsletters and using social media like Facebook. I'd hoped my next visit to Mary's house would signify the birth of a sibling for Ben but, in fact, the circumstances could not have been more different. My heart was breaking as I walked in the door to the house that had previously brought such joy. In an unthinkable twist of fate Mary was now terminally ill.

Mary had discovered she had cancer when Ben was one year old and, in typical Mary fashion, had taken the news with determined optimism.

'Oh, don't worry about me, Virginia, I am going to beat this,' she told me firmly as we chatted on the phone. 'I've had a lot of worse things happen to me than a bit of cancer.'

But no amount of fighting spirit could beat a cancer as aggressive as the one savaging Mary's body and I'd been devastated to learn it had spread beyond all hope of a cure.

It was Mary's mother, Margaret, who had called to warn me that she was out of the hospice and that I should come quickly if I wanted to see her.

As Tony lead me into the front room where I had so many warm memories of sitting and talking to a vibrant, excited and formidable Mary, it was a very different scene that awaited me.

This time Mary's mother and her sister, Elizabeth, who was pregnant with her own baby, clung to each other unable to hold back the tears while Tony held a wriggling, uncomprehending two-year-old Ben. It was heartbreaking.

As Mary lay too weak to talk or move in the bed that had been placed in the front room, as she no longer had the strength to climb the stairs, she was almost unrecognisable. She was a thin and frail shadow of her former self and all I could do was crouch down and hold her hand.

'You are an amazing woman, Mary,' I whispered, tears streaming down my face. 'I will never forget you.'

As I held her hand my mind was filled with flashbacks of all the happy times I'd experienced in that room. Mary had lain on the sofa in this very spot as I'd felt her tummy. I'd watched her move around the room with such energy and life. How could this be happening now?

Mary's funeral took place one week later, on a damp day in February, in a chilly, grey, stone church in the local village. There was no question of me not attending and I'd been honoured when Tony had asked if I might say a few words at the ceremony about Mary's pregnancy and Ben's birth. Kay and Sophie came along with me for support.

Walking to the pulpit, I cleared my throat and told everyone about Mary's determination not to conform to stereotypes and adhere to their medical and societal restrictions on pregnant women. As I replicated Mary's actions of jumping up and down, arm aloft as she instructed me how she was going to give birth, it even caused a ripple of laughter.

While it was terrible to bid goodbye to Mary, the circle of life always has an amazing way of bringing positivity to the bleakest of situations. So it was a real joy for me when just a few weeks after Mary's funeral I was invited to help Mary's sister, Elizabeth, begin her own journey into motherhood.

A gentle, calm and easygoing woman, Elizabeth had learnt a lot about birth from Mary but was not quite as self-assured in her body and the coming labour.

'Virginia, I am not like Mary, even though I look like her,' she told me. 'I have lived in France for a long time where they are very medicalised, so it has rubbed off on me a bit, I think. You will have to help me build the confidence I need to have a home birth because I know it's what I want deep down.'

'Of course I can do that,' I smiled and with every meeting I did my best to empower her, alleviating all her worries and concerns, and giving her plenty to read so she'd feel knowledgeable and in control.

It seemed to work and Elizabeth did labour at home, sitting on a birth stool with me there to support her throughout.

It was clear the arrival of a beautiful baby boy called Harry brought mixed emotions. There were tears of both joy and sadness as Elizabeth and Margaret gazed at the newest addition and thought about the precious sister and daughter who had died and was no longer part of their loving family.

Over the years I stayed in touch with the family and was able to help Elizabeth with her second pregnancy and the arrival of a baby sister for Harry who she named Angela.

The family continue to be very close and on visits to see Elizabeth and her brood, Mary's son Ben is often there. It has been nice to see him grow from a toddler into a happy, chirpy boy who looks upon his Aunty Elizabeth as a substitute mummy and plays well with his cousins.

Whenever I look into his eyes I cannot fail to see Mary looking back at me and I will always feel part of this very special family.

Chapter Thirteen

Sitting down with Jane, a former young mother now going through it all over again for the second time at 40, I felt very envious. Having celebrated my 50th birthday the year before, my child-bearing years were well and truly over but, while there would be no more babies for me, at least I had my children and my clients to live through vicariously!

My very first grandchild was on the way and I was beyond thrilled at the news. I'd been itching for grandchildren for a while – especially since my mother had already had six by the time she was my age! When Andrew and Charlott asked me to be their midwife and deliver their baby at home it felt like such an honour.

It seemed like only yesterday that Andrew had been tottering around with his blue blanket trailing behind him. Now he would soon be a father. Time moved so fast and it was hard to believe that both my boys were now in their 30s. Sophie, now in her third year of midwifery training, was very happy with her boyfriend Robert and had recently bought her own place close to our home. Courtney was home from her travels and working as a teacher's assistant at a school for children with learning difficulties. She hoped this experience would help with her future plans to go to university and study to be a social worker.

'I didn't even think to ask about my choices when I was young!' Jane confided as we chatted in her living room. 'They laid me on my back and gave me no information, no choices and left me alone while I was in labour. I went with the flow and even let them give my babies artificial milk!' Listening to her was uncanny as it completely mirrored my own experiences, despite mine being a decade earlier. What I'd give to go back and know then what I know now. A vibrant, curvy blonde, Jane had been a teenage mum like me, having had her first three children in quick succession. Now they were all grown up and she hadn't expected to have any more. After meeting her second husband, Ahmed, later in life, though, she was doing the mother thing all over again and I was determined to make her 'second-time round' experience amazing.

At each appointment Jane chatted openly about her former life as a young wife and mother, when she'd done the best for her family and continually worried about the bills. She did not speak much about her first husband and I got the impression that it was a case of growing up and growing apart until they eventually divorced.

Ever since then Jane had busied herself looking after her children, keeping house, running her elderly day care business and socialising when she could.

'I'd pretty much given up on meeting anyone else,' she told me. 'I was happy being single! I'd even had my fallopian tubes tied so I couldn't have any more children!'

But then she met her prince – Ahmed, a handsome, devoutly religious Muslim man from Pakistan, who also worked in the elderly care business. They fell instantly and immediately in love and exchanged vows at a beautiful wedding mixing East and West traditions. But with no children of his own, Ahmed was desperate to be a father.

By now Jane wanted another child, too, so the couple had sought medical help. Jane had agreed to have eggs harvested from her ovaries in order to begin IVF. It had taken just one monthly cycle for her to fall pregnant. I'd eagerly looked forward to caring for Jane but unfortunately it was not to be on this occasion and she suffered a miscarriage.

Determined not to give up on their quest to have a child of their own, Jane and Ahmed began another round of IVF as soon as it was possible. Once again, it worked very quickly and I was soon back in their sitting room filling in notes and booking Jane for my care.

This time all was well and, as her pregnancy progressed, Jane had a clear birth plan. She had reflected long and hard on how she had given birth in the past and knew what she wanted now.

'I want a home birth with soft music this time and I want to do it under my own steam, not being told what to do and what position I should be in,' she said. 'I just have to convince Ahmed, that's all.'

As a fourth-time mother I was confident Jane would have no problems giving birth but because she was pregnant by a new partner her risks of developing pre-eclampsia were raised. While it is still unknown exactly why it occurs, when a woman falls pregnant by a new partner her risks of developing pre-eclampsia are raised back to that of a woman going through her first pregnancy. Throwing Jane's age into the mix and the fact this was an IVF baby, she had already been informed by her doctor that this should be treated as a high-risk pregnancy under obstetric care.

Ahmed, being very traditional, adamantly believed in the doctor's word being final. He thought that hospitals were the safest places in the world to give birth and seeing as his baby, along with Jane, were the most precious things in his life he did not want to take any chances with their health. As a result, Jane had a battle to convince Ahmed that having a home birth was the best route.

If he'd had his way, Jane would be placed in a gilded cage and put on watch in a laboratory until the baby was born safely. But he loved and trusted Jane, so he was willing to at least listen to her plans and to consider what she was saying.

I was well used to having the mothers-to-be do all the talking while their husbands sat and listened but during my visits it turned out to be Ahmed who said the most.

Having read seemingly every childbirth book published as homework, Ahmed was at each appointment with a long list of questions, some of which shocked and surprised me due to their depth and complexity.

As he asked me question after question Jane watched him fondly, her eyes shining with love. The queries ranged from why I was taking his beloved's blood pressure to what I might find in her urine sample.

'How is the baby lying, Virginia?' he asked, watching with a furrowed brow as I prodded Jane's stomach.

'How do you know the cord is not round the neck?'

'How do you know that the baby is growing properly?'

'Why are Jane's feet swollen?'

As Jane looked on fondly as the two of us discussed the subjects he raised, it never occurred to me that I was devoting too much time to him at the detriment of her care.

Then at 36 weeks I arrived at the couple's house to find Jane alone.

'Where's Ahmed?' I asked.

'He's running late seeing a business client,' she said. 'But I'm glad he's not here actually.'

'Is everything all right?' I asked, noticing that she seemed less upbeat than usual.

'It's as if I don't matter anymore,' she admitted. 'It's all about the baby for Ahmed and you seem to be caring more for him than me.'

'Oh no, Jane, I am so sorry,' I replied, mortified that I'd been so absorbed in educating Ahmed that I'd sidelined Jane in the process. 'I thought you were enjoying the way things had been going; I felt like it was the two of us teaching Ahmed.'

'I know, Virginia,' she sighed. 'I thought it was OK, too, and I wanted Ahmed to know everything but I want it to be about me now. I am beginning to get a little scared and I am not so confident anymore.'

My heart sank as her bottom lip began to tremble.

'I just don't think I can do it,' she added as tears streamed down her cheeks.

'Of course you can do it!' I said, doing my best to rally her. 'Now tell me what is worrying you.'

'I feel like I've lost my confidence,' she said, sniffing. 'Maybe I'm wrong to think I can do things differently this time. Maybe I'll need an epidural.'

'No, Jane, you are strong,' I told her firmly. 'You were made to do this. I wouldn't be saying this if I didn't believe it. It's normal to have worries, that's all about developing as a mother and being aware of danger so you can protect your baby.'

Determined to put right the situation, I spent a lovely afternoon with Jane addressing her fear, worries and self-doubts, and then speaking truthfully about my own life and dreams.

'I envy your life,' I told her. 'I had my children young, too, and wish I could have that time over to have a baby at home with a birth plan I'd decided on. You're going to feel so empowered when you have this baby!'

As a smile crept on to Jane's face I could tell she was starting to believe in herself once more. After a few hours I left feeling much better about the situation but also having given myself a firm telling off. I'd never put the needs of a father before a mother again, that was for sure.

Over the next few weeks I kept in touch with Jane via phone. We had one more routine antenatal check before her due date and when I arrived full of goodwill to lavish Jane with my attention I was a little concerned to see her looking tired and drained.

'Are you OK?' I asked.

'I've been having pains all night,' she said. 'But they're irregular, not like proper contractions.'

'Right,' I said. 'Let's check you out shall we?'

After checking her blood pressure, urine and feeling to find that the baby was in a good position for birth, we sat down to have a chat.

'All this pain is normal – it's pre-labour pain,' I explained. 'Your body gearing up to labour actively. The best thing to do is be strong and wait it out, or I could do a membrane sweep to try and encourage it along but it's not entirely necessary. Waiting is best but a sweep can work if a woman is good and ready.'

With Jane wanting to go ahead, I did a good digital stretch of the cervix to help the labour hormone oxytocin to be released and get the labour going. In the process, I found that the cervix was very stretchy and the baby's head was low down – both very good signs that strong active labour was not too far away.

'I don't think it will be long now, Jane,' I smiled. 'Try to relax. Rest as much as you can, eat when you want to and keep a positive mind. Maybe go for a walk if you feel up to it and give me a call as soon as you get started.'

Sure enough, by 3pm Jane was calling me back to the house as her contractions were now strong and powerful and coming regularly.

I arrived to find her pacing up and down in the lounge, stopping to lean on Ahmed's desk, where a pile of childbirth books he had accumulated over the previous months had started to build. The labour was proving to be a quick one, as is usual for a multigravida woman (the term we use for mothers who have had more than one baby) and by early evening, Jane started to feel the urge to bear down. I helped her change position between contractions easing a birth stool under her bottom to take the place of her tired legs and she sat there with Ahmed behind her cuddling and comforting her. A birth stool is an old-fashioned device used throughout history that dates back to medieval times or before. It is a low, horseshoe-shaped seat that keeps the woman in an upright yet comfortable position. The baby's head descends amazingly well when a birth stool is used. It also enables a midwife to sit cross-legged on the floor in front of the woman in a low position so you can catch the baby with ease. With the woman physically raised above the midwife, it also puts her psychologically in a more empowered position.

Although Jane was blonde, I had no doubt that with Ahmed's dark skin, brown eyes and jet black hair it would be easy to spot the first signs of this little one as it began its downward descent into the world.

As Jane continued to push with determination, my eyes stayed glued to the spot as I looked out for black wispy curls protruding between pink flesh. But as the vulva widened I was shocked to see a white rounded flash of flesh covered in an even whiter creamy paste.

'The baby is bald?' I thought for a moment. But within seconds I knew this was not a head. It was a fleshy bottom! Oh my goodness I had been sure I'd felt the head during a vaginal examination earlier, hadn't I?

Only about five per cent of all babies present in the breech position and of those one in four will not be discovered in pregnancy. When women have either tight or very loose muscles they can be hard to detect and even the best consultants, without the use of ultrasound, are not infallible.

I knew breech babies could be missed by palpation or during vaginal examinations, but both? This was the first one I had ever missed completely.

'Jane, Ahmed,' I began. 'I do not want you to be alarmed, but this baby is coming bottom first. I have delivered breech babies before but, Jane, I do need you to change position. Can you get on to all fours for me, please, the baby needs room to hang.'

Staying calm, Jane got on to all fours while Ahmed started to pray out loud. They had their heads pressed closely together and were gazing into each other's eyes for strength. As the baby started to emerge, I clapped my hand in amazement and called to them over the words of Ahmed's beautiful prayers.

'There is nothing to fear,' I said. 'Your baby is on her way out and she is an amazingly healthy girl.'

Sure enough, as the baby's body was born it was clear she needed no help from anyone. Seemingly knowing her way out she brought her pink, chubby knees up to her chest in a peddling motion as she descended and then her arms dropped out, her little limbs flailing round as if to save herself from falling. Within minutes her head slid out easily from under her mother's pubic arch. There were those telltale black curls!

Catching her as she dropped, I lowered her to the floor in a forward movement so she lay in front of Jane. I laughed with joy as I watched Jane scoop her newborn daughter up off the floor and cradle her to her chest. As she flung her head back and let out a cry of pure ecstasy and joy, tears poured from Ahmed's eyes as he leaned forward and hugged them both, raining kisses down on Jane's sweat-dampened face. As stark relief hit me I, too, cried – happy tears of shock and joy cascading down my cheeks.

Not long after Jane delivered her placenta easily with no help from me. All that remained now was for the rest of the family to come and admire the brand new addition and hear the wonderful story of her birth.

With Jane now breastfeeding the little princess they'd named Afra, her face was radiant with delight and pride at having achieved the birth she wanted – even if it was breech!

Over the next week I was pleased to see both mother and baby doing well, as I carried out my postnatal checks. On my last visit I bid the happy family goodbye as Jane passed baby Afra to Ahmed.

'Can you wind her?' she asked.

We both watched as Ahmed held his tiny princess to his chest and patted her back with concentration.

'Am I doing it right?' he asked. 'How many times should she belch?'

Smirking, Jane threw me a private look.

'Here we go again!' I thought.

Meanwhile, Charlott's pregnancy had been a straightforward one and in the early hours of 14 June 2010 Andrew called me to say the labour had started. He had a slight panic to his voice and my immediate instinct was to rush to comfort my son rather than his girlfriend in labour, which was a very strange feeling.

I arrived at the house to find Charlott writhing in pain in the bath with very strong labour pains. As well as having Andrew there, she was also being supported by her own mum, Annette, and my daughter Sophie, who was months away from finishing her own midwifery training. Together we rallied round, keen to help Charlott during this amazing family moment.

Straightaway I could see that the bath was not deep enough to give Charlott much pain relief or comfort.

'Why don't we get you out and sat on my birth stool,' I suggested. She nodded in agreement and not long after we'd helped her out of the bath the baby started to emerge.

Knowing how wonderful it was for some men to catch their own babies, I didn't want Andrew to miss this opportunity. So grabbing his hands I pulled him in front of Charlott to catch his son.

Although he caught the little boy with me supporting him, he then immediately lowered the wet slippery baby to the floor, snatching his hands away to leave the baby lying there between his mother's feet.

'Pick him up, Andrew,' I said gently.

'No, Mum, I'm scared,' he replied. Seeing that the intensity of the situation had left him frozen to the spot, I gently picked up the tiny, bald baby and passed him up to Charlott.

'Hello, Luca,' she said, biting her lip with emotion as tears streamed down her cheeks. As everyone studied our newest member of the family there wasn't a dry eye in the room – except for me. For some reason I felt strangely detached and was confused at my lack of feelings.

Sticking to the job at hand, I helped Charlott as she delivered the placenta, having passed Luca back to a much calmer, smiling Andrew. Leaving him gazing smitten at his son, I helped Charlott into the shower and then to bed where Andrew brought Luca to join her.

Continuing with my tasks I cleared up the room and stowed everything back into my car. Then changing into a clean set of clothes I walked back into the room to check on Luca who was now laid in the crib next to Charlott.

'Can I pick him up?' I asked, my role now nothing but new grandmother.

'Course you can!' Charlott smiled.

As I gently scooped Luca up and held him to my face I breathed in that sweet baby smell. Then lowering him to my lap I marvelled at his little scrunched up face. It was at that moment that I realised that this sweet little boy was the absolute image of his daddy when he was a baby.

'The son of my son, my first grandchild!' I thought. In that moment I realised that my earlier lack of feelings were because I was being the midwife first and foremost, but now I was just Noonie the proud grandmother. My heart soared and I couldn't hold back the tears.

As much as I loved being a grandmother my thoughts often turned to Matt and Gemma who had been trying to conceive since the May before their wedding in August 2009.

When Luca had been born I knew how much they had wanted it to be them. Another six months had passed since his birth with no sign of a baby for Matt and Gemma and they were now saving up to start a course of IVF.

I knew how important it was to them so I started to plan a special Christmas present for them.

As the family gathered on Christmas Day I read out a poem I had written for the occasion which detailed the different funny stories of family life over the years.

But as I began to read the final verse, I could see Sophie and Courtney's eyes filling with tears.

There is just one glitch, one road to climb that may seem
    tough
But one we can commit to if we all try hard enough
Two of us need help right now, a pain to overcome
Two of us are not alone and we need to help as one

As everyone mopped their eyes I handed Matt and Gemma a box.

'You can open that now, you two,' I said. 'And hand out what's inside to everyone.'

As they unwrapped the box and pulled out several money boxes with the words 'baby fund' written on them, the realisation hit them.

Together, as a family, we were all going to save up to help them with their IVF treatment.

'I can't believe it,' Matthew said, wiping his eyes. 'I can't thank you enough.'

Just after Christmas the whole family were round for Sunday lunch. As we chatted in the kitchen Sophie cleared her throat.

'We've got some news,' she said, glancing at her boyfriend Robert. 'I'm pregnant!'

After I'd hugged her and Robert my eyes turned to Gemma. Although she was smiling I could tell how hard it was for her to hear it.

A little while later I found her and Matt cuddling in the front room and I put my arm round both of them.

'Don't worry,' I said. 'It will be your turn soon.'

Two months later in March the family once again arrived for Sunday lunch. Andrew and Courtney were laughing and chatting in the kitchen as I prepared the gravy and Sean carved the chicken while Sophie and Charlott cooed over Luca, who at eight months old was crawling all over the place.

When Matt and Gemma arrived, Matt seemed keen to hand me a parcel wrapped up in tissue paper.

'Ooh a present!' I teased. 'You must want something.'

As I opened the gift, I immediately recognised it as the wall plaque I'd given them on their wedding day. The one that read 'Nana's Kitchen'.

'Don't you remember, Mum?' Matt laughed. 'You told us you wanted it back one day!'

Suddenly the penny dropped. Gemma was pregnant!

'Oh my darlings!' I cried as I hugged them. There were tears all round as everyone rushed to congratulate them. Gemma and Matt would not need IVF after all. They had done it themselves!

'Great news!' added Andrew. 'I can now use the money I've saved in my "baby fund" box to buy a new suit!'

So, before the year was out, I was blessed with not one but two further grandchildren!

First of all, my beautiful Sophie brought her baby Jesse into the world at the end of August. Then three months later Gemma went into labour in November.

The plan had always been for Gemma to give birth at my house so that she could get all the TLC she needed and it would also give her some privacy away from their lodger.

So the night before active labour, with sporadic contractions indicating that Gemma was getting started, Matthew drove her over to ours.

With Gemma under my watchful eye, I advised her to manage her discomfort by bouncing and swaying on a birthing ball as she and Matt settled down to watch TV with Sean, Courtney and I.

Everyone eventually went to bed and at some time during the night I awoke to see a light on outside the bedroom door and, blinking my sleepy eyes, I crept along the corridor. I found Gemma was in the bathroom with Matt sitting on the floor next to her.

'You OK, darling?' I asked.

'Yes I am fine but I just couldn't sleep any more as the contractions are coming but they're still irregular.'

'Have faith, Gemma, they will become active soon, I promise,' I said.

'Are you all right there, Matt?' I said, turning to my tired-looking son. 'Do you want to go and get some sleep and I will sit with Gemma?'

'No, Mum, you go back to bed,' he told me firmly. 'We are fine here and we will need you more later.'

So reluctantly I went back to bed.

'Is she OK?' Sean mumbled as I slipped back into my warm spot.

'Shhh, go back to sleep, everything is fine,' I said softly.

I must have dozed back off because the next thing I heard was the front door closing as Matt and Gemma left the house to go for a walk. It was now light outside.

Sean and Courtney left for work with the instruction that when they returned that evening the dining room would be a no-go area until Gemma's baby had been born.

'Can you examine me, Virginia, please,' Gemma asked when they came back from their walk at 9am. 'I really want to know if I am dilating now.'

'OK, Gemma,' I said. 'But, remember, it doesn't tell the whole picture, OK?'

Getting her into a comfortable position, I took a look. Gemma was three centimetres dilated and active labour did appear to be underway with the contractions now stronger and coming more regularly.

I settled her in the dining room on a birthing ball then she moved on to her side on a cosy bed I had made up for her on the floor.

Meanwhile, Matt, who had inflated the birthing pool the night before in readiness, was busy filling it with relaxing warm water.

As I sat next to Gemma, I was joined by Matt and together we reassured her everything was OK and Matt whispered affirmations to her that they had learnt while doing hypnobirthing classes. During the classes Gemma and Matt had learnt about teaching the mind to control the feelings and sensations going on in the body and to use visualization to aid relaxation.

'Let the air fill your body like a balloon with each contraction and then let it go up into the sky and float away,' Matt soothed as Gemma concentrated on her breathing.

I was proud to see him being such a caring birth partner.

Unfortunately as her contractions got stronger Gemma was struck by a nausea which lasted pretty much throughout her labour. For some women it's the body's natural reaction to the flood of hormones or needing to rid the stomach of its contents.

Poor Gemma, even the contractions were easier to manage than the constant retching.

'It's OK,' I said, pressing a cold flannel against her forehead and offering her cool water. 'Just keep sipping on water so it keeps you hydrated.'

By lunchtime Gemma was ready to get into the pool and, despite being sick every 30 minutes, she was uncomplaining, floating around in the pool not making any sound. As the contractions appeared to die off around teatime, I felt that it was a sure sign her cervix was fully dilated.

'Would you like to get out of the pool and try sitting on the birth stool?' I asked. 'That may help the contractions to come back and then you may feel expulsive urges and start to push.'

Gemma duly climbed out with the help of Matt and before long she began to feel the need to push with a vengeance.

'It's burning!' she cried.

Soon a little head started to emerge and, just like with Andrew, I helped Matthew into position as Gemma pushed their son out into his strong hands at 16.37 on 16 November 2011. He and Gemma sobbed tears of happiness as they admired their much-wanted son Lex.

'He looks just like you did as a baby,' I told Matt.

Then helping Gemma up, I supported her to the spare room where I tucked her into bed with her baby.

'Keep sipping your water,' I instructed.

I've always felt very protective towards Gemma, who in turn calls me her 'other mummy', so for the next few days I pampered her just as I had wanted to. As she got to grips with breastfeeding, I brought her trays of nice food and helped her with the baby as much as she wanted.

Then, once she was strong enough, she and Matt headed home to a brand new life as proud parents.

The three cousins, Luca, Jesse and Lex, are all growing up together. They sometimes play really well and sometimes they fight over toys just as all little ones do, but no matter what their proud Noonie watches on.

*   *   *

When a young woman called Annabel first rang me to ask to book an appointment to discuss me being her independent midwife I had no idea that this would involve the kind of interrogation that one might expect to deliver the royal heir.

Annabel lived with her husband, Stuart, at a gorgeous family home in the Kent countryside, which included a working farm that had stables and grew hops. I'd arrived to meet her one wet Sunday morning in November and, as I got out the car, a pack of friendly dogs were there to meet me, sniffing around my ankles and escorting me, tails wagging, to the back door.

'Sorry, they're just very friendly,' Annabel, a pretty blonde in her 20s said by way of apology as she invited me into the utility room. Once inside she offered me a choice of a row of slippers laid out to encourage visitors to remove their muddy shoes before entering the main house.

'Thanks for coming to see me at the weekend,' Annabel, who was 25 weeks pregnant, smiled as I followed her down a long passage filled with saddles and other horse paraphernalia into a warm and inviting kitchen where her mother, Frances, was busy tending to a delicious-smelling Sunday roast.

'This is my parents' house,' she explained. 'Stuart and I are in the process of selling our place and have been staying here. Please make yourself at home,' she said beckoning me over to a large kitchen table in an adjacent conservatory overlooking fields that stretched as far as the eye could see.

As her mother poured me a cup of tea and placed a plate of chocolate biscuits at my side, a man introducing himself as Stuart appeared from a door in the corner of the kitchen.

At this point I'd expected Annabel's mother to take herself off discreetly as the three of us chatted but she sat down at the table with us and I realised she fully expected to be involved. And she wasn't the only one. One by one all the family – Annabel's father, her brother and his partner, her mother-in-law and finally her father-in-law – trundled into the conservatory and sat down facing me.

As they eyeballed me expectantly I felt akin to a convicted felon facing a firing squad. 'Wow, first time for everything,' I thought.

'The thing about Annabel is she has a severe needle phobia and is terrified of anything medical,' Stuart began, holding his wife's hand. 'But she's been told she can't have a home birth unless she has blood tests. Is this true?'

'No, there is always choice,' I said.

Stuart went on to explain how routine blood tests were out of the question for Annabel who would need to be sedated before anyone could approach her with a sharp instrument. As he spoke Annabel smiled sweetly at him and the rest of her protective family unit. I was pleased to hear that having undergone surgery (after being sedated under very difficult circumstances) earlier in her life Annabel's blood group had been identified. Seeing as it was a common one it made things a lot easier.

'As long as we have that, we should be fine,' I concluded. 'Everything else can be managed. The most important thing is to keep Annabel calm and relaxed.'

'I get panic attacks if I even go near a hospital,' Annabel said. 'So the only option for me is a home birth.'

That was fine with me but suddenly I understood why so many members of the family had congregated to meet me. Her army of supporters had serious doubts about home birth for their precious Annabel. Indeed, both sets of parents seemed highly suspicious of it.

'Is it even a safe option?' questioned Frances.

Having lost track of the number of times I have had to defend home birth I was only too happy to recount my usual facts, figures and statistics to prove it was a safe choice, if that was what Annabel wanted.

Throughout the questioning from the parents I was acutely aware of Martin, Annabel's brother, sizing me up with a stare, his body language leaving me in no doubt that the thought of birth was something very alien to him but his love for his sister required him to be there.

As everyone bombarded me with questions about what I would do if the baby failed to breathe or Annabel haemorrhaged I was able to allay their fears.

Then, as I saw Frances exchanging reassured smiles with Annabel's father, Piers, I knew that I'd finally won them over. After a couple of hours the Spanish Inquisition atmosphere went from intense to light-hearted as the family began to tease Annabel about her phobia.

'We should warn you that Annabel will jump out a window if she sees a needle,' Stuart added, recalling the time his wife had escaped from a dentist who, with an injection hidden behind his back, arrogantly thought he could cure Annabel of her phobia by tricking her into submission.

'Luckily for Annabel it was a ground-floor window,' Stuart added to snorts of laughter from his in-laws.

As the delicious smells wafting from the oven indicated that the family's roast was almost ready, I bid them farewell asking them to call once they had made a decision.

I was pleased to hear the following day that Annabel wanted to go ahead and, with everyone reassured, the close-knit clan proceeded to get very excited about the coming baby.

After reading all the information I'd given her, Annabel had settled on a water birth and had agreed that in the case of an emergency I was allowed to administer an injection, as long as I didn't tell her it was coming. Not wanting a repeat of the window episode I agreed to accept her consent in advance.

Everything was shaping up nicely until at 37 weeks I found the baby to be lying across her uterus, a position called transverse.

'It might not be a problem,' I reassured her. 'It is likely the baby will turn head down.'

We waited a week to see if baby would move to a longitudinal presentation but the next time I checked the stubborn little thing was still transverse. Knowing that there was no way a baby could be born in that position, I reluctantly had to bring up the subject of intervention.

'I'm afraid it may be that the baby needs to be turned to head down,' I said. 'An option is for you to visit an obstetrician to see if they can move the baby into the right position.'

This procedure was called ECV (external cephalic version) and involved the doctor pushing and moulding the baby into the head-down position using their hands on the outside of the tummy.

I knew it was the last thing Annabel wanted to hear but, to her credit, she remained calm despite realising this would mean a trip to the hospital to see a consultant obstetrician.

With her consent I made an appointment for the following day and it was agreed that I'd meet her and Stuart in the hospital reception so that I could be both Annabel's advocate and a familiar face at the hospital.

Dr Canet, the obstetrician we were seeing, was someone I'd worked with on occasions and I knew her to be a forward-thinking medic who believed the longer she could keep women out of the labour ward the better. I really hoped that she had the skills to keep Annabel out of it completely.

As the three of us walked along the corridor to the room made ready for our consultation, Annabel chatted away with excited nerves like a child about to ride the ghost train. However, knowing the whole picture, I was on tenterhooks as to how it all might go. It is rarely a joyous episode when a woman, having planned a home birth, has the need to visit an obstetrician at this late stage of her pregnancy. I really wanted Annabel to get the birth of her choice but I knew only too well that once a woman gets into the medical system choices can easily be swallowed up in hospital procedure.

Introductions made, we all sat down as Annabel and Stuart brought Dr Canet, a short, dark-haired woman in her early 60s, up-to-date on how the pregnancy had progressed and about Annabel's medical history. I occasionally filled in with any information that was needed to complete the picture.

'Please can you lie down on the bed so I can feel the baby,' Dr Canet asked.

Annabel duly removed her boots and manoeuvred her swollen, cumbersome body on to the examination bed. As Dr Canet moved her hands over the protruding belly she frowned.

'I'm just going to bring in the scanning machine,' she said.

After running the probe over Annabel's belly she pushed the equipment to one side and sat down.

'I am so sorry, Annabel, but in my opinion this baby will not stay down even if we do manage to turn it,' she said. 'I think you may have a heart-shaped uterus, which means the baby has more room lying this way. The only option is a caesarean section.'

As I listened to her describing the procedure – and Annabel's body tensed – it was clear Dr Canet really hadn't grasped the severity of Annabel's phobia.

'We can do the caesarean section in the next couple of days,' she said. 'But, don't worry, you won't feel anything! We will use a spinal anaesthetic, similar to an epidural.'

'Oh no, oh no,' Annabel began to mutter, her body rigid.

Pushing the doctor's hands away she sat up, shaking her head and breathing deeply.

'I'm sorry but needles are out of the question for Annabel,' Stuart interjected.

'I'm afraid this is the only option,' Dr Canet said firmly.

'If I need a caesarean section, I will need to be put to sleep,' Annabel said, the look on her face became more and more strained.

'Well, Annabel, we don't advise that, I am afraid,' replied the doctor. 'We prefer you to have a spinal anaesthetic which will numb you.'

By now Stuart was also beginning to look very worried as he glanced furtively between Annabel, me and the doctor.

'It is nothing to be concerned about, you'll see,' Dr Canet added as if it were a done deal. The stress in Annabel was palpable in the air.

In an all-too-familiar scene I watched as the usual medical dance ensued. The doctor suggested that Annabel speak to the expert when it came to anaesthetics and went to fetch one of her colleagues.

I was pleasantly surprised when in walked Dr Ralph the middle-aged chief anaesthetist I'd known as a student and had asked for advice about mobilising women after epidurals. I'd always liked him and found him very approachable.

But, once again, Annabel, now with tears running down her cheeks, was forced to tell her story, interrupted only by Stuart who explained with emphasis how Annabel reacted to needles – even throwing in the window leap story for good measure.

Although Dr Ralph listened, it was obvious to me he was merely waiting for Annabel to finish speaking in order to give his opinion.

'My advice, Annabel, is that you have a spinal anaesthetic,' he said.

'No but . . .' Annabel tried to intervene to no avail, tears now dripping off her chin quicker than she was able to wipe them away as she twisted and turned a tissue in her hands.

But Dr Ralph had started his monologue and was not going to stop until he had imparted his information.

'It's much safer,' he said. 'You maintain your own airway, you are conscious so you can talk to us throughout and before long you will have your baby. Really, we do it all the time, you will be fine.'

'I think being awake is a real problem for Annabel,' I interrupted. 'This is not a small fear, it is a lifelong phobia.'

'Yes, I understand that, but we have to keep Annabel as safe as possible and a general anaesthetic has added risks,' he said. 'We need to put a drip in your hand but we can put a little bit of cream on your hand, like we use for the children, if you are worried it will hurt when the needle goes in.'

It was no surprise when Annabel, who was still sitting on the bed, leaned over and picked up her boots. I thought she was going to put them on and leave but as she held them aloft I saw her face contort with frustration and stress.

'Nooo!' she screamed at the top of her voice hurling them as hard as she could across the room aiming at poor Stuart. The boots hit the wall behind him with a resounding thump as he simultaneously ducked and raised his hands in protection.

With that Annabel jumped from the bed and ran from the room. Time stood still for the two doctors as they sat jaws hanging and staring from the open door to me with shock in their eyes.

'Leave her to me,' I said and raced out after a fleeing Annabel. I finally caught up with her in the crowded corridor panting and sobbing against an opened window, her breath steaming up on the cool glass.

'It's OK, Annabel, no one is going to hurt you,' I said, holding her tight in my arms. She was shaking and trembling but slowly her sobs calmed and her voice became coherent once again.

'I must be asleep. I cannot be awake with all those needles,' she whispered. 'I just can't do it.'

'Come on, Annabel, let's go back, get you a cup of tea and find a way to get everything back into your control,' I said. 'No one can do anything to you if you do not agree to it and I think they now understand just how afraid you are.'

Annabel wiped her eyes and looked down at her bare feet.

'How embarrassing,' she said, biting her lip. 'I don't know what came over me.'

'You have nothing to be embarrassed about,' I said. 'They heard you but they did not listen and if they are not willing to devise a safe plan that is agreeable to you, we will go elsewhere until we find someone who will.'

Heading back into the room I encouraged Annabel to sit with the shocked anaesthetist who I had always known to be a very caring man.

'OK, Annabel,' he said. 'I can see this is something a little more serious than a fear of needles so let's make a plan. How about you come in and we give you something to relax you. Then once you are asleep we can put any needles in that are necessary in order to proceed with the plan to do the caesarean section and deliver your baby?'

'OK,' Annabel agreed meekly, biting her lip.

So a week later Annabel's story ended with a lovely healthy baby being born by caesarean section while his calm and peaceful mummy slept unafraid among a very experienced team of doctors.

Later when Annabel came back from theatre I walked into the room where she was recovering to find her holding her newborn son, James, and smiling as Stuart and her large family surrounded her.

'How are you?' I asked, glancing at the hand where the drip was still attached but had been hidden with a bandage by the kind anaesthetist.

'He's done a good job of bandaging my hand,' Annabel smiled. 'That was thoughtful of him.'

'Yes,' Stuart agreed. 'And just as well, too, because if she had awoken and seen it, she may just have thrown the vase of flowers at the wall.'

As a relaxed Annabel giggled at the good-natured teasing I was thrilled to see that things had gone so well.

While we'd got off to a rocky start it was wonderful to know that Dr Ralph hadn't let Annabel down. By acknowledging her fears and her right to individualised care, he had ensured that Annabel took home a new positive experience of hospital – and her bouncing baby boy to boot!

Chapter Fourteen

Driving along an oak-tree-lined country road, I took my time enjoying the glimpses of the expensive houses just visible behind tall ornate gates.

I loved visiting Trudy and Timothy in their beautiful house near the sought-after town of Sevenoaks in Kent. Often, if the gates were closed, I would park in the lane and walk along their long driveway, enjoying the views of the gardens and approaching house.

Trudy, who up until recently had been living in Cheshire, had previously had a very positive experience giving birth at home to her two-year-old son. When she'd moved south she wanted to use an independent midwife again. She found me and we'd hit it off straight away.

As we chatted over tea, Trudy, a glamorous blonde in her early 30s, would tell me about her high-end florist business, rattling off the names of the lavish blooms arranged perfectly on her exquisite furniture.

Occasionally Timothy, who worked in finance, would be home and the three of us would laugh and discuss all things related to pregnancy and birth.

Apart from some extra monitoring due to an eye infection, Trudy's pregnancy had gone really well and she made my task of caring for her very easy.

It was towards the end of the pregnancy, when Trudy was 38 weeks, that I found myself questioning the position of the baby.

I couldn't be certain but rather than feeling a bottom at the top of her uterus it felt like my fingers were prodding against the hard round lump of a baby's head. Running my fingers from top to bottom and back to the top again I checked several times hoping that I was wrong.

'I think this baby is breech, Trudy,' I finally said.

'But I can feel hiccups in my pelvis,' Trudy said shaking her head from side to side. 'Are you sure my baby is breech?'

Continuing my examination I used my Pinard stethoscope to locate a heartbeat. It appeared to be just above the pubic bone which slightly confused my thoughts as to where the baby was positioned, seeing as a loud heartbeat here could indicate the head was facing down. I felt Trudy's tummy again, questioning her about movements and kicks.

With Trudy convinced that she could feel the head I thought that perhaps I had got it wrong. After all it wasn't too long ago that I'd missed Sally's breech baby. Given my uncertainty, I suggested we took her in for a scan.

'No thanks, Virginia, I really do not want a scan now. I'm tired, it's snowy and I'd just rather not,' she replied to my surprise. 'I'm just going to hope that the baby's head is down. I wouldn't do anything different even if it was breech anyway.'

I discussed the situation with Kay later that day because if the baby was breech I would need her to attend the birth with me, so I needed her full support. This was one of the reasons I loved working with Kay. Over the years we'd developed a mutual respect and trust that we could always rely on the other for help and assistance. When working as an independent midwife presented its challenges, it was good to know that Kay always had my back and likewise I'd always be there for her.

Just a week later I received the call from Timothy to say that Trudy's waters had broken, at 39 weeks.

Often I would tell a client to try to sleep before I snatched some more kip myself, but as this was a second baby, and as I noticed snowflakes were starting to fall outside I decided to leave straight away.

It took 40 minutes for me to drive to Trudy and Timothy's home and I arrived just before 10pm and ahead of the snow.

Parking up I saw that the main house was dark but the lights of the couple's self-contained guest apartment to the side of the house, were illuminated – I knew this was where Trudy had decided she wanted to give birth.

Just as I was getting out the car I was shocked to see Leanne, another client's name on my caller display. A call this late at night could only mean one thing. I had another woman in labour – the thing that I most dreaded and which had only happened to me on one previous occasion.

When I book women they often ask me, 'What happens if you have two women in labour at the same time?' My answer is always honest. I tell them that I can never, nor can anyone, give them a 100 per cent guarantee that I will be with them for the birth.

'Life has a way of throwing curve balls,' I admit. 'But it is a very rare occurrence and ninety-nine per cent of the time I will be there for the birth.'

'Hi, Leanne,' I answered cheerily. 'Is everything OK?'

'I am having contractions,' she replied, confirming my worst fears. 'I think things have started.'

Not wanting to worry her I told her a little white lie.

'I'm just in the bath, Leanne,' I said. 'I'll get out now but can I call you back in a few minutes?'

I hated telling lies but at least it would buy me five minutes of time to check on what was happening with Trudy.

Walking across the gravel drive to the apartment, I climbed the stairs which led me into a warm, cosy living space. I found Timothy sat watching TV and Trudy in the bath. At first glance, she did not appear to be in very strong labour as her contractions were irregular and she was chatty and chirpy.

With relief I quickly assessed that this was latent labour. With active labour not yet underway I should have time to go and see Leanne, while waiting for Trudy's labour to become established.

My brain rushed with thoughts of everything I needed to juggle – an urgent call back to Leanne to say I was on my way and an alert to Kay. Oh, and the snow!

'Please don't let it settle,' I prayed to the birth angels, but retaining a cool exterior I smiled at Trudy.

'It's going to be a while before active labour starts,' I said in my most soothing voice. 'Get some rest if you can and give me a call when the contractions get stronger. I just need to go and assess another woman who is having a headache but I'll be back as soon as you need me.'

I then speed-walked back to my car, trying not to notice that a light sprinkle of snow was beginning to materialise on Trudy's lawn.

As soon as I opened the car door, I was dialling Leanne's number.

'I am coming to check on you now,' I said. 'See you in around thirty minutes.'

Setting off on the 20-mile drive to Leanne's house, I called Kay to fill her in, sighing with disbelief as large flakes of snow began to spiral across my windscreen.

Together we began to form a contingency plan but with all the commotion of the night we had completely forgotten Kay was going to be called to Trudy's birth as backup in case the baby did happen to be breech.

'So I'll go and check on Leanne and call you back,' I said in conclusion. 'Then we can make a decision about whether you need to take over one of the births.'

This would mean a heart-breaking choice for me. I wanted to be with both women and knew that they, in turn, would want the midwife they had built up a trusting relationship with. Although my clients rarely met Kay, they all had her information in their notes and I always made a point of explaining how we shared our philosophy on midwifery and how she cared for her own clients every bit as much as I cared for mine.

Arriving at Leanne's terraced town house, I knocked on the door. It was opened by Leanne herself and she certainly did not seem to be in very active labour but, knowing this was her second baby, I was aware that things could be unpredictable.

I sat with her for a while drinking tea and assessed that she was in much the same situation as Trudy – experiencing early labour with irregular contractions but otherwise all was well.

Then when Leanne went upstairs to have a bath, I called Kay to discuss the situation on the phone.

'I'm going to stay here for a while,' I said. 'If Leanne goes into active labour and Trudy also calls, I will call you back to decide which labour to send you to.'

A call from Timothy just a minute or so later revealed that things had suddenly changed. Trudy was having strong contractions. Swiftly I made up my mind. I'd go back to Trudy and send Kay to watch over Leanne.

In order not to distress Leanne, I told her that I was going to assess another client who had a headache but that my lovely and experienced colleague Kay was on her way to care for her until I got back. I could only pray that would indeed be the situation and that I would not let Leanne down.

I drove slowly back to Trudy's house remaining on high alert as my car trailed black tyre marks in a thick blanket of snow.

'Oh please,' I sighed, staring in dismay at the ever-growing, cotton-wool-sized flakes that obscured my view. The double-lane roads were down to just one slow lane and cars appeared to have been abandoned at the kerbs where side roads were impassable.

Arriving back at Trudy's house, I left my car at the end of the long drive, which was now very deep in snow, and, equipment bag in hand, scuttled down the long drive where, having left the door open for me, Timothy was calling for me to come upstairs.

My heart racing, I ran up the steps to be met at the top by Trudy who was sweating and panting as the weight of her contractions riveted her to the spot. There was no doubt that she was now in strong labour.

A quick assessment showed that Trudy was well and the baby's heartbeat was a healthy 130 beats per minute. Running my hands over her tummy I tried to palpate, to determine the lie of the baby but it was too uncomfortable for Trudy to keep still.

'Can I do a vaginal examination?' I asked. Wincing in pain, she nodded.

As she manoeuvred herself on to the carpet, I slipped on a pair of gloves. I could feel that the cervix was thin and stretchy and at least seven centimetres dilated which was good.

But as my fingers brushed across the peachy sensation of a centrally placed left buttock and dipped down to feel the start of the right my heart fell. I instantly remembered my earlier suspicions and knew with no doubt that this was a breech-presenting baby.

The situation was far from ideal, given that I was alone and the roads were so bad, but at least the baby appeared to be in the right position for a straightforward breech birth.

'Trudy,' I said calmly, looking into her eyes. 'Remember I thought baby was breech? Well . . . it is. I don't want you to worry, please stay calm.'

As a straightforward second-time mother, I would have been happy to support Trudy to birth her baby breech – as I had done unexpectedly with Jane. But in such circumstances I preferred to have another midwife present.

I explained to Trudy that I could either call Kay to assist me with the birth or we could get an ambulance for her. Still taking in the news that the baby was indeed breech, Trudy was anxious. Worried how long it would take Kay to get to us given the weather, she replied, 'I want to go to hospital.'

Grabbing my phone I called an ambulance, praying that there would be one in the vicinity and we would not have to wait while it travelled a distance in the snow.

'OK, Trudy, try and stay calm,' I said. 'I have told them we are coming in.'

To my utter delight and relief, within minutes of finishing the call, I heard tyres crunching along the lane and the flicker of blue lights illuminated the dimly lit room.

Trudy, also hearing the ambulance, started to walk determinedly down the stairs. She then proceeded to march up the long drive in the snow in not much else but her thin dressing gown and slippers with Timothy tailing behind her.

Having been in active labour almost consistently for four hours now, I was pretty amazed at how quickly she moved along that driveway in the deep snow. Soon she was climbing into the back of the ambulance and Timothy and I got in behind her. Following the ambulance driver's advice, she sat in a seat and strapped herself in. Timothy sat with his back to the driver and I sat down in the seat next to her and off we set.

As we began the slow journey to the hospital on one of the worst weather days of the year, it was clear Trudy's contractions were still coming thick and fast. She was coping really well, though, breathing through them silently with her head slumped down.

We had not been in the ambulance for more than ten minutes when Trudy grabbed my hand, her fingernails digging into my flesh.

'It's coming, Virginia. The baby's coming!' she said, her eyes wide with panic.

'Oh shit and bugger,' I thought. 'These ambulance men are not paramedics. Why didn't we stay at home?'

Had we stayed put, I could have requested a paramedic to come to help. Now here we were in a much more precarious situation – in the back of a cold ambulance on a snowy night with a breech baby about to be born and not much help.

'Please stop the ambulance,' I called out and the vehicle immediately came to a halt.

I helped Trudy on to the stretcher in front of us and then on to all fours. I pulled up her dressing gown and rested it on to her back and there right before my eyes was a tiny pair of buttocks protruding at the vulva.

So many things went through my mind and I had seconds to make a decision. We were in the middle of nowhere, 20 minutes from the hospital. Did I get the ambulance guys to keep driving in order to get to the hospital quicker or did I tell them to stay put and get on with delivering the baby? I decided on a mixture of both.

'Can you carry on driving very slowly to the hospital,' I shouted through. 'The baby is on its way so I need to remain standing. You need to radio the hospital and tell them they need someone at the door to assist,' I told the technician in the back with us, who, judging by the look of fear on his face, was definitely not going to be much assistance.

As we trundled along and the baby started to be born I did not touch it. I just let the contractions do their work, watching as first the left and then the right leg dropped down, then the arms dropped out like clockwork with no help needed from me. It was a little girl!

Then, with baited breath, I waited to see the all-important chin so that I would know that the head was flexed. Trudy had been hardly pushing for the body to be born but once I saw the chin begin to emerge I urged her to go full throttle.

'Now, come on, Trudy, I want you to give the biggest push you can,' I said. 'Push now and your baby will be born.'

'I can't, I can't,' said Trudy. 'I can't push anymore.'

Timothy joined me in encouraging Trudy, and started to shout very loudly.

'Push! Push!' he yelled.

I could see the baby's mouth and then the nose which meant she could breathe if need be! Was her chest moving? My stomach lurched as for a minute I thought not. Then suddenly I noticed the lovely pulsations still coursing through the attached cord giving her the much needed oxygen to sustain this final part of her birth. Then slowly her eyes and brows were visible creating the illusion of this tiny baby wearing her mother's body as a hat.

The baby finally plopped down into my waiting hands. There followed an anxious couple of minutes, while we waited for her to take a breath. We were still a little way from the hospital so it was a tense moment. It took a few breaths from my oxygen bag to inflate her lungs but to our relief soon she was crying lustily at the indignity of having to hang there quite naked till her mother relinquished the tight hold on the top of her head.

After helping Trudy to turn over and get as comfortable as she could on the ambulance stretcher, I handed her the baby for a well-deserved cuddle.

The last five minutes of the journey to the hospital were calm and relaxed and we all had a huge grin on our faces as we pulled up at the doors. As the vehicle came to a stop, the ambulance doors were flung open by Jessica, a midwife I knew, who leapt aboard ready to assist.

'Oh,' she said, clapping her hands at the sight of a happy Trudy sitting snugly with her baby. 'Looks like everything is under control here!'

After helping Trudy and her baby into the awaiting wheelchair, Jessica wheeled them along the hospital corridor to the maternity unit with a shell-shocked Timothy trailing behind. There, in a quiet side room, Trudy was able to deliver the placenta in considerably calmer circumstances.

'These breech babies, eh?' Jessica said. 'Sometimes as midwives we definitely don't know our heads from our arse!'

Before I even had a chance to feel indignant, I saw Trudy glancing at me with a sheepish grin.

'No, Virginia knew,' she said. 'It was me who refused to believe it.'

'Sorry, Virginia,' she added, grabbing for my hand. I patted hers and placed it back on to her baby where it belonged.

'I would not have had it any other way, Trudy,' I said. 'You made your choices; I supported you and did my best.'

Remembering Leanne, I grabbed my phone and stepped outside to call Kay. By now it was almost 4am.

'She's in early labour,' Kay confirmed.

'Tell her I'm on my way,' I smiled, having already called Sophie, who'd now qualified as a midwife and worked with me from time to time, to collect me. When Sophie arrived ten minutes later she drove me quickly back to Trudy's house to collect my car. I silently thanked the birth angels that it wasn't snowed in and I was able to make it back to Leanne's house in time to relieve Kay.

I found Leanne pacing the house, well into strong labour. Then after four hours, as she sat calmly on a birth stool, Leanne was able to breathe her baby out without a sound. As the head emerged very slowly I recalled the incredibly different scenes in the ambulance the night before. Then after snuggling Leanne up with her healthy baby daughter my work was done. All that was left to do was thank the birth angels for guiding me through the snow to two safe births in one night!

In the summer of 2011, I was really surprised to get a call from Tonia to say baby number nine was on its way.

After assisting her with the birth of all eight of her bouncing babies, I'd come to think of Tonia as family and had gently suggested that the birth of little Carneya would be a good point to end her nine-year baby marathon.

'We really planned to keep to eight,' Tonia, now 38, told me sheepishly. 'But then I got pregnant and had a miscarriage.'

With the end of the unplanned pregnancy leaving Tonia and Jason upset, they'd decided they could not finish their baby birthing career on such a sad note.

I totally understood their need to leave childbirth with a live baby and I was excited to be their midwife for the ninth time.

When I arrived a week later at Tonia's warm and welcoming family home it was to be greeted, like all the other times, to a calm, quiet atmosphere. You'd expect a house that contained eight children under ten to be noisy and overwhelming with the shrill sound of loud, boisterous voices all trying to compete with each other to get heard. But that was not the case with Tonia's abode. As I walked in the door there was nothing out of place. Everything looked clean and tidy with nice furniture and ornaments around and a special area at the far end of the front room filled with a neat array of mini-kitchens, DIY workstations and no end of different dollies and prams.

The television was playing a children's movie quietly in the background with Markeeta and Anelka, who were not yet old enough for school, playing quietly in front of it.

Meanwhile mummy extraordinaire Tonia was stood in the middle of the room with 18-month-old Carneya clinging to her legs. The blonde youngster eyed me curiously, peering at me from under long lashes with big blue eyes.

'How are you, Tonia?' I asked, smiling at my old friend who was now 16 weeks pregnant.

'Not bad,' she said. 'Still renovating! We're as far as the hallway now!'

After a cup of tea and a catch-up, I got down to business checking Tonia's blood pressure. I saw in my book that it was higher than the last time. With Tonia's advancing age and increasing weight, it was not a surprise that she was classified as borderline hypertension. However, we had time to do things to counter it and monitoring Tonia's health and the growth of the baby was all that was needed at this stage.

'Can you cut down on sugary things?' I suggested. 'And maybe you could fit in a brisk walk every day?' I asked.

'As if I've got time for that!' Tonia scoffed.

At our next routine appointment I arrived at the house to find Markeeta, Anelka and Carneya in cute matching dresses.

This time I had brought the birthing pool, which we looked at together while Anelka flitted between her mother and me. Then as I began to examine her mother, Carneya decided to get in on the action happily passing me items out of my bag.

Although the majority of Tonia's observations were fine, I was concerned that at 27 weeks pregnant her blood pressure was far too high to leave untreated and she required a visit to hospital. As I relayed the message, I watched her sigh. We both knew that a visit to the antenatal clinic would take a military operation for her to arrange. Tonia ran a tight ship with everything held together with a strict timetable. With Jason busy at work providing for his family, it was down to Tonia to rise at 5am to get started on the endless piles of washing and preparation of packed lunches. As everyone prepared to leave the house by 8.30am, the older children were relegated to helping the younger ones and did so without complaint.

Then after transporting the school- or playgroup-age kids safely to their various destinations, Tonia would return with her youngest charges to hang up the daily washing load to dry. If all had gone to plan there was time to tidy and clean the house before the midday trip to pick up the smaller children from playgroup. Then it was home for lunch and to prepare dinner for the evening meal before picking up the older ones from school.

With so much to think about, the prospect of getting someone to care for the children in her absence was pretty much a non-starter.

'Do I really have to go?' she said, screwing up her face. 'Even if I take the kids with me our minibus won't fit under the car park overhead barrier! Can't you take my blood pressure again? Maybe you made a mistake.'

We tried several more times, changing arms and changing machines, but there was no error.

'You really do need to go to hospital, Tonia,' I told her firmly. 'There's a real danger that this could now be pre-eclampsia.'

Like me, Tonia was only too aware that although rare pre-eclampsia is a serious condition that some women experience when they are pregnant. It typically occurs during the second half of pregnancy and starts to show itself with symptoms of high blood pressure and protein in their urine. If not monitored carefully and action taken when necessary, it can lead to problems with the woman's liver and kidneys and can also affect a baby's development.

Somehow, between waiting for Jason to come home from work and calling on Tonia's sister and mother, a plan was organised and a very put-out, flustered and upset Tonia was, at last, able to get to the hospital for a medical assessment. But if she'd hoped to be in and out that night Tonia was in for disappointment. Instead, to her utter annoyance she was kept in hospital for several days.

Consequently Tonia was on the phone to me on a daily basis moaning about waiting day in and day out for various results or for doctors to come and see her.

'I speak to one person then a shift changes and I wait around all over again to speak to someone else about something that could already have been done,' she complained.

But eventually Tonia was prescribed medication to control her blood pressure and returned home to the familiar surroundings of her abode.

While Tonia remained well at home, it was important to keep a close eye on her blood pressure and when she received an appointment for a medical assessment on Christmas Eve I knew that she was steeling herself for another stint in hospital.

Sure enough with her blood pressure still only just within the realms of acceptable – despite the medication – she was unsurprisingly advised to remain in hospital.

'There's no way I am staying in hospital on Christmas Eve!' Tonia announced as she relayed the situation down the phone. Suddenly I felt sorry for any medic who'd tried to impart this advice to Tonia. Wild horses would not stop her from heading home to her family.

Finally, seeing as her baby was deemed to be growing well and there was no sign of pre-eclapsia, common sense prevailed and Tonia was supported in her decision to return home.

Tonia got her family Christmas but in the second week of January, eight days before her due date, her blood pressure was once again worryingly high. With Tonia at serious risk of having a stroke she reluctantly agreed to stay in hospital for observation. As we kept in constant telephone contact over the next few days I was saddened to hear Tonia growing increasingly distressed.

'They want to induce my labour and interfere with me,' she sobbed down the phone. 'Please help me, Virginia, I don't want all this. I want my baby to be born like the others, at home, with you and me and Jason, not strangers who don't know me or care about me as a person.'

This became a very difficult, heart-breaking situation for me, I wanted to help Tonia achieve her dreams and make her own choices but I also wanted her and her baby to be safe.

Not long after speaking to her I had a call from the doctor at the hospital asking if I would come in.

'She will listen to you,' he said. 'You can convince her to be induced can't you?'

'I am coming to the hospital because I am aware of Tonia's distress,' I replied. 'But I should tell you that, as her midwife, I am coming to support her and whatever decision she makes. Let's have a chat once I'm there.'

As much as Tonia was a private and quiet person who could think of nothing worse than a hospital birth, I knew that ultimately she would not go against medical advice. Her baby was of paramount importance to her, as was her own life.

Arriving at the hospital I found a very tearful Tonia, crying in a machine-filled windowless room complaining of a headache. Tests suggested she was passing protein in her urine, an indication that her kidneys may be affected. However, seeing as her blood tests for pre-eclampsia were still coming back as borderline, it was clear she needed more monitoring.

From looking at the whole picture I could see some obvious immediate remedies to calm Tonia down and get her in a better physical and mental state in order that she could make an informed choice. After chatting to her about the options available to her, I asked to speak to her doctor.

'I'm not surprised she is complaining of a headache,' I told him. 'She is all puffy and crying in a stuffy, clinical room with no natural light and hasn't slept due to having her blood pressure checked hourly throughout the night. Even the strongest of people would have had a headache under such circumstances. She is prepared to think about having an induction but believes, as I do, that she is in no state to make that decision without first getting some rest.'

With Tonia's tests showing no immediate danger the doctor agreed to her wishes to be moved to a new room with a window, where she'd be given some painkillers for her head and left alone for a few hours to sleep.

'Great,' I said. 'Once she has had a rest I will see how she feels about inducing her labour.'

So after sending Jason – who'd also spent an uncomfortable night on a hospital chair – home to rest and to check on the kids, I took guard outside Tonia's new room for three hours making sure that no one disturbed her as she got some much-needed sleep and fresh air from the open window.

'How are you feeling?' I asked her when she started to stir.

'Much better,' she said. 'My headache has gone. Thanks, the fresh air has really helped.'

'So what are we doing then, Tonia?' I asked gently. 'What's your plan? Are you going to go for the induction?'

'Well, I don't want to,' Tonia sighed. 'I wanted it to be just the three of us at home but I know that this time things are different.'

'We can't risk your health,' Jason agreed, having just returned to the hospital. 'We've got to think about what is safest for you and to think about all the other children.'

With Tonia now calm, rested and able to think clearly we all agreed that she was ready to begin the induction of labour process.

It was far from the labour any of us had wanted Tonia to experience. With the induction commencing as she lay on the bed, she appeared to be in more pain than with her previous eight births and was also unsettled by the steady stream of midwives and doctors walking in and out of the room without introduction.

Tonia also did not labour very well or very fast as her contractions continued for the rest of the day, all night long and well into the following day. None of her labours, not even her first, had been this long or this difficult.

Although Tonia's labour was being artificially induced, I suspected the stress she was feeling was having a counter effect and she was not producing oxytocin. I knew Tonia better than any other woman I'd cared for, and I knew how she laboured. I knew what position she needed to be in and I knew she craved privacy in order to let go and birth her baby.

Finally, when yet another person came in the room, this time another midwife and only to ask for the labour ward key from Sarah, the plump, dark-haired midwife now assigned to us, I knew from the look on Tonia's and Jason's faces that I needed to advocate for them.

'She needs to get up off the bed and be left alone for a while,' I told Sarah. 'She just can't labour lying on her back or with so many people all around her and with so many interruptions.'

I was met with a disapproving glare from the latest doctor to come on shift; a small, dumpy, middle-aged woman who had unfortunately looked at the notes more than she'd looked at Tonia when she'd taken over on her 'rounds'.

'I will leave you to it then, Sarah,' she said coldly as she walked out of the room.

With just Sarah left with us, we were finally without an audience and I was sure I could appeal to Sarah's better nature for she was, after all, a midwife with a duty of care to support a woman's needs and wishes and was being quite kind and friendly.

'Sarah,' I said. 'Please can you make sure no one else walks in the room. I am going to help Tonia up and into the position she wants to be in.'

'No problem,' she agreed, glancing at Tonia who looked angry enough to combust should there be another interruption.

'What position would you like to be in?' I asked Tonia as I helped her off the bed.

'The usual one,' she said, indicating that she wanted to adopt her down on one knee 'Will you marry me' pose. I put pillows on the floor to make her comfortable.

After helping get Tonia settled, Sarah quickly headed off to answer a bell that was ringing from another room.

'I'll be back in a moment,' she said.

The minute she left I saw a change come over Tonia. As a glazed look came over her eyes and I saw her body soften, I knew that we'd turned a corner.

Now that Tonia was in charge of her body, oxytocin was coursing through it and with the privacy she craved at last her labour was properly underway.

Just 15 minutes after a vaginal examination from Sarah had found her to be only five centimetres dilated and 'not progressing', Tonia was displaying the signs that I knew so well, swinging her hips with a grunt and a low, deep moan. I busied myself preparing the area around her for the birth.

'Oh hi, Sarah, I think we're underway,' I said as the midwife came back into the room. 'I don't think you will be able to see the

259

baby from the position Tonia is in, though. I don't suppose you have a mirror do you?'

'Yes, we've got one of your mirrors,' she laughed. 'I'll go and find it.'

As she duly went off to hunt for it, Tonia, Jason and I were alone in the room once more. Tonia turned and looked at me. I knew that look – I had seen it eight times before.

'The baby is coming, isn't it?' I whispered, she nodded slowly, closing her eyes and lowering her head. A loud moan escaped her lips, a trickle of blood ran down the inside of her thighs and with a sharp thrust of her bottom out slid a wet, pink, breathing baby. Together Jason and I caught the beautiful little girl and gently passed her through and up to her waiting mother. We had done it again, just the three of us!

Finally, Tobella, baby number nine, named after the Italian painting *La Bella* of a beautiful lady in a blue dress, had completed this amazing wonderful family. As we cooed over her I observed that she was very small, the smallest yet, but looked just like her older sisters.

'Oh dear, how am I going to document that?' Sarah said when she returned to the room a few minutes later.

Easy! Baby born, mum, dad and midwife present. The record remains!

With Tonia back home with her family I made the last of my postnatal visits to their happy home. Although there was some discussion and laughter about whether Tobella would really be the last baby, I knew that the pre-eclampsia had scared both Tonia and Jason.

As I waved goodbye to an amazing family I promised myself that it would not be the last time I saw them.

Tonia and I still stay in touch via email and text messages and I am the proudest midwife in the world to have been such an important part of her family's life.

Chapter Fifteen

'Dylan is so excited about the new baby!' my new client Julie smiled as we watched her eight-year-old son playing outside the kitchen window.

'You should have seen him at the ultrasound. When we found out the sex he was shouting, "It's a boy! It's a boy!" He was just so happy!'

'Will he be there for the baby's birth?' I asked.

Dylan, Julie's son from her first marriage, had already struck me as a very intelligent and socially polite little boy who would really enjoy seeing his brother or sister arriving into the world.

'Oh I hadn't thought of doing that,' Julie said. I could tell she was already mulling the idea over in her mind. With her perfect home birth all planned – deliberately a world apart from the stressful forceps birth she'd had eight years earlier in hospital – Julie had been filling her days reading stories of calm, quiet births with candlelight and soft music. She and Anthony were in the midst of long-term renovations to their three-bedroomed, semi-detached house but were determined to create a lovely, tranquil birthing area in one corner of the living room. Having Dylan there for his sibling's home birth would complete her dream of a much more natural birth where she was in control.

While it is easy to assume an older child will be traumatised by the sight of blood and gore or their mother screaming in agony, I have witnessed children at births on several occasions.

'As long as the child is well prepared and everyone is happy with it, then it can do wonders for sibling relationships,' I told Julie. 'Even if their mother is yelling or crying, if they have been told she would do so and all the adults around are maintaining an air of calm then the child will remain calm, too.'

I recalled one birth where a mother had been on all fours with her husband supporting her in front while I got ready to catch baby. As we neared the crucial moment their little girl, who was sitting off to one side, had started to creep round towards me fascinated by what was going on.

'So, first comes the forehead. Can you see her little eyebrows?' I'd explained as the little girl watched, her eyes widening like big round saucers. 'Look, here come her eyes and now her nose and, there you go, a little chin.'

Eyes glued to her emerging sister, the six-year-old looked completely awestruck as there was a gentle jolt and the whole baby's head was born. Then, as the baby did its final turn and the body slithered out into my hands, she immediately bolted round to the front of her mother.

'We did it, Mummy, we did it. We had a baby!' she cried jubilantly.

'That's so lovely,' Julie agreed as I shared the story. 'I'll have a chat with Anthony and see what he thinks.'

As I made to leave I smiled at the sight of Anthony inflating the Jacuzzi pool Julie planned to give birth in, flanked by a curious Dylan.

'Do you know what this is for?' Julie asked showing him a sieve. Her son shook his head.

'Sometimes women who have babies go poo in the water!' Julie confirmed, laughing as Dylan scrunched up his nose.

A few days later Julie called to say that Anthony liked the idea of Dylan being present at the birth and I was delighted.

There was going to be another special element to Julie's birth as well – she'd agreed to have it filmed for a documentary on home birth called *Home Delivery*.

I'd had my reservations when I'd been approached by the makers of the show. There were already too many birth programmes on TV, most of which I hated because they revelled in showing midwives sitting around drinking tea while screaming women lay on their backs being left alone in labour and the voiceovers made it sound like everyone was about to die if the doctor didn't save the day. I had been very vocal about the fact that cameras at a birth can be invasive and it was hypocritical of me now to take part, but there had to be some balance. Birth needed to be shown in a different way and it was also a wonderful way to promote independent midwifery and my own business so, all things considered, I agreed to speak to the documentary makers.

After spending time chatting to the director, Jenny, and producer, Michael, I'd been assured that the programme they wanted to make was one of calmness and positivity around birth.

'We don't want to make a sensationalised film,' Jenny, herself 16 weeks pregnant, reassured me. 'We want it to be sensitive and touching. We won't be scaring the audience or taking explicit shots. If any birth turns into an emergency or you give us the instruction, we will immediately stop filming.'

I was also impressed by her colleague Michael who was so interested in everything I told him about home births. Maybe this could be an amazing opportunity to tell the real story about empowered women giving birth?

I knew how slippery some members of the media could be but with Jenny and Michael seeming very earnest I pushed aside my fears, not to mention the disapproval from some midwifery colleagues, and began to ask my clients if they'd like to be involved.

I'd already recruited one couple called Lindsey and Phillip when I broached the subject with Julie.

'Absolutely not,' said Julie, giggling when I first brought it up. 'I do not want my body on TV!'

I laughed, because, despite her outburst, it was obvious Julie meant not a word of what she was saying. In fact, she looked pleased as punch to be asked.

'Will you just meet with Jenny and Michael?' I cajoled. 'If you don't like them, I won't say another word about it.'

'I will speak to Anthony and we will think about it, OK?' she said.

'OK,' I smiled, secretly knowing that I'd already got her in the bag. Julie was just so proud of her plans for the perfect home birth that I knew she would say yes.

Sure enough, when the couple met Jenny and Michael they liked them immediately and with the reassurance Julie's bottom would not be making its debut on TV they agreed to go ahead.

The final few weeks of Julie's pregnancy were hard going as she was suffering from a trapped nerve and acute pelvic pain and needed crutches to get around. When I turned up to check up on her one morning I found her fighting back tears as her sweet, friendly faced husband Anthony fussed over her.

'It is just getting so painful, Virginia,' she said. 'I don't think I can manage it for much longer. I'm trying not to be negative, though; I'm thinking positive thoughts.'

As she spoke she looked quite flushed and when I tested her

blood pressure there was a slight elevation, which can sometimes mean that labour is imminent.

'I don't think you'll have to wait much longer,' I said.

My last appointment of the evening was to see a first-time mum called Caroline who had only just booked me for her own home birth. We had just sat down to discuss one of the gazillion questions women have to ask the midwife when my telephone rang. Glancing at the caller display I was surprised to see it was Julie who I had only left an hour ago. Apologising to Caroline I asked to answer the call.

'Hi, Julie, what's up?' I said.

'It started just after you left, Virginia,' Anthony's voice came down the line. 'Suddenly it's got really strong.'

'OK, Anthony, how far apart are the contractions?' I asked.

'They are about every three minutes and they're really strong, Virginia,' he said, sounding excited.

'OK, Anthony, I am still around your area, so I won't be long.'

I hung up the telephone, already starting to stand up ready to call time on my current antenatal visit. Caroline, who had obviously heard the exchange, was rushing to reassure me that it was fine. We could reconvene another day. It would be her turn soon and she would certainly want me to prioritise her when her time came!

I was about five miles down the road on the way back to Julie's house when I suddenly remembered I had to call Jenny and Michael! Oh my, I had nearly forgotten! I gave a quick call to Michael who said they would set off straight away.

Arriving at Julie's house I went inside to find her sitting on a birthing ball and bouncing up and down as the waves of pain came. The contractions seemed to be coming really fast and I was worried that Jenny and Michael might not arrive in time for the birth.

'Can you help me get to the toilet?' Julie asked me. She was still very much immobilised by her sore hips and I could see it was going to be a struggle to get upstairs.

'Can we use the downstairs one?' I asked, nodding to the nearby loo which was in the middle of renovations and, despite having no toilet seat and door, appeared to have been put in that day.

'Wait! I'm not even sure if it's connected,' Anthony said. 'I will call the plumber.'

That was easier said than done for poor Julie, who was struggling to stand and walk on her crutches and was already lowering herself on to the newly placed white porcelain loo.

'Right now, I don't care if I pee on the floor,' she cried as the floodgates opened.

From the lack of leakage we could safely assume it was indeed plumbed in and we all heaved a big sigh of relief that Michael and Jenny had not been there for this funny but private moment.

As I helped Julie back to the makeshift birthing area it was clear that Anthony had been very busy making everything perfect for his wife. Indeed, in the short time since I'd last visited Julie, he'd transformed the area where I'd seen him inflating the Jacuzzi into a soft, dreamy setting with a garden gazebo and atmospheric lighting to complete Julie's plans for a romantic birth. Meanwhile Dylan was sitting quietly on the sofa, playing with his laptop and soft music was on in the background.

As I began to help Julie into the water Jenny and Michael arrived.

This was the first birth Jenny had seen or filmed and I'd wondered how she'd find it being pregnant herself. Sure enough I saw the blood draining from her cheeks as the labour progressed fast and furious, and Julie got louder and louder.

Many women make noise when they are in labour, while others are very quiet and most are somewhere in between. On a scale of one to ten, Julie was definitely a number ten. With the windows open to let in the mild June breeze the neighbours were left in no doubt that Julie's baby was coming that night. Dylan, meanwhile, took it all in his stride, occasionally running over to the pool to look inside.

Despite all the noise she was making, Julie was able to relax between contractions and was quick to reassure us that she was fine. 'This is much better than my last birth,' she said.

With Anthony now also in the deep pool cuddling and stroking her back, she began to push.

Armed with a mirror I shined my torch into the water where I could see a tiny bit of head.

'You all right?' I asked Dylan, who was once again by my side.

'It is funny hearing Mummy sound like an animal and watching her squeezing Anthony's hand sooo tight!' he laughed, hitching himself up on to the side of the pool.

'Ergh, yuk, what's that?' he asked, wrinkling his nose, as a large amount of blood-stained liquid floated up through the water.

'That's normal birth mucous and it means baby is coming soon,' I said. 'Look, can you see him?' I shone my torch down into the water and on to the top of the baby's head.

'Wow, oh wow, MUUUUM!' shouted Dylan. 'I can see his head!' He then did a full 360-degree lap of the room in amazed excitement. It was a joy to see.

The plan had always been for Anthony to catch his newborn son and as the baby's head was out I indicated for him to take a look. As he gazed mesmerised into the water the body emerged.

What we hadn't accounted for was the fact that the inflatable Jacuzzi was larger and deeper than a conventional birth pool. Julie and Anthony had chosen it deliberately given Julie's statuesque height but its grey colour and the romantic lighting meant visibility was not good.

'Where has he gone? Where has he gone?' Julie shouted in a panic, feeling all over the bottom of the dark pool.

Looking into the water the baby was nowhere to be seen. I reached down into the water as Julie and Anthony were both feeling around looking for their newborn son. We all appeared to locate him together and each grabbed a limb, pulling him gently up through the water. All this activity was merely a few seconds at most and at no time was the baby in any way compromised.

It wasn't till the baby was safely wrapped in his mother's arms that we all realised Dylan had been hopping around calling out advice of his own.

'It's OK, don't worry, the baby doesn't breathe till it comes up, remember,' he said. He was right, of course! The baby won't breathe until it hits the cool air and I once witnessed a film where they kept a baby under water for 10 minutes or more. While it was uncomfortable to watch it gave me lots of confidence that time was on my side.

This was not the end for Julie though, because just when we thought things could not have gone better with the birth, and after Jenny and Michael had switched off the camera and left the house, to our surprise we had to transfer to the hospital. We had waited and waited and I had tried every trick in the book to get a very stubborn placenta to come out, but it was staying firmly put and the contractions that were trying to do the job were very painful for Julie. Eventually enough was enough and I advised some medical intervention. The transfer by ambulance was calm and not traumatic, as Julie was not bleeding or compromised in any way, but it was certainly a disappointment for Julie, Anthony and Dylan who wanted nothing more than to cuddle up to their new baby Ryan. We were welcomed by the staff at the hospital, the placenta was removed without too much medical input and we were on our way back home in a very short time. The trip to the labour ward had caused memories of Dylan's birth to resurface and, despite it being only a short episode, it had reinforced for Julie just how pleased she was not to have been there for Ryan's birth. Eventually all the drama and laughs of the lost underwater baby, the filming and the transfer to hospital came to an end and before the new day's sun had begun to warm the early summer morning, Julie, Anthony, Dylan and Ryan were all together at home at last as a loving happy family.

'What was it like seeing your first birth?' I asked Jenny.

'The screams scared me at first,' she admitted. 'But seeing you so calm and Julie smiling between the contractions made me feel better. I think I actually feel more confident about my own birth.'

As the filming continued over the next few weeks Jenny would often travel in my car with me on my way to see someone and film me as we drove, listening to me talk and nodding in approval when I was 'on a roll' as she called it.

'You are a natural,' she said on many occasions as we shot scenes of me performing my usual activities of life and work. I would often start tentatively as everyone does when being observed or filmed, but soon I would relax and my thoughts and opinions would flow naturally as I chatted away as if no camera existed.

It wasn't long before Jenny was able to attend her second birth – this time with Lindsay, who I'd recruited to be filmed for the show prior to Julie's birth.

Lindsay, a pretty and outspoken American brunette, lived with her husband Philip in a remote four-bedroom cottage in Lower Halstow in Kent with their two-year-old son, Henry.

When she'd been pregnant with Henry, Lindsay had badly wanted a home birth but after getting a long way into labour she'd been advised to go to hospital and ended up having a forceps birth.

'When I got transferred to hospital Philip couldn't go in the ambulance with me,' she told me sadly. 'I didn't know the staff treating me and I was so upset I took an entire can of gas and air.'

The whole experience had left Lindsay feeling as if her body had failed her. Rebuilding her self-belief was an important part of my job.

When I got the call to say that Lindsay's contractions were three minutes apart Jenny was with me in the car filming. I immediately put my foot down to get there. After a slight problem parking, due to a tractor making its way down the country lane, I rushed inside primed to give Lindsay all the encouragement she needed.

Lindsay was not one for expressing her emotions easily but seeing her floating in the pool looking almost childlike it was obvious that she was fearful things could go the same way as last time.

'Forget your last birth,' I whispered, leaning in over the side of the pool. 'This is this birth. Your body knows what it is doing. Relax your brain.'

'Is it OK if I poop!' she asked, acknowledging that other fear that many labouring women have.

'Yes, it's OK if you poop,' I reassured her as we both laughed. 'You know I get excited when I see a bit of poo.'

Jenny remained subtly in the background filming as Philip topped up the water in the pool and I continued to champion Lindsay.

'Shit it really hurts,' she told me, gripping the sides. 'I want it to come out now.'

Then as she rested her head on the side with her eyes closed I had some news for her.

'Lindsay, I'm excited!' I said, grinning at her.

'Why, did I shit myself?' she retorted.

As I'd explained to her earlier, the bowel movement was a good indication that the baby's head would be coming into sight shortly – and sure enough within ten minutes there it was.

'Fantastic! There you go!' I told her as she breathed out the baby's head.

'That's the best feeling in the WHOLE freaking world,' she shouted.

As Philip took photos Lindsay achieved the magic moment she'd so longed for by pushing out the body and lifting up her baby. Then, with pure animal instinct, she let out a jubilant cry of exhilaration.

Later, as the baby lay blinking in her arms, I watched her visibly melt as she gazed at her. 'I can't believe I did it,' she said, smiling softly. As I turned to Jenny I saw that she was in floods of tears as she watched the emotional scene unfold.

'I was crying so much I had trouble looking down the lens,' she sniffed.

With Lindsay's baby's birth making two I just needed to get one more couple to feature on the show. Having your baby on national TV is not something many women could do and I'd treaded carefully in recruiting Menna and Stephen.

Like their predecessors, Menna and Stephen were hesitant at first. However, once they'd met Jenny they had no qualms whatsoever and eagerly agreed to take part in the programme.

Menna's pregnancy progressed without problems and during all my visits we'd become very close. I'd liked her from the minute I'd met her when, sitting in her small front room, while my mouth had dropped open.

'Oh my goodness what is that on the wall?' I said, standing up and walking over to a large wooden structure with loops of rope hanging from it. It looked like some sort of medieval torture contraption.

'Stephen is a yoga teacher and he uses it for stretching exercises,' Menna explained.

'Oh, I see, but it really looks like it could be used for . . .' I began.

'Yes, yes, I know but we're really not into all that *Fifty Shades* stuff,' Menna interrupted quickly.

'I was actually thinking of childbirth,' I confirmed. Looking at each other we both started to laugh, if nothing else, the ice was well and truly broken.

'You could use this to hang off when you are pushing your baby out,' I said, demonstrating as I put my hands and arms through the loops of ropes and let myself hang from it. As I dropped into the ropes and let them take my body weight, I grimaced and panted hard, mimicking a woman in labour, which only made Menna laugh harder. Untangling myself from the strange-looking contraption, I looked up and there walking exaggeratedly slowly past the window with a direct view of my silly antics was an elderly man, mouth open in shock.

Well that did it, all professional composure vanished and tears of laughter poured from my eyes at the thought of what must be going through his mind. From that day on, the relationship between us was very special and, as the pregnancy progressed, the closeness grew and grew.

About a week before her due date, Menna and Stephen had moved house to a lovely part of Folkestone with cliff-top views over the English Channel, which was about 30 minutes from my own home. Menna had strict instructions from me not to get involved in any of the heavy work and when I called in to see her the day after they moved it was clear to see that she had taken me at my word. There she was perched on a packing box, gently rubbing her swollen stomach and giving out the orders.

Once all the furniture was in place and the boxes unpacked, we set up the birthing pool in a spare downstairs room and finally all was ready for baby to put in her appearance.

Andrew was getting married to Charlott that weekend so I just hoped I wouldn't get the call from Menna in the middle of the ceremony. Everyone in my family knew that births took precedent and I'd even cancelled a Christmas holiday to Vegas with Sean the year before when a woman needed me. But Menna didn't call and I was able to see my son walk down the aisle.

It was two days after her due date that Menna started to get signs that her labour was beginning. Jenny and Michael immediately drove down from London and booked into a local hotel. Seeing as Menna was a first-time mother it was likely to be a long wait but, wanting to get footage of early labour this time, they decided to base themselves at the seaside town.

Every night for a week I laid out my birth clothes only to put them away again each morning as Menna's contractions stopped and started. Eventually Stephen called to say the contractions had begun in the night and were now regular and often. It was time for the real thing.

I arrived at their home to find Menna walking around and breathing calmly through her contractions. Jenny was already there with her camera, which by now I was quite blasé about and took no notice of at all.

Soon Menna's contractions were picking up in intensity and I massaged her back while she leaned against the bedroom wall moaning low and quiet as the tightening of her uterus took her breath away. Seeing silent tears trickling down her cheeks I hoped, for her sake, this labour would progress well and the time would not be prolonged until she had her baby in her arms.

Before long Menna wanted to get into the birthing pool and we headed downstairs with Jenny slowly trailing us. As I helped Menna into the water, Jenny remained outside to ensure she wasn't imposing. Then, as agreed, from time to time, she would quietly open the door to the room and film unobtrusively from the doorway.

In doing this she got one of the most intimate and moving shots that would be broadcast on the show as Stephen whispered words of love to Menna, kissing her face as tears coursed down her cheeks. This was a very private moment but the besotted couple, who had been together since university, were proud to share their love.

Everything had been very straightforward and normal but then I noticed something irregular. There was a deceleration of the baby's heartbeat. Initially I put it down to the fact that Menna was in the second stage of labour. If the baby's head is being squashed it is normal for the heart to slow down only to go back to normal quickly.

Although the heart rate rectified itself after a few minutes more, it happened again and this time it seemed more slow to recover. Most babies this happens to are born perfectly healthy but on rare occasions it could indicate the baby is in difficulty and possibly not getting enough oxygen. Not wanting to take any chances I decided to call an ambulance for assistance with the view to a possible transfer to hospital.

Gently explaining my concerns to Stephen and Menna, I suggested she get out of the pool as it is much easier to deal with an emergency situation, should one occur, on dry land. I also expressed to Jenny, who was after all a pregnant woman herself, that the ambulance would be there as a precaution.

As Menna got out, I placed my small birthing stool next to the pool so she could quickly sink down on to it. Stephen steadied her as she sat, then he knelt down behind her to support and comfort her in his strong and loving arms.

It only took about ten minutes for the ambulance to arrive, by which time the baby's head was visible, albeit only a very small amount. As the baby's heartbeat was presently strong with no further signs of problems, I asked the paramedics to wait outside but close by in case we needed any help. I listened to the heart almost continuously as Menna strained and pushed to her utmost capacity. The sweat was pouring from her brow and the strain was evident on her face.

Jenny had by now moved to just outside the door and I could see her from where I sat. At this position she would film the baby's birth but, thanks to the angle, Menna's dignity would be maintained.

The baby's head was advancing steadily but not quickly. At any other time I would have smiled and marvelled at the wonder of nature unfolding before me but, on this occasion, having heard the earlier heart decelerations I wanted this baby born as quickly as possible.

As I prepared all the birth equipment I might need, I never once took my eyes off the advancing mass of black hair. I had towels to dry baby off if she needed stimulation and my stethoscope and oxygen bag and mask were right there next to me. I always prepare an area for resuscitation at every birth because even when the vital signs have been as normal as can be, you have to be ready for every eventuality.

Listening once again for the baby's heart I discovered I could not find it. I stayed calm, knowing that in all probability this was likely due to the baby's position deep in the pelvis. But when I tried again after the next contraction and still could not find it I had to presume there was a problem. This baby needed to be born as quickly as possible.

'Menna, I don't know if baby is coping well with labour as I am unable to hear her heart rate,' I said. 'Can I cut an episiotomy?' Menna knew what this entailed, as we had discussed it at one of our many antenatal visits.

'No,' she said. 'Let me try to do it myself.'

Her face straining as she began another push.

'OK, Menna,' I responded, watching as she put every bit of strength she had into getting her baby born. Seconds felt like hours, as I waited for that contraction to pass. There was no way I could do the episiotomy without consent but maybe I hadn't made her realise the urgency.

'Menna, I would not ask if I didn't think it was necessary,' I said, already drawing the anaesthetic into a syringe ready for if she consented. 'I have not heard the heartbeat for a couple of minutes now and, while I am sure it is there, I am concerned because the longer we wait the harder it will be to help baby breathe if she needs it. Please can we do the cut?'

'OK, yes, do it if you think that's best,' she panted, as Stephen, who sat behind her, wiped the sweat from her brow.

I did not need to think about it and in an instant, the needle was in and the numbing liquid was doing its job. I pulled on a sterile pair of gloves and opened a pair of sharp scissors. It was not easy to get my fingers in and alongside the baby's head to protect it against the sharp instrument but I managed and with a small cut, out flew baby into my hands along with a big gush of very fresh meconium. While it can be normal for some babies to pass meconium – their browny-green-coloured first poo – while they are still inside, it can also be a sign of distress.

My assessment of Menna and Stephen's daughter was instant. As she lay all white and floppy in my hands she needed help.

'Jenny, turn off the camera and call in the ambulance crew please,' I called out, surprised to hear my voice so steady and calm. Inside I was like jelly, my heart racing. No amount of training, practice on dollies or equipment can prepare a midwife for the total responsibility of resuscitating a baby.

I quickly dried the baby off with the towel but still she made no response. I grabbed for the bag and mask that I had checked just a few minutes before and put beside me. But the mask was gone from the end of the bag. My stomach lurched. It was the piece needed to put on the baby's face and the equipment was redundant without it. Somehow I had to get air into that baby to inflate its lungs.

It took a second, less even, for me to make the decision what to do. Leaning my head down I covered my mouth over the baby's nose and mouth and gently breathed into her lungs. I could clearly see her tiny body expanding and as I lifted my head after five gentle breaths, the paramedic came into the room. From the baby's birth to this point it must have been less than minute, but it felt like hours. As I continued to assess and resuscitate the baby I asked the ambulance crew to check her heartbeat.

'It's fine,' came the wonderful confirmation. 'Well over a hundred beats a minute.'

It wasn't very long, just a few mind-curdling minutes, before the tiny little girl started to gasp and breathe for herself.

I later found my missing piece of equipment under the corner of a towel and realised that it must have accidentally come off as I grabbed for a towel to dry the baby.

With little Rhiannon remaining a little floppy, we made the decision to take her to the hospital for an assessment by a paediatrician. Thankfully everything was fine but she was kept in for observation.

After I'd stayed long enough to ascertain that all was well, Jenny and Michael picked me up from the hospital. My thoughts drifted back to the filming and my concerns that what Jenny had witnessed might make her worry about her own baby.

'Are you OK, Jenny?' I asked, giving her a hug.

'Yes, I am fine, Virginia, don't worry about me! What I saw today just showed me that help is on hand even for a home birth.'

'Yes,' I agreed. 'I just feel sad about all that wasted footage. All that filming, the house move, the visits, the labour. Now it will end up on the cutting-room floor.'

'I don't think so,' Jenny smiled. 'But first you need to see it and decide what you think.'

Then Jenny proceeded to show me the footage. Although she had, as requested and agreed, turned off the camera just after the baby was born, what I had not realised was that I still had on my microphone. In fact, looking down there it was still poking out of my t-shirt where I had clipped it on this morning.

As I listened to what had been captured I was amazed. Where were the sounds of rushing and panic and paramedics diving in to save the day? That was what was in my mind when I thought back over the events of Rhiannon's birth but in reality it wasn't there. Instead what you could hear unfolding was a calm and straight-forward resuscitation of a newborn baby. And so with Menna and Stephen's permission, Jenny was able to use the footage to show how home-birth midwives are more than capable of dealing with an emergency situation.

When the documentary aired eight months later the response was amazing.

I was touched to get so much positive feedback from friends and other midwives I knew. Professor Lesley Page, President of the Royal College of Midwives, praised the programme in the *British Journal of Midwifery* calling me 'a midwife in her community of her community', which pleased me no end. But by far the best honour I received was from the Head of Midwifery at Darent Valley Hospital in Dartford and Gravesham NHS Trust who wrote me a very appreciative letter about the way she felt I had portrayed midwifery and the profession as a whole. As I had never met her, I was truly honoured for her to take the time to write to me. I really hoped that my old NHS colleagues thought the same and was pleased to read complimentary reports in the midwifery press.

The complication with Rhiannon's birth, Menna has said, was

awful and shocking at the time, but brought the family closer to me. As the person who gave their child vital assistance with her first breath, they feel a special connection with me and we have kept in contact.

Far from being frightened by the unexpected and unfortunate end to their home birth, Menna and Stephen have told me that they will plan for a home birth for their future babies. Though their transfer to hospital was not what they planned, the couple were thankful for all the support they received and told me that they were impressed by how smoothly independent services collaborated with the NHS staff.

In a happy ending, not only was baby Rhiannon given a clean bill of health and soon able to go home to begin life with her loving parents but she is still thriving. She is 16 months old now and there have been no effects of the hypoxic episode whatsoever. The whole experience also gave Jenny lots of food for thought.

'I've loved seeing you work, Virginia,' she told me at the time with a smile. 'In fact, so much so that I've decided to have a home birth myself!'

Her baby Harvey is more than a year old now and when we met up recently I was thrilled to hear about Jenny's own wonderful experience of home birth.

Chapter Sixteen

Warming my toes up in the blissful comfort of my bed and snuggling up to Sean I was just about to drift off after a long day attending a home birth when my phone rang.

Sighing I reached for my mobile. Much as I loved my job, the prospect of going out again on a cold January evening was not very appealing. With snow warnings on the news I sincerely hoped it was just Lauren, the mother from the home birth I had already attended earlier that day, fretting about something that would be easily solved.

No such luck. As I flipped open the cover to answer a call to an unlisted number I soon realised it was Johnny, the partner of my client Ruby Lee, an R&B singer who was due to have her baby at home in a week or so.

'Virginia,' he said, 'Ruby Lee's waters have gone but we're not at home.'

Feeling a lot more alert I tried to take in what he was saying.

'Where are you, Johnny?' I asked.

'At a hotel,' he said. 'It's Ruby Lee's birthday treat but her waters went when she got into bed.'

'Johnny, can I speak to her?' I replied, my mind going ten to the dozen but secretly hoping that no contractions had started and I could carry on with my plan to get some sleep.

281

'The phone signal is terrible so I'm outside,' Johnny said. 'Ruby Lee is in the bath, she says she can't get out as it's too painful.'

'Go back inside, Johnny,' I instructed. 'Ask her to get out of the bath and come to speak to me. It's important.'

I lay back down in my bed, now very wide awake, imagining the scenario of Ruby Lee inside the hotel in a bath and sending Johnny out to call the midwife. It was like days gone by when husbands had to run to the phone box at the end of the road.

But only by talking to Ruby Lee would I get a feel for the situation. If she could chat away in a normal voice then we likely had a long way to go. But if she took the phone puffing and panting and stopping for each wave of pain then I knew it was action stations.

As I waited I pondered whether I should get up and start getting dressed. The phone rang again.

'Yes, Johnny? Is she there?'

'No, Virginia, it's no good,' he gasped down the phone. 'She says the contractions are too painful to get out the bath.'

I was out of bed in a shot.

'Where are you, Johnny,' I asked. 'What hotel?'

'It's called the Marquis,' he replied. 'It's in a small place near Dover.'

'I know it,' I said. 'It's very near to me. If the hotel know what's happening don't let them call an ambulance. I am on my way.'

Putting down the phone I sighed heavily. Of all the hotels in the area it would have to be THAT place. Sean, Sophie and I had been turned away from the hotel's restaurant a few months earlier because we'd had one-year-old Jesse with us. With such 'child unfriendly' rules how on earth would they react to a baby being born in the building? I knew how much Ruby Lee wanted a home birth. If the hotel forced them out via ambulance then there was no doubt Ruby Lee would be hospital bound.

As I set off on the 15-mile journey to the hotel in Alkham my mind was racing as I formed a contingency plan. With Ruby Lee and Johnny living a good hour's drive from the hotel, the next best option would be to transport her back to mine.

With the roads empty at that time of night my journey took just 15 minutes. I parked up and pulled out my briefcase containing all the antenatal equipment needed for an initial labour assessment. Walking into the hotel reception I stood up straight ready for a confrontation. On reception was the very manager who had turned us away on account of my grandson!

'Oh dear, here we go,' I thought.

'I am a midwife,' I began. 'My client . . .'

'Yes, yes, through here,' he interrupted, much to my surprise. 'Let me show you where to go.'

I duly followed him along a small corridor and up some stairs.

'Here we are,' he said and I knocked gently on the door.

'Wow, you were quick,' Johnny, a black guy originally from the Caribbean, remarked as he swung open the door. Walking into a lavishly furnished room with mirrored-glass dressing tables, pretty, pale-blue soft furnishings and white crisp sheets, I followed Johnny into the bathroom.

There in the hot, steaming water lay the willowy and beautiful Ruby Lee, her eyes closed and face clenched with pain. Looking up to see me through half-closed eyes, her face softened into a smile.

'How often are the contractions coming?' I asked.

'About every five minutes, I think,' she said. But as I squatted and watched for a few minutes, it seemed they were coming a lot more frequently than she thought.

'I think it would be a good idea to know exactly how far dilated your cervix is,' I said after waiting for a gap in the contractions.

'Then we can make a decision about what is going to happen from now, because we need to get you home if we have time, don't we?'

Ruby Lee nodded her consent and so I went to my briefcase to fetch some sterile gloves. I was able to perform the examination while she remained in the bath.

Although Ruby Lee was only two centimetres dilated, her cervix was paper thin and the baby was very low. My instinct was that this labour was not going to be a long one. Whether we stayed put or everyone went home was really her call, though.

'I want to go home,' Ruby decided.

'Come on, then,' I replied. 'Let's get you out of the bath and dressed because the longer you leave it, the more difficult it will become.'

And so began the long, slow process of Ruby hauling her tired, heavy body out of the bath. Every movement and turn caused the next contraction to hit and we needed to wait till it passed to carry on. After 20 minutes she was finally out of the bath, with one of the huge, white, soft, fluffy hotel towels wrapped around her body.

She began to move into the bedroom, but as a pain ripped through her, her knees doubled and she was forced to lie curled up on her side on the bed. With the contraction wearing off, Ruby closed her eyes and dropped her jaw in relief.

'Just give me a minute to recover,' she said as she drifted off momentarily.

'Come on, Ruby,' I whispered after a few seconds of rest. 'If you are going home we need to get you going. It will only get stronger the longer you wait.'

'OK, OK', she said and once more began to pull herself up from her drowsy state. But then the next contraction spasm arrived and she'd flop back to the previous position. Eventually, after about half an hour we'd coaxed her to stand up long enough to pull on knickers but at this rate it would take an hour or more just to get her dressed.

'I can't do it,' she said, shaking her head wearily. 'I can't manage the journey.'

'Do you want to stay here?' I said.

'Yes,' she replied. 'I just want to stay here and go to sleep.'

The decision was made, we were staying put. Getting Ruby Lee back into bed, I pulled the cover over her and watched as once again her eyelids drooped. Now I would need to go and speak to the manager. I took a deep breath and steeled myself for a discussion that would likely have me working hard to appeal to his better nature. In reception I found the manager who seemed eager for an update.

'She still has a long way to go but she doesn't want to leave yet,' I explained. 'She needs to sleep then we can re-evaluate the situation in the morning.'

I watched his face, waiting for the protesting to begin.

'Of course she must stay,' he said smiling.

'Blimey, am I dealing with the same person?' I wondered.

'Do you have a room available for me to sleep in?' I asked, seeing as he suddenly seemed so supportive. 'That way, I will be on hand in case she needs me.'

'Yes, of course,' he replied. 'And would you like some food before you retire for the night?'

Well knock me down with a feather! Before I knew it he had led me to a freshly cleaned, vacant room across the way from Ruby.

'If there is anything else you need, just let me know,' he said pushing the key into my hand.

So having doled out instructions to Johnny to call me at any point if Ruby needed me I, too, sank into the softest, cosiest bed I have ever had the pleasure to sleep in.

I quickly drifted into that light, half-sleep that occurs when your brain is on high alert and awaiting the expected call from a woman about to give birth. When Johnny knocked on my door a few short hours later, at 4.30am, I was up, out of bed and at the door, in seconds.

'She says she is ready now,' he said, as I squinted into the light of the corridor, his voice breathy with nerves.

'OK, give me a minute and I will be there,' I replied.

After quickly splashing water on my face and pulling on my clothes, I darted across the corridor and found Ruby Lee once again in the bath but this time it was obvious that her labour had progressed a lot.

'The pain's in my bum,' she cried. 'I don't think I can do this anymore.'

I nodded at those telltale words that all women whisper or shout when the time is near, knowing that, thankfully, she wouldn't have to do it for much longer.

'I couldn't sleep,' she said. 'So I got back in the bath and did it by myself for a while. That's what I wanted but now it's hurting too much.'

I could see the bath was bringing her little comfort and the water was getting a bit too cold for my liking.

'I think we should get you out the bath and into a more comfortable position,' I said. 'Can we get you out to warm you up?'

With help from Johnny, Ruby Lee heaved herself to a standing position and stepped gingerly out of the now tepid bath water. As she shivered and closed her eyes, I wrapped her in towels warm from the radiator. Then after waiting for the next wave of pain to pass, I led her to the bed.

Adopting the most comfortable position, she got on to all fours and I massaged her aching lower back with some oil to alleviate the pain. As my hands moved over her skin I noted a bulge at the base of her spine as her pelvis widened to allow the baby even more room for its ever-advancing journey. From this angle, behind and to the side of Ruby, I was able to observe the advancing pink line that starts at the anal margin and ascends up between the buttocks to indicate the ever-increasing dilatation of the cervix. I did not need to perform an invasive and painful vaginal examination to know that the second stage of labour was not too far away.

As yet, Ruby had made no noise other than soft mewing sounds that could not be heard by the other guests in the hotel who were bound to be sound asleep at this time. With no one presently aware of the event about to unfold, I offered up a little prayer to the birth angels for the status quo to continue.

It was not very long before Ruby Lee began to omit the familiar grunts and long, deep breaths ending on a low moan that herald the second and exciting stage of labour.

'Oh God, I am going to poo, I am going to poo,' she suddenly exclaimed, her face full of panic. 'Quick get me up.'

'It's OK, Ruby,' I soothed. 'It's just the feeling of the baby pushing against your back passage.'

However, her outburst did make me wonder what disarray the room would be in following the birth. Birth can be a messy business and unless there is plenty of protection for carpets and soft furnishings, body fluids and secretions can be the ruination of beautiful things. The bed linen was likely doomed but I also feared for the light carpet, cream sofa and pastel chair.

Suddenly remembering that I had some disposable waterproof mats in my car, I dashed out to procure them from the boot. Back in the room, I spread the plastic-backed sheets around and under where Ruby was kneeling just in time to catch the bloody mucus that was dripping from her. Every sign was indicating that the time for the baby's birth was getting closer and closer.

'The bath,' groaned Ruby Lee. 'I must get back in the bath.'

Brilliant idea, I thought, the bathroom had no carpet!

Dashing into the bathroom, I ran the bath till it was as full as it could be without overflowing and flooding the floor. Then, returning to Ruby Lee, I helped her up off her knees and supported her on her wobbly walk to the bathroom.

Catching sight of the inviting warm water, she immediately sped up her pace, sinking down into the calming, warm depths with ease and obvious pleasure before the next contraction ripped through her body.

Seeing as the bath was almost free-standing in the large double bathroom with three accessible sides. Johnny was able to sit quite comfortably at one end of the bath leaning back on to the wall with a pillow as Ruby put her head against him and gripped his legs in preparation for the next contraction.

Meanwhile as I listened to the baby's heartbeat I found it to be strong and regular and as healthy as it could possibly be.

With no worry about mess and spillages now we were in the bathroom, the only problem were the acoustics. While Ruby Lee was merely moaning for the moment, the splashing sound as she alternated between being on her knees and in a squat was already being amplified by the echoey tiles on the walls and floor.

Before Ruby had been back in the bath for even a minute she began to push and heave as the contractions did their work.

'Yes!' I thought. 'We have lift off!'

Grabbing my mirror it was hard to see much in the limited space of the bath but observing the stretching and opening between Ruby Lee's legs I knew the baby was indeed approaching. I could see the veins in Ruby's neck straining with her efforts until at last

I spied the black hair of her precious baby curling out of her vagina. I indicated to Johnny that I could see the baby now and he, too, leaned over to catch the first glimpse of his son.

'It's burning,' Ruby Lee shouted with a look of panic on her face. 'I feel like I am being torn in half.' As she let out a short scream of pain, I cringed as it echoed loudly around the room. I bit my lip waiting for the banging on the door to confirm disturbed guests.

Fighting the temptation to stick my finger to my mouth and tell Ruby Lee to 'Shhh!', instead I whispered words of encouragement.

'Find your courage, Ruby Lee,' I urged. 'Dig deep, you are nearly there. Have faith in your body, it is nearly done.'

By now Ruby Lee was in a squat position with her knees pointing to either end of the bath. Looking down in front of her, beneath her bulging stomach I could see dark, black hair emerging further and further until finally, with a thrust forward of her hips, the head was born.

I leaned over Ruby Lee to see the water shimmering around the baby and ample hair swayed gently like water grass in a lily pond. To my reassurance the baby looked pink and healthy.

There was a minute of relaxation for Ruby Lee to take a breath, then the next contraction began to build. I watched as the baby rotated its shoulders round in order to manoeuvre them up and under the pelvic arch. Out popped one shoulder, then the other, and with the most powerful and final push he tumbled out into the welcoming warm water.

His little body was wrapped tightly in his umbilical cord so, arms submerged, I quickly turned him one way, then the other, releasing him under the water before lifting him up to surface for his first life-giving breath.

'Oh my baby, my darling baby boy!' Ruby Lee cried out as she eagerly took him and held him close to her chest.

'Turn off the lights quickly, Johnny,' she instructed, shielding her newborn son's eyes from the glare of the artificial light in the bathroom.

I helped her into a comfortable position lying in the bath with baby on her chest. Then fetching a pillow from the bedroom I put it behind her head and turned on the hot tap in order to warm up the water and keep both mother and child cosy.

'He's a good-looking little chap,' Johnny said smiling as he knelt down to kiss both Ruby Lee and the son they'd named Max.

'I love you. Happy birthday, my darling,' he whispered, reminding a delighted Ruby Lee that today was indeed her birthday, too.

Keen to let them have their moment, I sat quietly on the edge of the bath furthest away from the couple. There were tears in my eyes as I offered up a silent thank you to the birth angels for keeping them all safe.

With all the towels in the room wet we definitely needed more so walking out to the telephone I rang reception. It was now 7am and the call was answered in one ring by a female voice. Just three or four minutes later a knock on the door told me they had arrived. When I opened the door, I could not believe what I was looking at. The smiling girl carrying them was not even visible behind a pile of at least ten fresh fluffy towels.

Back in the bathroom, Ruby Lee was still cuddling Max but beginning to squirm as mild contractions indicated the placenta had separated.

Seeing that the umbilical cord was now empty of blood, I opened a cord clamp and snapped it on to the cord, passing the scissors to Johnny who expertly cut away at the tough sinewy tissue.

Once separated, I wrapped Max in one of the newly delivered towels and passed him to his daddy to hold while Ruby Lee, allowing gravity to assist her, stood up to let the placenta plop into the already blood-red-stained bath water.

Then, for the final time, she exited the bath, walked into the bedroom and got into bed, her arms outstretched for her baby. As we shared smiles of joy and some celebratory hugs, I left them to get acquainted and headed into the bathroom to clear up.

Standing at the door I surveyed my work with pride. Now that I had emptied the bath of its bright red contents and wiped the wet floor, there was no clue a baby had been born in there. I went downstairs to the reception to see if I could order us all some breakfast. The same woman who had brought the towels looked up eagerly as I entered the reception area.

'I think you may be pleased to know that around half an hour ago a baby boy was born and today is also his mother's birthday,' I said.

The receptionist looked at me aghast and her eyes welled up. 'Oh, my goodness,' she said. 'I have gone all goose bumpy, how lovely!'

Within ten minutes she and another member of staff appeared back at the room carrying trays of breakfast fit for royalty.

'Congratulations,' she beamed, taking a long, lingering look at the tiny guest sleeping peacefully in his mother's arms. 'The management would like to offer you an extended stay and invite you to remain here for another night.'

So Ruby Lee and Johnny did get the nice, relaxing stay they had planned, albeit with an extra guest. It was certainly a birthday to remember.

As for the Marquis Hotel, I know they were delighted with the night's events, especially given the nice bit of publicity generated by the baby being born there, who the parents subsequently named Max Marquis.

Chapter Seventeen

'Virginia, it's Adrian,' an anxious voice filtered down the phone as I felt Sean stirring in the bed next to me.

'Kim-Ly's contractions have started. They're coming every ten minutes. She is in labour!'

Adrian was a tall, skinny man who had employed me to assist his pregnant wife who had recently moved to the UK from her native Vietnam. Kim-Ly hadn't been allowed into the country until the care had been set up with me so I'd first met her when she was 24 weeks pregnant. Although I did my best to teach her about how her labour contractions may start, her English was not good. Sometimes even Adrian seemed to have a problem understanding her.

'Hello, Adrian, that's good news,' I said, rubbing my eyes as I sat up in bed. 'First babies take their time so it'll probably be a while yet. Call me back in a couple of hours when they're stronger.'

Ten minutes passed and I'd just closed my eyes to drift off back to sleep when the phone rang once more. It was Adrian again and this time he was sounding very panicked.

'Virginia, her waters have broken and they're going all over the floor!' he said.

In the background I heard Kim-Ly's voice.

'I want her come!' she was crying out.

Immediately I jumped out of bed, pulling a jumper over my head.

'Drive carefully,' I heard Sean mutter as I started to make my way downstairs with the phone still clamped to my ear.

'Oh no, I can see something coming out,' Adrian continued, his voice sounding an octave higher.

'I'm coming,' I said. 'Please try and stay calm.'

'Oh sweet Jesus, no,' I heard him cry. 'I can see a head. Oh God. Oh God. Oh God! I can see the baby, what should I do?'

Jumping in my car I set the phone to hands-free and set off on what would be a 20-minute drive to Adrian and Kim-Ly's home in Maidstone.

'Adrian, tell me exactly what is happening,' I instructed, hearing lots of moaning and groaning in the background from Kim-Ly.

'Now the head has come out. It's out. But it's not breathing,' Adrian's commentary continued, his panicked words flying out in high-pitched squeals.

'It's OK, Adrian, the baby won't breathe until it's born,' I said. But as he continued to hyperventilate, I was sure he was not listening due to his panic.

'Has the body come out?' I asked.

'Oh God, oh no! I need to call my mum! What do I do?'

I could not get a word in edgeways. By now I was on the motorway and ten minutes from my destination.

'Adrian,' I said raising my voice. 'Please calm down and listen to me.'

But all of a sudden the voice changed.

'Oh hello, my darling!' Adrian trilled in a gooey voice. 'You're sooo beautiful!'

The temporary calm was over in a matter of seconds.

'Oh my God!' he began again. 'The baby's here! I don't know what to do. I don't know if it's breathing yet!' I had to laugh because

293

judging by the ear-splitting cries radiating down the phone the baby was making very good use of its lungs.

With the baby's shrill cries indicating that all was well, I put my foot down, willing the remaining minutes of the journey to fly by.

'It's all OK, Adrian, just pick the baby up and pass her to Kim-Ly,' I said. 'Cover them both up to keep them warm and then go and open the door for me. I am nearly there.'

Pulling up outside the house I dashed in to see a tiny baby girl cuddled as I had instructed in her mummy's arms under a warm blanket. Adrian had listened to something at least!

After helping Kim-Ly to deliver the placenta, the three of us sat down to a welcome cup of tea.

'What happened, Kim-Ly?' I asked. 'Why didn't you let me know earlier that labour had started?'

'I say him call mewife,' Kim-Ly exclaimed. 'He say no, too soon. I say him baby coming! He say no baby no comin! He say mewife say pain come lots. I say yes pain come lots. He say me no, too soon!'

Adrian had obviously heard me teaching Kim-Ly that contractions come more and more often, but what he had not taken in was my advice to 'listen to what Kim-Ly says', as women know their own bodies. Whether she has been in labour for five days, five hours or five minutes, a woman knows when her baby is coming so LISTEN to her!

Having seen the ease with which Sophie had taken to motherhood with Jesse, it was no surprise when she announced she was expecting again within a year of giving birth to her son.

Sophie went into labour with her second child on a cold February evening in 2013 and it happened very speedily.

Unlike Jesse's birth, Robert was very blasé when Sophie suddenly sat up in bed at midnight announcing that the baby was on its way.

'Oh, Sophie, try and sleep a bit more,' he'd mumbled sleepily before nodding off once again.

'No, Robert!' Sophie had insisted, shaking him awake. 'Get up now and call Mum!'

Seeing her grimace as a huge contraction gripped her tummy, Robert sprang into action and within ten minutes I was on the doorstep – this time with Courtney, who was going to be the photographer.

I found Sophie doubled over the couch with tears streaming down her face.

'My waters have just gone, Mum,' she said when the pain had passed.

'OK, darling,' I said, taking her in my arms as the next contraction made her knees buckle.

As I sunk down with my arms wrapped tightly around her, Sophie squeezed me back. We stayed like that facing each other on our knees rocking with each pain and holding on to each other while Robert got the pool ready.

After I'd helped her into the pool, it wasn't very long before Sophie felt the urge to push and we saw a faint wisp of dark hair beginning to emerge. I couldn't believe it – Jesse had been bald and blonde, the image of his father, but this baby had undeniably dark hair and I wondered if it would look like Sophie, who'd been very dark when she was born.

Within a couple of pushes the baby was born and with a cry of relief Sophie took hold of her new baby.

Knowing that there was no rush and the baby would not breathe until it was out of the water and felt the rush of cool air on its face, she slowly guided it up through the water as Courtney snapped away. Later we would admire the amazing photographs of the baby still under the water as Sophie reached down to help her new child into the world.

Hugging the baby to her chest Sophie gazed up at us with a look of wonder. Robert, Courtney and I hugged her and smiled, kneeling by the side of the pool to wait.

Sophie had no intention of rushing and wanted to take time to gaze at her new baby, Jesse's sibling. For a long five minutes she just gazed and stroked the baby while she hugged it tightly to her body so there was no chance any of us could see whether it was a boy or girl.

'Oh come on, Sophie, let's see what it is!' Robert finally said, no longer able to contain his excitement.

Smiling, Sophie slowly looked down and peered between the baby's legs, then she looked up at us her chin wobbling as she started to cry.

'It's a girl,' she called out.

Well that was the undoing of me and I immediately sobbed into the towel I was holding. Sophie loved Jesse with all her heart, as we all did, but ever since being a little girl herself she had longed for the day when she, too, would have a daughter and her joy was palpable in the air.

Arriving in a speedy three hours, little Connie had joined our family and I felt truly blessed to have four beautiful grandchildren.

Just like the proverbial bus I had waited for years and now here they were all coming at once.

A few months later, as I took a much-needed break at our holiday home in Turkey, I answered the phone to an unknown number on my mobile.

'Hello, Virginia, this is Suzie from Sky News,' a voice trilled down the line as I continued to water the garden. 'We wondered if you could be our midwife in the studio when Catherine Duchess of Cambridge goes into labour next weekend?'

'You do realise the new royal baby could come anytime – tomorrow or even in three weeks?' I asked, utterly amazed that this female researcher didn't seem to realise that baby birth dates can be rather unpredictable.

'Oh no, we have been told she is due on the thirteenth – so that's next weekend!' she replied with conviction.

Sighing I gave up. 'Well, give me a call when it happens,' I said. 'I am due to fly home in a few days and will come if I can.'

Strangely enough the Duchess didn't go into labour on the thirteenth and, as I had predicted, was still pregnant and awaiting labour with all the paparazzi camped outside the Lindo Wing at St Mary's Hospital in London for a good while longer.

I was actually enjoying a day out at the seaside with all the grandchildren, Sean, Matt, Gemma, Andrew, Charlott, Sophie, Robert, Courtney and her boyfriend Chris, who'd she'd been dating for a year, when I got the call on 21 July to say that Kate's waters had broken. But it wasn't 'that' Kate – it was my client Kate, who was also aged 31 and about to become a first-time mother, just like her royal counterpart.

'Oh fantastic news, Kate,' I said, disguising my disappointment that I might need to change my plans and miss out on my day with the grandkids. 'Are you having any contractions?'

'No, nothing,' she said.

'Are the waters clear? Are you feeling well? Is the baby moving?' I continued. With positive confirmations to all my questions, it seemed my day of candy floss and sandcastles would be saved after all.

'It may take a little while yet,' I told Kate. 'So stick to showers and no baths now until labour starts as we don't want any risk of infection. Don't have intercourse and check your temperature regularly. If it stays the same, there is no problem. I will come and see you first thing in the morning but if anything changes or you are concerned call me immediately.'

With Kate primed to call me the minute things changed, I was able to relax and get back to a lovely day out enjoying the glorious summer weather with my family. As I ate candyfloss, with Connie perched on my hip and watched my three grandsons squealing with delight as they went on the dodgems with their dads, I was grateful that I hadn't had to rush off to a birth.

The next morning, having not heard anything from my Kate, the news was filled with reports that the Duchess of Cambridge had gone into hospital in labour. How exciting! What were the chances of both Kates giving birth on the same day?

As Kate's husband Sam and I chatted about what great publicity it would be if their little treasure was born on the same day as our future king, I found myself smiling. Getting news coverage for the work of independent midwives was high on my agenda as my counterparts and I faced the toughest time of our careers. As 2013 drew to an end it was set to become illegal for independent midwives to practise without insurance thanks to a new law being brought in as a result of an EU directive. The new legislation will make it mandatory for all health care professionals to have Professional Indemnity Insurance (PII), which is easier said than done.

At present around 170 independent midwives in this country work without insurance when they attend births, putting their whole financial lives at risk every working day should they get sued personally. It's not that we don't want to be insured, the issue is that the commercial insurance market cannot make a profit from independent midwives due to our small numbers.

The organisation to which I belong, Independent Midwives UK (IM UK) has searched worldwide for workable and affordable PII for many years with no success. Historically, claims against midwives are overall very low but unfortunately insurers lump midwives in with all maternity claims – whether they be mistakes made by sonographers during scans, surgeons during caesarean sections or misinterpretation of CTG readings (fetal heart monitors) – and they conclude that the risk of a large claim is far too big.

So up until now independent midwives like me have worked without insurance while explaining the situation to our clients.

So what can we independent midwives do? Give it all up? Stop offering the gold standard care that women choose to have and evidence has shown is the safest and most satisfying for women and babies? Deny women the choice of any care other than the NHS?

I have taken on a client as late as 38 weeks into the pregnancy, when she has felt disempowered by midwives determined to make her conform to the care they were prescribing. Instead I was able to uphold her choices safely and respectfully and her birth and post-natal period was just as she wanted. Recently I had the honour of caring for a woman whose baby was incompatible with life. The NHS suggested she terminate her baby at 34 weeks and induce the labour. Her GP believed the best place for her was in hospital, despite this not being what she wanted. The woman and her partner loved and valued their baby as any other and decided not only to continue with the pregnancy but to have a peaceful home-birth. This woman is now grieving of course, but she is not destroyed because her choices were met and her home birth was empowering.

I truly and utterly believe that my approach has saved the lives of women physically, mentally and socially. To stop now due to politics would leave my life bereft of meaning. I will fight on, I will stand with others or if necessary alone. I will face any consequence of breaking a law in order to say my life's work has had meaning. I will not betray the women I care for.

While it is a great thing that this country has free healthcare there are unfortunately times when women are not always supported in their choices and are swallowed into the 'one size fits all' system. This is not the fault of any individual midwife, rather the crisis of a failing, understaffed system that cannot achieve what evidence points to as being best for women – one-to-one continuity of care with a known and trusted midwife.

A workable and affordable solution to the ongoing and long-term problem of lack of indemnity insurance for self-employed independent midwives has been sourced – the product is Captive Insurance, where an insurance company is created and wholly owned by a non-insurance entity and is used to insure the risks of its owner. So IM UK becomes the insurer!

Captives are usually formed if the parent company is unable to source insurance from the commercial market, as happened with IM UK. The product, as of today, is licensed and capitalised but is lacking in adequacy. IM UK is eagerly awaiting a response from our government for a one-off payment to secure the future of our Captive and therefore the future of Independent Midwifery.

Independent midwives presently care for 3,000 women annually and if we can get this insurance protection in place then the likelihood is many more midwives and mothers will feel able to take this route and opt out of the NHS.

Last February, determined to fight for the rights of future generations of birthing women, I joined the board of IM UK and began a campaign in the media to draw attention to our plight.

On the board of IM UK we all have our various roles in this amazing battle to survive and, while my colleagues have been beavering away working with insurance brokers and meeting with Health Minister Dan Poulter, my fellow independent midwife Meg Miskin and I are working on setting up a charity, The Independent

Midwifery Trust. The goal of the trust is to raise money to support the ongoing aims and ideals of independent midwives, including a hardship fund for women who would benefit from one-to-one care but cannot get it.

Since I have been on the board of IM UK I have put my loud and outspoken personality to good use organising rallies and events and even dressing up as a stork, along with other midwives and supporters, to travel to London to deliver a letter asking for help from the Prime Minister in Downing Street. I have written a song called 'The Baby's Coming' for our group The Midwives, which has been recorded as a downloadable track in the studios of one of my most famous clients, Tim Rice Oxley from the band Keane, and all proceeds will go to the Independent Midwifery Trust.

Whenever a public figure or celebrity can get on board to champion and support natural and positive birth experiences the effect can be far-reaching. Likewise, how birth is portrayed by the media can have a huge impact on women.

As I'd followed the media coverage of the Duchess's impending birth with baited breath I prayed that she would not go the route of some celebrities and book a planned caesarean section.

When I began to hear stories in the news about her interest in hypnobirth, where mind control manages the sensations and pain during labour, I applauded her plan to use it to achieve a natural birth. I really hoped she was strong enough not to let control be taken away from her, for the outcome would have a worldwide impact on the message women receive about birth.

While we may never know the details of the Duchess's birth, she was obviously well informed about natural birth. Her labour was quite quick and she appeared to be so well standing on the steps of the hospital the following day that I can only guess that it was, indeed, the birth of her choice. If it wasn't, Kate, please give me a call for your next one!

Meanwhile, my blonde Kate was still awaiting her own baby's arrival, which was due to take place in her mother's house in Whitstable, Kent.

As the anticipation grew for Prince George's first public appearance, Kate and Sam made their own fully informed choice. Twenty-four hours had passed since Kate's waters had broken but she would not be induced.

As I visited Kate at home during that long wait we both watched as Prince William and his Kate stood beaming outside the Lindo Ward showing off their own bundle of joy.

'I bet I won't look that good after I give birth,' Kate scoffed.

'Of course you will,' I replied. 'But I'm sure the last thing Kate really wanted was a beauty team and the world's media descending on her during a time when she just wanted to be with her baby and husband in private.'

With Prince George having been whisked off home, my Kate's labour eventually started 56 hours after her membranes had ruptured and six hours after I arrived at her house she was almost fully dilated. But after days of intermittent contractions that wasn't speedy enough for Kate!

'Can't you see him yet?' she gasped as she lay back in the birthing pool.

'You need to start pushing and then push for a while before I can see him, Kate,' I told her. 'You will feel him before we see him.'

As another hour passed Kate grew increasingly tired and stressed.

'It hurts too much,' she cried out. 'I need something more for the pain.'

I suspected this was a sign of transition. Many women say things they do not mean or are out of character at the end of the first stage of labour – asking for more pain relief is often one of them. Even if it was just transition, though, I needed to respect what Kate was saying.

'Do you want to get out of the pool, Kate?' I asked gently. 'You always have the choice to go to hospital for an epidural.'

A look passed between us and I had the confirmation of what I already knew. She had no intention of getting out of the pool or going to hospital, she was a strong woman and it was just the normal stress and worry of a woman in labour.

Situations such as this demonstrate the importance of continuity of care. The mother trusts the midwife and the midwife knows the mother through and through, and knows if she does not mean what she is saying. I had none of the doubts that I had in my earlier career that, by encouraging a woman to keep going through the pain, I many in any way be denying her the choice of using an epidural.

Despite that earlier wobble, Kate battled on with the second stage of labour proving quite tough as she pushed with as much gusto as any woman I have ever witnessed. I began to think the baby could be bigger than I'd thought but as the head advanced I could see it was at a slight side angle making the dimensions bigger than they needed to be and progress slow and tough.

By now Kate had gotten out of the pool and was sitting on a birth stool with her mum and Sam behind her offering support. I was sat cross-legged on the floor in front of her as I watched the baby coming closer and closer to the point of birth.

'OK, Kate, the baby's head is nearly born,' I said, as I wiped the sweat from her face with a cool flannel. 'You will get a minute's rest once the head is out while baby does its normal turn before the next contraction. Then the body will come and it will all be done. There will be maybe two or three more contractions. OK?'

'Oh God!' she began to moan as the next contraction began to build. 'I can't do one more let alone three!'

Well, the birth angels must have been listening. As the contraction took over her body with full force, out shot her eight-pound baby as fast as a steam train.

'Wow,' I said, having caught him unexpectedly in my hands. I quickly passed him up to Kate who grasped her tiny son to her chest, with cries of relief and happiness from her mum, Cathy, and Sam.

We all sat there for a few minutes not moving and just admiring the little chap they'd named Jasper. Not a royal baby but equally as beautiful and as precious as the Prince himself.

'Great catch,' announced Sam. 'You should play cricket.'

'I never take my eyes of the ball, Sam,' I replied. 'Now about that name – we could still get some publicity if you change it to George?'

I never made it on to TV to talk about Prince George but I'm holding out for Royal Baby number two in a few years!

As I anxiously await the fate of independent midwifery I look back on my 17-year career with pride and gratitude. It has been a real privilege to watch and help amazing women to give birth, stay strong, beat the odds and be empowered as the circle of life goes on.

I still remember those women at the beginning, who were my learning tools as a student and a newly qualified midwife. I can recall like yesterday the worrying, sad and distressing times when I felt belittled by the Bison, and even thought I had no more to give and that this job was too big a mountain to climb. But mostly I treasure the memories of the women who taught me to be the midwife I am today. And like those women who keep going through a long and difficult labour, I, too, have kept going because the joy, smiles, satisfaction and tears of elation have outweighed all those tough moments.

All women have different ideals, dreams and choices about their baby's birth and as an independent midwife I have loved helping them to have the power and confidence to make the choices that I never had.

I am still every bit as excited and proud of what I do as the day I qualified. I want to tell the woman at the checkout at Tesco I am a midwife and how much I love my job.

I still pinch myself when I walk up a garden path or into a house where a baby will be born and someone says, 'The midwife is here.'

And I still get the biggest thrill at those magical and timeless words:

'Virginia . . . The baby's coming!'

Epilogue

'It's going to be a brother,' my eldest grandchild, Luca, told me, his brow furrowed with a serious expression as he placed his little hand on his mother's belly.

Laughing, I swung Luca, now three, up into my arms.

'It might be a sister in Mummy's tummy,' I told him as he shook his head in protest.

'No, it's a boy,' he frowned. 'Don't want a sister. I want a brother.'

'He's just like Matt, you know,' I said turning to my son Andrew. 'When you were coming he would not even entertain the possibility you might be a girl.'

'We'll see,' Andrew said, smiling at Charlott. 'We're going to find out at our scan today.'

Just as I'd got used to the idea of four grandchildren, Andrew and Charlott had revealed they were expecting a little brother or sister for Luca – and like their cutely excitable son they, too, were hoping for a little boy.

'We want Luca to have a brother and for them to be as close as Matt and I were,' Andrew explained. 'For them to be the best of friends, too.'

But when Charlott was just a few weeks pregnant she'd started to bleed and for a while it looked like she might miscarry.

The Baby's Coming

'It may be nothing,' I said as I hugged her in my arms. 'Many women have bleeding and go on to have a healthy baby.'

'But it could also be a miscarriage, right?' she'd asked grimly.

'Yes, darling, it could be,' I replied. 'But, if so, you must see it as nature's clever way to recognise when things aren't right.'

I hoped my words would reassure her either way and bring some comfort but it was with stark relief all round that we discovered our fears were unfounded and a scan showed Charlott was carrying a healthy baby.

Thankfully the bleeding soon settled down and Charlott's pregnancy progressed as normal. Now, finally, the day had come where we'd find out the sex.

Later that afternoon, as I saw Andrew's name calling, I quickly snatched up my phone.

'Well?' I asked.

'Luca is right, Mum!' he laughed. 'He really has got a brother on the way!'

'That's brilliant news!' I said. 'Those two will be as thick as thieves!'

Seeing as both Luca and Charlott's daughter Amelia (who was now 14) had been born at 42 weeks, we were not expecting this new baby to come any earlier than the end of September.

But as October slowly ticked away it was a wonder whether this sleepy baby was ever going to put in an appearance.

Fourteen days after her due date I reminded Charlott of her choices and asked whether she'd like to be induced.

'I just want it all to be natural, Virginia,' she said. 'No interference.'

So day 15 arrived with no sign of the baby, then 16, 17 and 18.

'He really has got comfy!' I said.

Finally, 19 days past her due date, Charlott's contractions started on 14 October 2013 and Andrew summoned me to the house.

I arrived to find Amelia and Charlott's mum, Annette, already there.

I was amused to see Charlott kneeling on the floor and laughing at the TV – clearly in between contractions. Sure enough, as I sat down next to her it wasn't long before the giggles were replaced by groans and she rested her head on the sofa and gripped my hand.

'I want the birth stool,' she cried out.

Like many women, Charlott found the familiarity of doing the same as her last birth comforting and, having anticipated this, I quickly grabbed my stool from where I'd left it in the hall and slipped it into place under her.

The night carried on and with Charlott making good progress, Andrew sat behind his beloved while Annette crouched down on the floor next to me.

'Are you going to catch him?' I asked Andrew.

'No, you can, Mum,' he replied, his face white as he recalled the feeling of being overwhelmed that he'd had during Charlott's previous birth.

At that moment Charlott let out a cry and to everyone's shock a large white balloon started to emerge.

'Oh look!' I cried in excitement. 'He's going to be born in the caul!'

This was the term used for a baby being born in his bag of membranes when the waters have not yet been released. It really was a rare occurrence to see the membrane sac around the baby still intact at this late stage in the birth, but there it was!

Astonishingly, as the sac squeezed out of the birth canal we could see the baby's head inside it giving the strange illusion that he was being born encased in a space helmet.

'Come on, Annette,' I said. 'Do you want to catch him?'

As she nodded eagerly, I grabbed her hands and placed them under the baby in readiness. Then, as the baby's body started to emerge, his two grandmothers moved together to catch him as he slipped on to the floor.

Carefully I peeled the membrane away from his face so he could take his first breath. As he let out a tiny spluttering cry, we all gasped in collective joy and I lifted him up and passed him to Charlott.

'Hello, Cody,' she said. 'We have waited ages for you!'

Weighing in at a massive 9lb 6oz, Cody took his place as the heavyweight of the Howes family going back for several generations.

And, as usual, I thanked the birth angels for his safe passage into life.

'That was amazing,' Annette said, wiping away tears of joy as she reflected on helping bring her daughter's baby into the world.

'Yes,' I agreed as we stood listening to the happy gurgles of our newest grandson enjoying his first ever feed.

'It always is.'